Religion, Politics, and the Origins of
Palestine Refugee Relief

# Religion, Politics, and the Origins of Palestine Refugee Relief

*Asaf Romirowsky and Alexander H. Joffe*

RELIGION, POLITICS, AND THE ORIGINS OF PALESTINE REFUGEE RELIEF
Copyright © Asaf Romirowsky and Alexander H. Joffe, 2013.

First published in 2013 by
PALGRAVE MACMILLAN®
in the United States—a division of St. Martin's Press LLC,
175 Fifth Avenue, New York, NY 10010.

Where this book is distributed in the UK, Europe and the rest of the world,
this is by Palgrave Macmillan, a division of Macmillan Publishers Limited,
registered in England, company number 785998, of Houndmills,
Basingstoke, Hampshire RG21 6XS.

Palgrave Macmillan is the global academic imprint of the above companies
and has companies and representatives throughout the world.

Palgrave® and Macmillan® are registered trademarks in the United States,
the United Kingdom, Europe and other countries.

ISBN: 978–1–137–37816–3

Library of Congress Cataloging-in-Publication Data

Romirowsky, Asaf.
    Religion, politics, and the origins of Palestine refugee relief / Asaf
Romirowsky and Alexander H. Joffe.
        pages cm
    ISBN 978–1–137–37816–3 (hardback)
        1. Refugees, Palestinian Arab—Gaza Strip—History—20th century.
2. Palestinian Arabs—Gaza Strip—History—20th century. 3. American
Friends Service Committee. 4. United Nations Relief and Works Agency
for Palestine Refugees in the Near East. I. Joffe, Alexander H. II. Title.

HV640.5.P34R66 2013
362.87′809531—dc23                                      2013026220

A catalogue record of the book is available from the British Library.

Design by Newgen Knowledge Works (P) Ltd., Chennai, India.

First edition: December 2013

10 9 8 7 6 5 4 3 2 1

# Contents ❧

# Figures ❧

# Acknowledgments

We gratefully acknowledge Donald Davis, archivist of the American Friends Service Committee in Philadelphia, Pennsylvania, for his exceptional help with this project and for permission to cite the materials used here. We also thank our families for their love and support throughout this project.

# Introduction: The Palestine Arab Problem and the International Community ᘛᘚ

The Palestine Arab refugee problem has been at the forefront of the Arab-Israeli conflict and international affairs since 1948. In the twenty-first century the refugee issue looms as one of, if not, the most intractable issues in the conflict. The political role of widely dispersed Palestinians, including those defined as refugees who remain in camps in Lebanon, Syria, and in the West Bank, and even more dramatically, the concept of a "right of return" to their previous residences now in Israel, remain constant challenges to any negotiated peace proposals.

In the meantime, the international community, through the United Nations Relief and Works Agency for Palestine Refugees in the Near East or UNRWA, created by the United Nations General Assembly in December 1949,[1] and through non-governmental organizations (NGOs), provide for the health, education, and welfare of those it defines as refugees. Though UNRWA has now existed for some sixty years, it was not the first international program addressing the Palestine Arab refugees.

This book examines UNRWA's lesser-known predecessors and the role of NGOs in shaping the international response to the refugees. International involvement came in stages. From September through December 1948, limited relief efforts were undertaken for Palestine Arab refugees by the small and overwhelmed United Nations Disaster Relief Program, which like many observers at the time, warned of looming disaster. On November 19, 1948, the United Nations General Assembly created a larger-scale, but still a temporary relief mechanism. Resolution 212 (III) stated "the alleviation of conditions of starvation and distress among the Palestine refugees is one of the minimum conditions for the success of the efforts of the United Nations to bring peace to that land." The resolution then directed the establishment of the United Nations Relief for Palestine Refugees (UNRPR), "to relieve the desperate plight of Palestine refugees of all communities."[2] It is this organization, and specifically its most successful NGO, the American Friends Service Committee (AFSC), which are the subjects of this book.

The UNRPR was a coordinating and funding body for temporary relief provided by autonomous voluntary organizations such as the International Committee of the Red Cross (ICRC), the League of Red Cross Societies and the AFSC. Each group, with separate regions of responsibility, staff and bureaucracies, delivered food, shelter, and other rudiments in a chaotic wartime and postwar environment. Other United Nations organs were deeply involved during this period, notably the United Nations Children's Fund (UNICEF), which provided limited food relief, and the United Nations Conciliation Commission for Palestine that facilitated negotiations and acted as the UN's primary reporting and as analytical entity on the conflict.

The UNRPR program marked the beginning of the international community's permanent involvement in the refugee issue. Before the United Nations developed any meaningful capacity to administer itself or deliver food, health, education or other forms of relief and aid, private aid organizations, the precursors of modern NGOs, were vital and indeed indispensible.

The AFSC was long established as an international relief organization and was invited by the United Nations to play a central role in the early years of the Palestinian refugee relief. But the path to this role was not straight, and was built on a deep foundation of Quaker involvement in the Middle East, the unique postwar politics of the American Protestant community, and the failure of the AFSC's own efforts at religious diplomacy. Despite uncertain beginnings, and countless difficulties and constraints along the way, this early NGO executed its mission in the Gaza Strip with great effectiveness and economy throughout 1949 and early 1950. The AFSC attempted to shape UNRWA's policy towards the refugees, but the Quaker group's involvement was fated to be short-lived, and its influence on UNRWA was minimal. The AFSC's sense of failure and retreat from future refugee projects in the Middle East and elsewhere is a key to the story of international efforts to help Palestine Arab refugees.

AFSC's approach to the Palestine Arab refugees was the road not taken. Despite long experience in European refugee relief, the AFSC had never experienced anything like the Palestinian situation. The steadfast refusal of the Arab host countries to accept Palestinian refugees as anything other than the segregated wards of the international community was unique. So too was the equally steadfast refusal of the refugees themselves to resettle or assimilate into their host societies. Faced with these problems, the growing inefficiency of the United Nations, and motivated by Quaker religious ideology that stressed pacifism, aid and moral dignity, and the economic rehabilitation of families and communities, rather than open-ended relief, the AFSC accommodated the refugees as best they could. But seeing no possible endpoint, the AFSC terminated its efforts in 1950. Ultimately, UNRWA became the sole provider and facilitator of the Palestinian refugees.

The internal story of the AFSC involvement demonstrates the complex politics and morality of relief work. Quaker doctrine shaped the AFSC but internally the organization was divided by conflicts between expectations and realities, idealistic and realizable goals, and between leadership and field workers. Differing attitudes toward the refugees themselves, toward Israel and Jews, and other political involvements, split the leadership and the field and yet resulted in a shared decision, that to go on with refugee relief in Gaza was wrong.

But the AFSC's involvement had political ramifications that went beyond the refugee situation. The opportunity to participate in the UNRPR project and to provide Gaza relief came at a pivotal time for the AFSC, one of both unique success and painful failure. After receiving the Nobel Peace Prize in 1947, the leadership made the conscious decision to take explicit political stances regarding Cold War politics, an approach that saw the AFSC drop its carefully cultivated stance of neutrality and criticize the United States in increasingly harsh terms. At the same time the leadership made an unusual bid for leadership within the American Protestant community, and a public appeal to American society as a whole regarding nuclear disarmament and the pacifist cause.

This seemed an opportune time for the AFSC and the Quakers to assume a new role within the Protestant context. The primary political concerns of Protestant denominations, including British Anglicans and their American Episcopalian counterparts, American Congregationalists, and British and American Quakers, were the protection of Christian communities in the Holy Land and their own prerogatives as missionaries, educators, and overseers of Christian holy places. All of these were profoundly threatened by the partition of Palestine into Arab and Jewish states. Though Quaker theology was much less anti-Semitic than that of other Protestant denominations, American and British Quaker attitudes toward Jews and Israel were complex and tinged with theological, interdenominational, and practical considerations. The Quakers' traditional friendship toward the Jews was to be tested in many ways. One was the fact that other American Protestant figures were leaders of anti-Israel groups and worked alongside State Department and oil industry personnel from similar backgrounds.

But the offer for the AFSC to participate in Palestine Arab refugee relief also came after the failure of three separate AFSC efforts at religious diplomacy during the first months of 1948 and with increasing pressures later that year within American Protestant denominations for action regarding the Palestine Arab refugee crisis. Though the AFSC aimed for higher geopolitical and ethical ground, as a large and experienced relief organization, it could not escape from the Palestine Arab crisis. It also badly needed a success.

But once involved, the AFSC quickly confronted what seemed to be limitless needs and growing goals, both from the refugees and the international community. The AFSC's tradition of helping refugees through relief and vocational training was only half welcomed by the refugees themselves. As the scale of the refugee problem grew to encompass ever-increasing numbers of non-refugee Arabs, the United Nations itself sought to do more. When political settlements proved impossible, the international community imagined ever-larger regional development schemes, such as those proposed by the United Nation's Economic Survey Mission and the American Point IV program. Though the AFSC leadership may, in fact, have played a small role in instigating and promoting such schemes, these ran counter to the organization's doctrines, capabilities, and interests. The final result of deferring a political solution in favor of refugee employment and works was the AFSC's withdrawal, and the permanent welfare regime of UNRWA. In modern parlance this was a "humanitarian trap" where interventions and then a huge welfare infrastructure substituted for hard political decisions and compromises.

The AFSC was constrained—or trapped—by local and international political contexts, realities for which they were arguably unprepared. The AFSC's programs and decision-making took place in several larger political contexts over which it had no control. The United States was rapidly moving to contain the repercussions from the British withdrawal from its empire, including the Palestine Mandate, and contain Communism and Soviet influence in the Middle East and northern Mediterranean. At the same time the British, still reeling economically and stung by the withdrawal from Palestine, were attempting to retain what influence they could afford in newly independent Arab states. For Western governments, the overarching concerns were a peaceful resolution to the Arab-Israeli conflict, continued stability of friendly Arab governments and the control of rising Arab nationalism, and fear of Soviet expansionism in the context of the early Cold War. These were among the largest political realities that the AFSC had to navigate.

Like other participants in the Palestine refugee crisis, the AFSC became caught in a contradiction: the only political solution to the refugee crisis was resettlement in Arab host countries or repatriation to Israel. These were unacceptable to Arab states and Israel, respectively, who in response, encouraged pursuit of political solutions to other issues such as borders. This in turn refocused debate onto the refugee issue, where the same two possibilities (resettlement or repatriation) loomed. Regional development schemes, especially large-scale ones, had similar political implications and were largely understood by proponents and commentators as means to facilitate refugee resettlement. For Arab states, however, these proposals primarily offered a means to extract development aid first and consider the refugee situation later, if ever.

As this study shows, the AFSC recognized these contradictions early on. It also demonstrates the extent to which voluntary organizations like AFSC were coaxed and even manipulated into becoming instruments of American diplomacy. But at the same time, one of the important and surprising conclusions, based on the study of State Department documents, including some only recently declassified, is that the regional development concept, and above all, the idea of resettlement of refugees in Arab counties, were firmly understood to be the only viable approach from 1949 through the early 1950s. This is in spite of countless public pronouncements regarding a balanced approach that would include repatriation, resettlement, and "rehabilitation," or "reintegration."

Thus the AFSC withdrew but Palestine Arab relief continued. During the 1950s, after the failure of development schemes and anxious regarding its own survival, UNRWA followed the lead of the Arab states. These states had prevented Palestinian refugee resettlement in their own countries, and engineered UNRWA's open-ended mandate while carefully excluding the Palestinian refugees from the United Nations High Commissioner for Refugees (UNHCR). As a result, UNRWA and other NGOs have soldiered on for six decades. By giving up on resettlement and repatriation and accepting the roles of providing refugee housing, education, and health, and more recently as legal protector and advocate, UNRWA has, in reality, perpetuated the refugee problem. Moreover, since UNRWA's mandate was constructed by the United Nations General Assembly, which retained for itself the sole responsibility for declaring the Palestine refugee crisis resolved, UNRWA is virtually permanent.

In the meantime the AFSC had long abandoned the arena. But its experience, the warnings of its personnel, and the subsequent history of UNRWA, stand as harbingers of the modern NGO dilemmas regarding accountability and transparency, rent-seeking, and moral hazard and the "humanitarian trap." These were the AFSC's lessons that were not, in the end, learned.

# 1. Studying the Palestine Arab Refugee Problem ✑

The scholarly literature on the Palestine Arab refugee problem and UNRWA is vast but deeply uneven and highly politicized. Despite many thousands of published items, only it may be argued that only a handful are truly scholarly works or display penetrating insights. Moreover, despite countless diplomatic and political histories of the period, refugee relief—as opposed to the real or putative origins of the refugee crisis—plays only a small role in the narrative.[1] And yet refugee relief, in the form of UNRWA, has become one of the primary engines of both continued international involvement and modern Palestinian identity.

Another difficulty in writing about Palestine Arab refugee relief is the unevenness of the documentation. Surprisingly, publicly available United Nations materials are not extensive. Available records include, for example the General Assembly and its various debates, and public discussions regarding the many United Nations organizations and commissions, including the UNPRP, the Economic Survey Mission, Conciliation Commission for Palestine, and the early years of UNRWA. These provide superficial descriptions of the politics surrounding the refugee issue. But internal UN documents such as field reports, memoranda, planning, budgeting, and personnel files remain difficult to access. The UN's internal decision-making processes thus remain obscure.

There is, however, no lack of such primary documentation for the UN's Palestine Arab refugee programs. The Ford Foundation funded an inventory of UNRWA documents in 1985 by the Refugee Documentation Project at York University that located hundreds of meters of UNRWA documents. These included various refugee registration files, photographic documentation, and administrative documentation.[2] But unlike archives maintained at the United Nations in New York, access to UNRWA archives remains carefully controlled by the organization itself. These archives have been primarily used by a small number of sympathetic scholars and by UN personnel writing in advocacy or academic capacities, such as those documenting Palestinian property claims in anticipation of eventual repatriation or compensation schemes,[3] or allegedly restoring the "lost visibility" of pre-1967 refugee society.[4] Research on Palestinian society, UNRWA itself, and the evolution of relief organizations have not been priorities for those accessing UNRWA documents, to the detriment of historical understanding.

But any look at the modern debate over Palestine Arab refugees—both the origins of the problems and international responses—must take into account two facts that are not often recognized. First is that the debate was originally shaped by scholars with direct experience with refugee relief, including with the AFSC. Second, and more significantly is that in recent decades two entirely parallel, competing narratives have developed that are drawn from many of the same materials but shape them to reach utterly different conclusions. The competing narratives over the Palestine Arab refugee problem are a microcosm of those that describe and shape the Arab-Israeli conflict as a whole.

## EARLY SCHOLARSHIP ON THE REFUGEE CRISIS

In-depth studies of the Palestine Arab refugees emerged in the early 1950s, some of which still have unique value, since they do not suffer as greatly from the overburden of later polemical scholarship. One early work was a doctoral dissertation by Channing B. Richardson,[5] written at Columbia University under the supervision of the important Middle East historian J. C. Hurewitz. Richardson had been a conscientious objector during World War II, serving in the Civilian Public Service program, and later joined the Quakers. In 1945 he joined the United Nations Relief and Rehabilitation Administration and worked in displaced persons camps in Germany.[6] After returning to the United States, to begin his doctoral work, he accepted an assignment with the AFSC to administer a refugee camp in Gaza under the auspices of UNRPR.

While in Gaza, Richardson published a piece that described the origins of the UNPRP.[7] He stressed the inadequacy of the United Nations Disaster Relief Organization and the originality of the UNRPR approach, with respect to the public-private partnership, the speed of implementation, and both the autonomy and political independence of the organizations providing aid on the ground. But most significantly, already in 1950 Richardson clearly stated about one of the most vexing problems facing the relief organizations:

"What is a 'refugee'?" Since no official definition has ever been given, the agencies interpret the word as best they can in the field. Thus arises a series of problems which few, if any, international organizations might answer satisfactorily. Are Bedouins entitled to United Nations relief if they are cut off from some of the lands in which they used to roam? Are fellahins refugees if they used to be migrant workers deriving 40 per cent of their livelihood from lands now in Israel? What about villagers living in their own homes but separated from their lands by mines and barbed wire? Or settled residents of an area who are now destitute and hungry because the presence of hordes of refugees has cut off their labor?[8]

Richardson articulated problems that were well known to AFSC, United Nations and governments, but that were not understood by either scholars or the public. Had they been, it is possible that other policy choices would have been made. These problems, however, would confront UNRWA and other relief organizations for decades to come. UNRWA would also continue to construct its own definitions of "refugee."

In 1952, Richardson summarized UNRPR's operations.[9] His view of the origins of the refugee problem shows the Quaker mindset of even-handedness at work; "Over 1,000,000 Arabs and about 625,000 Jews were apparently determined to use violence to enforce their claims."[10] This mentality, where cause and effect were of less significance than the results, has helped subtly shape the history of the refugee question ever since.

Another early work on the refugees was a doctoral dissertation by Don Peretz,[11] also written under the supervision of J. C. Hurewitz at Columbia University. Peretz had worked in 1949 for the AFSC in Israel, and later traveled through the Middle East on behalf of the Ford Foundation that was then in an early stage of adopting an international focus.[12] As will be shown below, his Jewish background and "un-Quakerly" sympathy for Israel was to be a source of controversy with the AFSC leadership. Peretz remained involved with the Palestine Arab refugee issue, authoring several studies during the 1970s through the 1990s.[13]

Peretz's dissertation was published in 1958 and remains significant today, especially for his succinct presentations of the numerous international negotiations and plans to address the refugee problem, including repatriation, the shift to ever-larger economic development solutions, and internal Israeli political debates.[14] One of the most controversial aspects of his book, however, was his relatively brief analysis of the origins of the refugee problem. He contrasted, for example, the Jewish community's "quasi-government" with the Arab community's near complete lack of autonomous institutions. With the British withdrawal there was a breakdown of all services to the Arab sector, a collapse of morale, and "the community became easy prey to rumor and exaggerated atrocity stories. The psychological preparation for mass flight was complete."[15] Such explanations have been strenuously downplayed by many recent historians.

Another contribution to early scholarship is Rony Gabby's 1959 hugely detailed book *A Political Study of the Arab-Jewish Conflict. The Arab Refugee Problem*, based on his doctoral thesis for the Graduate Institute of International Studies in Geneva.[16] Although largely descriptive, it remains one of the most useful and comprehensive studies of the problem. Born in Baghdad, Gabbay was a Jewish refugee in Israel from 1950 to 1955. Although written long before the declassification of official Israeli, British, and other documents, Gabbay's discussion of the social structure of Mandate era Palestine, as well as the circumstances of the flight of the refugees, remains unmatched as a model of scholarship and even-handedness.

Gabbay's treatment of Palestine's pre-1948 politics and demography is concise and direct, and his use of the voluminous United Nations documentation is especially helpful. Like Peretz's book, however, his discussion of the origins of the refugee crisis emphasized Palestine's abandonment by the wealthy Arab class, chaotic wartime conditions, and the disorganized flight of lower classes.[17] The title of his book also speaks to an understanding of a basic religious dimension to the conflict that was lost in the rising nationalist polemics of the later 1950s and 1960s. For these reasons, the book has been rarely cited in recent years. For his part, Gabbay himself never wrote about the Arab-Israeli conflict again.

## 1970s AND 1980s

The Palestine Arab refugee issue, and a general consciousness of the Palestinians as a separate group, entered the academic and popular consciousnesses during the 1960s. But the critical literature on UNRWA and international organizations dealing with the Palestine refugee problem remained surprisingly small through the 1980s. The few perceptive analyses that were produced are important in their own right and also help show the way in which subsequent scholarship has been dramatically polarized.

One such contribution was an article by political scientist and former United Nations official David Forsythe in 1971.[18] Forsythe argued that UNRWA had come to be viewed as a de facto "peacemaking" organization when in fact it had "been limited to peaceservicing roles of an administrative nature which have indirectly facilitated the success of movements that seek to use coercion not authorized by the UN."[19] He pointed to the manipulation of the language that created UNRWA, where Western states initially sought to emphasize "practical" and "realistic" solutions and Arab states read this as code for refugee resettlement. In response, they insisted that "repatriation" be included in the founding resolution, as well as the term "Palestine."[20] In Forsythe's view the organization was constrained from the moment of its creation and thus gravitated toward direct relief and other forms of assistance and maintenance. In doing so, the organization "is having a political impact on the Middle East not expressly intended by the General Assembly and directly contrary to Security Council efforts to facilitate peacemaking."[21]

Political scientist Amos Perlmutter responded to Forsythe in a piquantly titled paper, "Patrons in the Babylonian Captivity of Clients: UNRWA and World Politics."[22] He lamented Forsythe's uncritical assessment of UNRWA's political involvement, saying, "the agency's existence formed a structural addition to the international institutionalization of the Arab-Israeli conflict. At the mercy of the refugees, while at the convenience of Arab states and their anti-Israeli machinations, the agency's "bypassing" of the conflict became a structured aspect of this conflict."[23] Perlmutter argued that this "turned UNRWA into a structure that further institutionalized the Arab-Israeli conflict."[24] In response,[25] Forsythe disputed specific arguments but did not address the fundamental issues raised by Perlmutter. Forsythe also produced the only monograph to date on the often-neglected United Nations Conciliation Commission for Palestine.[26]

Edward Buehrig's book, *The UN and the Palestinian Refugees, A Study in Nonterritorial Administration*,[27] is a structural analysis of UNRWA and its position within the United Nations system. Buehrig usefully pointed to several areas, namely funding and personnel, which remain among the organization's most contentious problems. Unlike most analysts, he emphasized the unique and changing nature of the organization's legal status, including its formation under Article 22 of the United Nations Charter that authorizes the General Assembly "to establish such subsidiary organs as it deems necessary to the performance of its functions."[28]

Two other agencies, the United Nations Childrens' Fund (UNICEF) and the United Nations High Commissioner for Refugees (UNHCR) were also created under Article 22. These were in contrast to a treaty-based approach under Article 59 of the Charter that were funded by mandatory contributions from UN member states, while subordinate organs of the General Assembly were funded by voluntary contributions.[29] Buehrig emphasized the difficulties of a voluntary contribution system for organizational budgeting, and that UNRWA budgets, unlike those of UNICEF and UNHCR, are not subject to formal approval by UN supervisory committees.[30] The UNRWA advisory committee also has no executive or operational responsibilities and only makes recommendations.

Another area that Buehrig stressed was UNRWA's inability to police activities that go on in its camps. Lacking territorial authority, UNRWA has no law enforcement or police protection powers, which puts it at the mercy of host governments or, as later experience has shown, non-territorial groups. At the same time, however, UNRWA has historically insisted on the inviolability of its premises but lacks any mechanism to protect itself beyond imploring for help from the host government or other local authority, such as terrorist groups.[31] These issues became particularly important during the 1970s and after with the rise of terror organizations operating inside UNRWA camps and facilities.

Though written in the 1990s, Benjamin Schiff's *Refugees into the Third Generation. UN Aid to the Palestinians* (1995) remains the best history of UNRWA.[32] Schiff stressed many of the same structural issues as Buehrig, but took pains to emphasize the political circumstances that UNRWA found itself in during the 1950s and after 1967. His sympathy with the refugees and UNRWA as an organization was clear, but did not significantly compromise his presentation. Schiff also used a limited number of AFSC documents to discuss the birth of UNRWA.[33]

## THE "NEW HISTORIANS"

By the 1980s, declassification of Israeli documents and new trends in historiography brought renewed attention to the issue of the Palestine refugees, particularly the origins, circumstances and scale of their flight. The primary figure associated with this trend was Benny Morris of Ben-Gurion University of the Negev. In an initial revisionist work in 1984, Morris made extensive and arguably tendentious use of newly available documentary evidence to suggest that the scope of the Palestinian refugee flight of 1947–1948 was larger than previously thought.[34] Moreover, he suggested that much of the flight was deliberately engineered by Israeli forces, who also committed various atrocities against civilian populations.

Morris was challenged vigorously on these points by Efraim Karsh of King's College London, who pointed to the selective use of documents and quotes, many of which often demonstrated the opposite of what Morris alleged.[35] With repeated critiques from Karsh and other scholars, and thanks to a difficult-to-explain political conversion in recent years, Morris has modified and retracted many of his initial claims regarding the refugees in later revisions of his book and in subsequent works.[36] He has also usefully dissected the contentious historiography regarding one of the most troubling events of 1948 war, the Deir Yassin massacre, demonstrating how the systematic misrepresentation of the incident and inflation of the number of casualties by Arab propagandists backfired and hastened the flight of refugees.[37]

These and many other historiographic battles over the creation of Israel were embedded in larger Israeli and Israeli-Palestinian debates over the use of history to generate and bolster, or conversely to dissolve, national narratives and identities. The refugee issue remains central to these debates. Many Israeli scholars, the second or third generation beyond that which had participated in the state's creation and written the first versions of its history, felt their predecessors had created an unduly glossy image of the Zionist enterprise, including the integrity of its diplomacy and execution of the War of Independence. At the most extreme, some believed Zionist idea itself and Israeli state were irretrievably corrupt.[38] The "New Historians" sought to explore the dark side of Israeli history, particularly with regard to the refugee issue. Their motives ranged from straightforward challenges to official history, the desire to undermine Zionism, the Israel state, its international standing, and to aid the Palestinian cause. These "post-Zionist" efforts also took root in controversial revisions to state educational curricula and in popular culture. The refugee issue was thus placed at the center of debates regarding Israeli identity and the "original sin" of Israel's creation, particularly by Israelis who would become far more extreme than Morris such as Ilan Pappé and Avi Shlaim.[39]

Yet in a sense Morris and others were also participating in a uniquely lopsided binational project. A parallel revisionist effort had long been conducted by a cadre of Palestinian historians headed by Walid Khalidi and Ibrahim Abu Lughod.[40] Since the 1960s, they and others had spearheaded efforts to present a Palestinian counter-narrative that moved beyond the initial lachrymose conception of Palestinian history as one of failure and flight to a more historically grounded, albeit tendentious, one that emphasized Palestinian victimization. The earlier narrative had lashed out at all parties, Arab and Palestinian leaders, the United Nations and the West, Israel, and the Palestinians themselves. The later narrative focused far more on alleged Israeli wrongdoing. In the broader sense it coincided with the "Orientalist" critique of Edward Said and the rise of post-colonial theory in Western universities, which stressed victimization of the Middle East and its historical consciousness by the West.

Palestinian revisionist history writing also had quasi-official status since the Palestine Liberation Organization provided support for research institutions and conferences. It placed exclusive blame for the refugees' flight and continuing plight on Israel but did so, however, using far more detailed if deliberately skewed historical evidence and arguments. Allegations of Israeli "war crimes" and deliberate "ethnic cleansing," based on selective readings of old and new Israeli sources, were buttressed (and seemingly legitimated) by the assessments of Israeli scholars such as Morris, Pappé, and Shlaim, and became the central explanation for the Palestine Arab refugees. The quasi-academic nature of this effort amplified those of earlier journalists such as Erskine Childers and polemicists like Fayez Sayegh.

For example, Khalidi's studies of the Haganah's "Plan Dalet" (originally published 1961) claimed that this prewar planning document, part of which called for the expulsion of Palestinian civilians from certain areas if they resisted capture by Israeli forces in case of war, had in fact been consciously implemented. Khalidi, in fact, deemed Plan Dalet the "Master Plan for the Conquest of Palestine."[41] Though this claim has been repeatedly refuted,[42] it has become part of the popular conception of the refugee problem. These and other claims of widespread "ethnic cleansing," "war crimes," and Israeli "racism" are now central to revisionist studies published outside of Israel by individuals such as Ilan Pappé and Rosemarie Esber, as well as those inside such as Oren Yiftachel, all of whom deliberately straddle and conflate scholarship and advocacy.[43]

The origins of the refugee crisis, and the question of refugee relief are central to the scholarship-advocacy pioneered by Khalidi and Abu Lughod. By and large, however, the international response to the Palestine Arab refugee crisis is largely taken for granted, and the insights of the earlier generation of scholars such as Richardson, Gabbay and Peretz, into both the politics and the culture of the refugees, are either dismissed or ignored.

## SCHOLARSHIP-ADVOCACY

During the 1970s and 1980s, there was a huge expansion of scholarly articles on Palestinian refugees, most written from an advocacy standpoint. The Institute for Palestine Studies was created in Beirut in 1963 by a number of Palestinian intellectuals and became a focal point for the creation and dissemination of Palestinian narratives and viewpoints. The creation of the Association of Arab-American University Graduates in 1967 by Ibrahim Abu-Lughod, and the general upheavals that accompanied the years between 1967 and 1968, also boosted scholarship that was explicitly favorable to the Palestinians and their narratives.[44] The result has been the creation of an entirely separate literature that presents the Palestinian narrative on the entirety of the Arab-Israeli conflict, without making any reference to other sources, with the exception of Israeli "New Historians."

The founding in 1971 of the *Journal of Palestine Studies*, supported by a mainstream American academic publisher, the University of California Press, and the *Middle East Report* by the Middle East Research and Information Project collective, and the *Arab Studies Quarterly* in 1977, were additional turning points that gave pro-Palestinian writers their own platforms with a respectable imprimatur. The *Revue d'études Palestiniennes* was also established in France in 1982 and disseminated the Palestinian viewpoint through the generally sympathetic French speaking world. These, along with newer journals such as *Holy Land Studies* (created in 2001 with a strong Liberation Theology and Replacement Theology orientation) have been important vehicles for the revitalization of the Palestine refugee issue. It was also during this period that a great number of studies regarding Palestinian nationalism were published.[45]

The growth of academic specialization also helped the Palestinian cause. The creation of academic sub-disciplines and eventually journals in areas such as refugee studies, human rights, and international law became venues to generate a new and tremendously large literature on Palestine Arab refugees and UNRWA. Legal studies purporting to establish the necessity of repatriating Arab refugees and their descendents to their erstwhile homes in Israel, and supporting mechanisms for compensation, are now especially common. As will be discussed below, the timing of these studies, as a reaction to the Oslo peace process that seemed poised to settle the Arab-Israeli conflict and resolve the refugee issue, was not coincidental.[46]

Similar focus on Palestinians is seen in other academic fields and journals, for example those devoted to international public health.[47]

The growth of academic specialization has been accompanied by the even more explosive growth of local and international NGOs, many of which are supported by the United Nations system and by European governments as extensions of their foreign policy, addressing issues such as democracy promotion, human rights, and development. A global network of institutions to promote the Palestinian cause generally, and that of the refugees specifically, has been created that interlocks with academia and media as personnel cycle through all these locations.[48]

The amount of attention focused on the Palestinians in refugee studies is such that some scholars have expressed concern that "Palestinian exceptionalism" has led to insufficient attention on other Middle Eastern refugee populations.[49] Many of these journals are also used regularly by quasi-academic NGO professionals, including those from UNRWA, to present analyses and advocacy pieces.[50] Typical of this scholarship-advocacy position are defenses of UNRWA in *Refugee Studies Quarterly* by UNRWA officials Lance Bartholomeusz and outgoing Commissioner-General Karen Abu Zayd.[51] Equally one-sided is the extensive literature in legal and human rights journals on the Palestinian "right of return," that proponents typically find support for in United Nations General Assembly Resolution 194.[52] Allegations of Israel's "ethnic cleansing" are stated as established and uncontestable facts, and the term "original sin" is employed without qualification.[53]

The pervasiveness of scholarship-advocacy in favor of the Palestine Arab refugees and UNRWA has spawned a small backlash. Studies from quasi-academic organizations supporting Israel and written from a journalistic standpoint have documented UNRWA's faults and called for its reform or abolition.[54] These have put the organization and its supporters on the defensive and resulted in lengthy exchanges in the opinion pages of primarily American and Israeli newspapers and magazines. More substantive critiques of UNRWA have also appeared, including by former staff members that have also been attacked by the organization and its supporters.[55] The issue of UNRWA's use of "soft power" to defend itself and its prerogatives will be discussed in the concluding chapter. The situation is such that any discussion of the origins of the Palestine Arab refugee problem is automatically enmeshed in a political debate. The value of returning to primary documentary sources, such as the AFSC's archives, is manifest.

## STUDYING THE AFSC AND
## RELIEF ORGANIZATIONS

As noted above, former AFSC personnel played important roles in creating the first literature on the Palestine Arab refugee issue, but the organization itself has been the subject of only intermittent attention. Archival materials from NGOs that had been involved with early refugee relief, including the AFSC, were surveyed as part of a project by the Institute for Jerusalem Studies.[56] Peteet's[57] brief survey of AFSC materials in Philadelphia, which are used far more extensively here, contributed several useful observations regarding the nature of the organization's experience with Palestinian refugees, and also provided a brief sketch of AFSC operations in Gaza in her 2005 book on Palestinian refugee camps.[58]

Gallagher presented a more substantive monograph on the AFSC experience in Gaza, Israel, and with UNRWA.[59] Her presentation of the AFSC experience in the refugee crisis made generally good use of archival materials and oral histories, but overall her approach was hagiographic and uncritical. There are also many situations where her tendentious conclusions were not born out by a fuller examination of AFSC documents. She provided a rich picture of AFSC activities in the field but she fails to discuss the AFSC's internal decision-making. She also does not consider the organization's interactions with patron governments and other organizations, the international political situation, its political evolution, or its theological and political relationships with other Protestant denominations.

The theme of the AFSC as an early NGO is more developed in a series of articles by Feldman. In one, she used the AFSC experience to examine how Palestinian refugees in Gaza were identified against the emerging concept of international refugee conventions. These culminated in the 1951 International Convention Relating to the Status of Refugees and the creation of the United Nations High Commission for Refugees.[60] In another, she used the AFSC data to suggest that the ethical demands of humanitarianism are necessarily compromised by the practical and political realities found in the field. In her view, the ethical contradictions of humanitarian work imply the need for more rather than less political involvement.[61]

Though Feldman made creative use of AFSC's archival materials, her goal was problem-driven analyses aimed at abstract questions of NGO practice and humanitarianism. Her discussions of AFSC institutional decision-making and its relationship to political circumstances were therefore inconsistent. She also failed to consider AFSC's political interactions with Western states, its evolving political stance, or its religious position with respect to other Protestant denominations. These are addressed by the more comprehensive historical analysis presented here.

Finally, no survey of the literature on the AFSC's approach to the Palestine Arab refugee problem is complete without mention of the memoirs and biographical sketches of personnel such as Executive Director Clarence Pickett, Elmore Jackson and Howard Wriggins, some of which provide useful insights into their personalities as well as perceptions of the organization and the refugee problem.[62] These materials, written for public consumption, must be contrasted with the documentary evidence from internal AFSC files, and with oral histories collected from AFSC field personnel. Contrasts between the external representations and the internal debates, and the senior decision-makers and the field personnel, are vital parts of the story of the AFSC's Gaza relief mission.

# 2. The Quakers and the American Friends Service Committee: Origins of the Quakers and Quaker Ideology ℘

The American Friends Service Committee (AFSC) was founded in 1917 by the Religious Society of Friends, better known as the Quakers. The Quaker movement arose during the mid-seventeenth century in England as one of the Nonconformist movements. The Nonconformists included Dissenters such as Puritans and Presbyterians, along with Congregationalists, Methodists, Baptists, Unitarians, and Quakers.[1] These stood in violation of the 1662 Act of Uniformity, which prescribed the Church of England's rites, prayers and doctrines, as well as membership in the church as prerequisite for public office.

Quaker doctrine, as articulated in particular by George Fox (1624–1691), held that there was an "anointing within man to teach him, and that the Lord would teach His people Himself."[2] The like-minded could therefore come together without the need for mediation through clergy or ordained ministry, although Fox himself was an itinerant preacher in England and in the American colonies. Quakers rejected all forms of sacrament, such as baptism, and the notion of the Bible as inerrant Scripture, believing instead that Christ was the Word. Quakers, who tremble or quake before God, "testify" or bear witness to their belief through "spirituality in action." Testimonies are shaped by Christian ethics as contained in the Sermon on the Mount and include opposition to slavery, conscription and oaths, and the promotion of peace, integrity, temperance, and relief of suffering. Quakers also oppose violence in all forms and reject compulsion in religion, a belief that has led them to not proselytize among Jews. Quaker doctrine calls for modesty in dress, speech, and lifestyle, the avoidance of amusement, including theater, games and music, an abhorrence of idleness, and demands scrupulous honesty.[3]

Quakers were persecuted in England and parts of North America for their beliefs. They were banned from sitting in Parliament from 1698 to 1833, and imprisoned and banished from the Massachusetts Bay Colony. But the Commonwealth of Pennsylvania, founded by Quaker William Penn in 1682, became a safe haven and for an extended period was governed directly by Quakers. In later centuries, Quakers founded a series of important educational institutions in Pennsylvania including Haverford College (1833), Swarthmore College (1864), and Bryn Mawr College (1885), as well as other charitable institutions. The Quaker influence on American life, values, and institutions has been deep and pervasive, if under-acknowledged.[4]

Several schisms during the nineteenth century produced conservative and modernist Quaker factions in both Great Britain and the United States. Debates over issues such as Scriptural authority and unprogrammed worship split the small community of Friends. During the twentieth century, liberal or modernist factions pursued social justice and peace agendas but schisms and unifications continued. Modern debates include authority and leadership, the place of Christ in Quakerism and the question of whether Quakerism is "primitive Christianity revived" or whether it is Christianity at all.[5] The movement's lack of institutionalized religious leadership, non-liturgical styles of worship, and schismatic nature have largely hindered the development of systematic theology. Though sharing certain aspects of Christian theology with other Protestant denominations, Quakerism is as much a methodology as it is a series of beliefs. Traditionally, modesty and self-reliance were central, and these underpinned the Quaker approach to refugee relief.

## FRIENDS AND THE AFSC FROM THE CIVIL WAR TO WORLD WAR I

Social justice, pacifism, and refusal to bear arms are central tenets of Quaker doctrine. The American entry into World War I thus posed a serious challenge to the Quakers, as well as to other "peace churches" such as the Mennonites and Amish. Conscientious objection, including from Quakers, had existed in America since the Revolutionary War. But during World War I, the system that had developed during the Civil War, when objectors who were conscripted could find a substitute or pay for one, was discarded, and objectors were required to serve in noncombatant roles.

Prior to American entry in the War, English and Irish Friends had formed a Friends Ambulance Corps, a War Victims Relief Committee, and an "Emergency Committee for Helping Aliens."[6] Willingness of conscientious objectors to participate in different levels of military training or related activities varied greatly, based on individual conscience and sectarian background. Seeing American participation coming, American Friends undertook a large-scale preparatory effort, even as thousands of conscientious objectors who resisted military service were imprisoned, including in military facilities.

The AFSC was formed on April 30, 1917 to provide alternative forms of "service" and to satisfy government and public opinion regarding the participation of Quakers in the war effort. As Rufus Jones,[7] the first head of the AFSC put it, "It was the unanimous sense of the group that Friends could not accept exemption from military service and at the same time do nothing to express their positive faith and devotion in this great human crisis."[8] Ultimately, AFSC partnered with their English coreligionists and with the Red Cross to deliver medical aid and help with reconstruction and resettlement in northern France, with a smaller mission in Russia. The Society of Friends in the United States was also mobilized to provide aid packages and to publicize the AFSC's relief work.[9]

Helping displaced refugees create temporary shelters and returning refugees rebuild was a particular emphasis for AFSC. This took place at practical levels, through the provisioning of food and tools, including such items as beehives, cows, and school supplies, and the contribution of AFSC labor, as well as reconstruction of the abstract sense of community through "love, affection, and friendly sympathy."[10] Teaching skills was as important as providing relief, since skilled refugees would contribute to the reconstruction of self-reliant families and communities. This approach was evidently successful; Jones' history of the AFSC's work in France modestly records the heartfelt gratitude of refugees.[11]

The success of AFSC in France as whole was such that after the end of World War I, the organization was providing medical aid and relief in Serbia, Austria, and Germany. Jones also noted the effect of AFSC's selfless approach and spirituality in Germany:

> Unexpectedly a group of representative Friends came among them with no reference to their wickedness, with no desire for vengeance, but, on the contrary,

breathing peace and kindness and bearing in their hands tokens of friendship and kindly human interest. The impression made upon all classes of people was profound, and though they desperately needed food they appeared even more eager to learn about the underlying religious faith and the spiritual message of their Friendly visitors.[12]

But after World War I, the AFSC stood at crossroads. The initial goals of helping provide alternative service for war resisters and relief to war victims had been met. Individual Quakers, above all Herbert Hoover, had also distinguished themselves in relief work. Hoover had been appointed by President Woodrow Wilson as director of the American Relief Administration in 1919, and that agency's efforts reached forty-five nations and millions of people in the four years of its existence. Hoover himself, though not a philo-Semite, was especially active on behalf of persecuted Eastern European Jews.[13]

Thus, in 1924 a group of Quakers met in Philadelphia and, under the leadership of Rufus Jones, elected to expand the mission of the AFSC with the establishment of the Interracial Section to address racism and the needs of African Americans, as well as to extend overseas operations[14] Doing so set them further on the path to becoming a preeminent American aid and relief organization with a political inclination toward controversy. During the 1930s, Clarence Pickett, executive Secretary of the AFSC, enjoyed a strong relationship with First Lady Eleanor Roosevelt, who supported the organization's works throughout the United States. The relationship gave the AFSC a tremendous publicity boost and gave Pickett a unique public profile and the unique ability to move in powerful political circles.[15]

This approach, in effect finding support for political action in the name of a Christian love that was above politics, found philosophical support in Jones' writing and those of Howard Brinton, a Quaker philosopher and close friend of Jones. His books and pamphlets, geared toward Quaker beliefs, philosophy, and education, are perhaps the closest thing to Quaker theology in the twentieth century. Brinton's influential 1934 pamphlet *A Religious Solution to the Social Problem* argued, for example, that excessive individualism was the key problem of the age, but that this could be solved through religion while still respecting the rights of the individuals. This was posited as the path to social reformation.[16] The question of the individual's responsibility to the collective, exercised through religious action, was to be key to the AFSC.

**Figure 2.1** Clarence Pickett.
*Source*: Courtesy of the American Friends Service Committee.

## QUAKERS AND THE THEOLOGY AND POLITICS OF AMERICAN PROTESTANT MISSIONS IN THE MIDDLE EAST

The Quakers' humanitarian approach to European refugees was not the only aspect of their religious theology and mission. The background of AFSC's relief efforts was also the many missionary and educational projects undertaken by Friends groups throughout the world, including in Palestine. Quakers had gone to Palestine as early as the 1650s in order to preach. Perhaps the best-known Quaker in Palestine during the early nineteenth century was Warder Cresson of Philadelphia who became the American consul in Jerusalem in 1840. After quickly being recalled from the position, he converted to Judaism in 1849, was famously tried for "lunacy" at the demand of his family in 1851, and he returned to Palestine in 1853 to live out his life as a pious Jew and farmer.[17]

Like many denominations, Quakers were especially active in the Middle East during the second half of the nineteenth century. Eli and Sybil Jones, aunt and uncle of AFSC founder Rufus Jones, opened a girls' school in Ramallah in 1869 and later in six nearby villages. In 1889 the Ramallah school was expanded into the Girls' Training Home that provided Christian education and vocational training. A boarding school for boys was also opened in 1901, and a Quaker meeting house was opened in 1910.[18] In Lebanon, the Swiss Quaker missionary Theophilus Waldmeier founded a coeducational school in Brummana, a Christian town east of Beirut, in 1873.[19] The Quaker schools in Ramallah would become an important center for educating Muslim as well as Christian girls. Along with other Christian schools, they became a target for animosity and public attacks from the Supreme Muslim Council during the 1920s and 1930s with allegations of missionizing.[20]

Specifically, Quaker efforts must also in turn be seen in the larger context of American Protestant missionizing in the Near East, which was undertaken by theologically liberal, rather than evangelical or fundamentalist, denominations, namely Anglicans and Episcopalians, Congregationalists, and Quakers. American Protestants had been sending missions to the Middle East since at least 1810 and a wide array of missions, schools, and clinics were established through the Ottoman Empire with particular emphasis on Anatolia and the Levant. In addition, American Congregationalists opened two major educational institutions, Syrian Protestant College in Beirut (now American University of Beirut) and Roberts College of Istanbul, a coeducational boarding school, which would become centers for developing new Middle Eastern elites, and in turn, nationalisms.[21] The American self-image as the Christian "new Jerusalem" profoundly influenced the progressivist and modernizing efforts of its missionaries. These in turn were situated in the still larger context of the deep fascination and identification Americans had for the Holy Land during the nineteenth century.[22]

During the latter half of the nineteenth century, as the United States slowly developed its diplomatic apparatus, missionaries became accustomed to acting as unofficial American diplomats and sources of intelligence overseas. The institutions they created often acted as the primary or sole representatives of American Republic and American Christian culture. Scholars have also long noted that American missions, particularly religious and educational institutions, tended to draw "converts" not from the

Muslim or Jewish populations of the Middle East but rather from Eastern Christian denominations. American Protestants had by necessity a practical and humanitarian rather than conversionist approach and American missionaries had particularly close, if frequently patronizing, relationships with Christians throughout the Ottoman Empire.

These relationships, however, had sensitized American diplomats, leaders, and publics to the suffering of fellow Christians during the last decades of the Ottoman Empire and through the Armenian genocide of 1915 and the expulsion of Greek Christians from Turkey after the Greco-Turkish war of 1919–1922.[23] Thanks largely to American Protestant denominations such as Presbyterians and Congregationalists, the tragedies of Assyrian, Armenian, and Greek Christians were front-page news and critical American foreign policy issues from the 1880s through the 1920s.[24] These experiences responding to Christian persecution were also crucial during the mid-twentieth century to convincing leaders of those same denominations that they had continuing political and technological roles in the Middle East, especially with regard to rising nationalisms. The tragedies also deeply sensitized American Protestants to the problem of refugee crises.

But if the sense of responsibility of these American Protestant denominations was shaped by their theology, their attitudes toward Jews were more complex. They were not Biblical literalists and held conventionally supersessionist view regarding Jews and Judaism. Missionaries and their supporting denominations as a matter of course de-emphasized the Jewish connection to the Holy Land. Quakers shared these elements of Protestant theology, which were complicated or tempered by pacifism, along with demands for modesty and self-reliance.

The fundamental contradiction for American Protestant missionaries was that from the Woodrow Wilson administration forward American foreign policy was supportive of national self-determination, including, in a desultory manner, Zionism. This ran counter to American theological conceptions of supersessionism and the Christian progressive mission of uplift, and for Anglicans and Episcopalians, the notion of a new Christian civilization in the Middle East that they would lead. Zionism and Jewish self-determination, in particular, were seen as theological and political threats. This had the effect of putting Christian missionaries on the side of the imperial status quo, where their prerogatives and those of their Christian charges were defended. For the same reasons American missionaries and their denominations later found themselves supporting Arab nationalism.

Faced with the realities of lack of success in promotion conversion and rising nationalism, a number of Protestant denominations including the Quakers participated in a sweeping reassessment of missionizing efforts. This culminated in the major 1932 publication *Re-Thinking Missions* in which the conversion efforts of missions were downplayed and the service aspects, such as supporting schools, hospitals, and social welfare efforts, were promoted. Though the superiority of Christianity was maintained, the report put the best face on the situation and stated that "the Christian way of life is capable of transmitting itself by quiet personal contact and contagion."[25] This tacit acknowledgment that conversion at any scale was impossible therefore formally aligned Protestant denominations not with missionizing but with their local infrastructures and prerogatives and with the imperial status quo and nationalist successors.

As will be shown below, as oil and Communism became paramount international issues by the mid-twentieth century, the concerns of American Protestant missionaries began to converge once again with elements of American foreign policy. For Quakers, the smallest American Protestant denomination, without formal clergy or liturgy, and nominally non-political, all these changing circumstances posed serious challenges. Under the leadership of Clarence Pickett and the AFSC, there was a brief bid for a Quaker leadership role in American Christianity, in which the Middle East and the Cold War were fundamental.

Spreading the faith through direct evangelizing was not as central to Quakers as it was to other Protestant denominations, but their theology of individual action led them to create institutions that would in effect speak for themselves. The accusations of proselytizing lodged against their schools in Palestine may have sensitized AFSC personnel to the problem in later years. But despite Quaker theological opposition to nationalism, it became unavoidable during the decades after World War I. For example, the boys' school in Ramallah became a hotbed of Arab nationalism and opposition to Zionism, particularly under the leadership of Khalil Totah. Educated at the school and at Columbia University, Totah became headmaster in 1927, taking over from A. Willard Jones as part of a deliberate policy of handing Quaker educational institutions over to local Arab Quakers.[26] Totah was a vociferous opponent of Zionism, which he regarded as the "chief attendant evil" of imperialism.[27]

Totah also provided an important link to the experience of British Quakers. The Religious Society of Friends had been far less active than American groups in Palestine with regard to missions in the Middle East. But in 1934 the Friends' Yearly Meeting of Palestine and Syria sent Khalil

Totah, and British Quaker Daniel Oliver from the Brummana School, to London to speak on their behalf to the London Yearly Meeting of Friends, and to give presentations to British officials. Totah returned saying "We accomplished nothing. England, including the English Quakers, were so sympathetic with the Zionists viewpoint, that our visit made no impression."[28] But Totah's testimony before the Peel Commission in 1937 on the topic of Arab education gave him an enlarged platform to state the same grievances and he accused British Mandatory authorities of neglecting Arab students.[29] The Peel Commission recommended the abolition of the Mandate and that Palestine be partitioned into Arab and Jewish states, but that Jewish immigration be restricted.

Totah maintained his contacts with British Friends through the Arab Rebellion of 1936–1939. In May 1936, Totah wrote to the Palestine Watching Committee in London to complain about measures being taken by the Mandatory authorities against striking Arabs, and to urge British Friends to approach Jews in London to seek negotiations.[30] In turn, the Palestine Watching Committee issued a statement urging that Jewish immigration to Palestine be halted.[31] The 1945 pamphlet issued by the Palestine Watching Committee on the Palestine question included two articles from an exchange that had appeared in popular magazines and newspapers. "A Constitution for Palestine," by Professor E. B. Castle, strongly opposed the resettlement of European Jewish survivors of the Holocaust in Palestine. In contrast, "Reconciliation in Palestine" by Sir Wyndham Deedes, Chief Secretary to the British High Commissioner Sir Herbert Samuel of the British Mandate of Palestine, argued in favor of a Jewish state.[32]

A professor of educational administration at the University of Hull and formerly headmaster of a Quaker boarding school in Great Britain, Castle had visited Lebanon and Syria immediately before World War II. Castle had also delivered the prestigious Swarthmore Lecture at the Britain Yearly Meeting of the Religious Society of Friends in 1941 and he was an outspoken pacifist. He and the long-time AFSC member James Vail were to be key figures in bringing the AFSC directly into the Palestine question in 1948.

These Protestant theologies, denominational histories, and varied experiences up to World War II were fundamental to shaping both AFSC's approach to the Middle East, to refugee crises and, in turn, their own expectations regarding how refugees would respond to crisis and to relief efforts. They would also help shape Western foreign policy as a whole.

## WORLD WAR II AND EUROPEAN REFUGEE RELIEF
### 1945–1948

Between the wars the AFSC became involved in providing famine relief in Russia in 1920–1921, poverty relief in the United States, and war relief to victims on both sides of the Spanish Civil War.[33] The AFSC also involved itself in global affairs in other ways. In 1933, for example, Clarence Pickett, recently appointed executive secretary of the AFSC, signed a petition, along with a number of other clergy and peace activists, calling for the US Congress to "grant the President authority to lay embargoes on American export of arms." The AFSC's "Peace Section" led a 1935 "Emergency Peace Campaign," a broadbased effort to mobilize anti-war organizations against American involvement in another European conflict. The campaign had some 1200 local affiliates.[34] These forms of pacifism were still within the American mainstream during the early 1930s, particularly for religious groups, but would no longer be by the later 1940s and 1950s. During these periods and thereafter, the AFSC redoubled its emphasis on pacifism.

With the rise of Nazism, AFSC became involved with what would become the greatest refugee crisis in history. The experience also demonstrated the organization's approach to religious diplomacy and relief efforts, where naïve idealism coexisted with practicality. With the rise of Nazism the Friends network in Germany, including Quaker Student Clubs, gave the AFSC in Philadelphia an unusually clear view of the nature of the regime and the growing persecution of Jews.[35] Shortly after *Kristallnacht* in November 1938 Rufus Jones and two other leading Quakers traveled to Germany to personally investigate the suffering of the Jews. There they pleaded the case with representatives of the Reich Security Main Office and Reichsführer-SS Reinhard Heydrich for Quakers to be permitted to investigate the condition of Jews and bring relief aid. In a written statement Jones stressed that the AFSC's aid to Germans in the past was completely non-political and non-judgmental, and had only come "to support and save life and suffer with those who are suffering."[36]

Jones reported that Heydrich's underlings "read the document slowly, carefully, and thoughtfully. It plainly *reached* them and we noted a softening effect on their faces, which needed to be softened." He credited the statement with having softened the hearts of the SS and facilitated later Quaker relief efforts for Jews. He also suggested that his interlocutors, who did not include Heydrich directly, were changed by the experience of encountering:

an unexpected new way of life which had at its heard another kind of force to which they, in a moment of softness, yielded and paid their respect. If that view is correct the outcome was a miracle wrought by the way of love. The gentleness of the men at the end of our meeting with them, the fact that they went and got our coats and helped us put them on, and shook our hands with good-bye wishes and with a touch of gentleness, made me feel then, and now in retrospect, that something unique had happened in their inside selves.[37]

Jones and his associates returned to the United States, along with a number of Jewish refugees. Under the leadership of Clarence Pickett and Rufus Jones, in February 1939 the AFSC supported the Wagner-Rogers Bill in the United States Congress that would have admitted child refugees from Europe beyond the quotas established under earlier laws. This effort was unsuccessful. The AFSC also supported the non-sectarian Committee for Refugee Children, whose honorary chair was Eleanor Roosevelt, and its successor, the Foundation for Refugee Children. These were established in 1940 to help refugees, in particular Jewish children, resettle in the United States.[38]

After the onset of war, AFSC operations in Europe became far more difficult. But participation in European relief during the interwar period gave them continued credibility even with the Nazis, and they were allowed to operate in Vichy France for a time. In cooperation with the American Jewish Joint Distribution Committee, the AFSC provided assistance to Jewish refugees in France, Spain, and Portugal, and in 1941 and 1942, the AFSC transported Jewish children from southern France to the United States. In general, the Quakers' reputation for having assisted Germany after World War I was an asset to the AFSC and to individual Quakers who sought to help Jews. But as a whole the experience of the Quakers and other peace churches within Germany with respect to the Jews differed little from most Protestant denominations. Numerous individuals of conscience helped imperiled Jews while the organized churches refrained from speaking out, in effect doing little or nothing.[39]

The AFSC remained active in refugee relief throughout World War II, but the creation of the United Nations changed the larger international political setting. The United Nations Relief and Rehabilitation Administration (UNRRA), founded in 1943 (and called a "United Nations" agency even though the organization as such was not founded until 1945), constituted an international partner for AFSC, which became immediately active wherever requested.[40] In early 1947, Pickett warned in a letter to the *New York Times* that UNRRA funding was running out but that the need for aid, which would be administered through voluntary organizations like AFSC, remained.[41] Pickett also noted in retrospect that

> as time went on, the relations between UNRRA, particularly its over-all administrators, and our Committee, were most cordial. Early in 1944 we lent an AFSC team to UNRRA for refugee work in Egypt, Greece and Yugoslavia. In the late summer of 1945, before AFSC as such had an entrance to Germany, part of the team served in Germany in UNRRA refugee and displaced persons programs. We carried out reconstruction projects in China with the aid of UNRRA funds and equipment. We co-operated in its reconstruction program in Italy. One had to recognize that relief and reconstruction needs over the world were of such volume that they could only begin to be met by government funds and international administration... In 1946–1947 we were sending large amounts of food, clothing and medical supplies into most of the war-devastated countries of Europe. In some of these countries we were picking up threads of fellowship formed in the days of the AFSC relief missions in the wake of World War I. In other regions the fellowship was new. Finland was new, and the associations there were heart-warming. Hungary was new to us, and Quaker food and clothing distributions bore fruit of warm friendships between Committee representatives and Hungarians of all shades of political belief. One couple returning from this mission told us, "As in so many countries now, group fears group... and all fear the future. Our presence—after they were convinced that we had no political ax to grind—had a healing, releasing effect."[42]

At the beginning of 1947, AFSC published an appeal that estimated their annual budget for relief work at $8,000,000.[43] Like Pickett had in his letter to the *New York Times*, the appeal not only warned Americans about continuing relief needs on the eve of UNRRA's end, but also chastised them saying, "As a nation we have mistaken victory for peace. We have failed to distinguish people from governments."[44] The appeal nevertheless explicitly addressed Americans as "citizens," "Protestants, Catholics or Jews," and as "members of our communities."

## THE AFSC AND THE POLITICS OF PACIFISM

By the late 1940s, AFSC occupied a distinctive place in American and international society. It was an established Christian organization with global experience and was recognized by national and international establishments. But it was also a universalist organization that went against the grain in support of unpopular causes, with a humanitarian ethic and pacifist ideology that were in most senses radical both in the American and Protestant contexts.[45]

But the postwar international scene, and the prospect of being awarded the Nobel Peace Prize in 1947, prompted major changes within the AFSC itself and launched it, under the direction of Clarence Pickett, toward an unaccustomed leadership role in American Christian circles and American society at large. Since its beginning, Quakerism had been oriented toward the individual exercise of conscience through positive acts that spoke louder than words. Historically, Quakers and the Society of Friends had also been nonpolitical. Pacifism was a form of political dissent but it was applied uniformly toward all nations. The Society of Friends itself was politically neutral and the AFSC was willing to work as best it could with any type of government in the interest of relief and aid for refugees. But at the end of European relief efforts the Cold War between the Untied States and the Soviet Union loomed as the pivotal conflict, one with the potential to annihilate humanity.

Thus in April 1947 a faction within the AFSC's leadership, led by Clarence Pickett and chairman of the board Henry J. Cadbury,[46] convened a meeting that was nominally intended to plan the organization's thirtieth anniversary celebrations. There, Pickett, Cadbury, and former AFSC staffer Eric Johnson forcefully argued that tensions between the Untied States and the Soviet Union were so extraordinarily dangerous that the AFSC should abandon its long-standing position of political neutrality. Instead, the organization should actively attempt to shape public opinion and spearhead a peace movement that in practical terms would be aimed at the United States and its policies.[47] No less a Quaker than former American president Herbert Hoover had commented, "that Pickett fellow was too much of a politician-more of a politician than a Quaker ought to be unless he's in the business."[48] This was evident in the transformation of the AFSC in 1947 and would become more apparent still during the 1950s.

In Pickett's genuinely radical approach, political neutrality, rather than an article of faith and an asset, was regarded instead as a crime. As Eric Johnson put it, only propaganda would "persuade Americans that the only way to save humanity is through cooperation." Another participant at the April 1947 meeting added, "Evolution is too slow. We need revolution in the Society of Friends."[49] Pickett and others also argued for de-emphasizing the role of volunteers in AFSC operations in favor of professional staff, and the hiring of more non-Quakers in these roles. Already by 1947 the AFSC was comprised of 597 staff members, only 32 percent of whom were Quakers.[50]

The efforts of Pickett and Cadbury were opposed by the AFSC's founder, the 84-year-old Rufus Jones. But Pickett and Cadbury carried the day, and their efforts were received enthusiastically by the Christian press. Immediately after the meeting, Pickett and Cadbury lobbied their British counterparts and the Nobel Committee, hoping for the 1948 Peace Prize. To their surprise and satisfaction, it was awarded to the AFSC and the British Friends Service Council in 1947. It also began the transformation of the AFSC from a religious group and "recast it as just one more pressure group within the secular political community."[51]

With this new direction firmly established among the leadership, and with the moral "halo effect" that accompanied the Nobel Peace Prize, the AFSC began to articulate a conventional left-wing pacifist message largely devoid of religious or Quaker content. The key manifestation of this was a 1949 pamphlet entitled *The United States and the Soviet Union: Some Quaker Proposals for Peace*, which recommended a strengthened United Nations, enhanced contacts between the United States and the Soviet Union, and a unified Germany.[52] The publication had little impact on the rapidly growing debates within the United States regarding the Cold War. Nor did the 1951 publication *Steps to Peace: A Quaker View of U.S. Foreign Policy* or the 1952 pamphlet *Toward Security through Disarmament*.[53] Dissatisfaction regarding its weak reception prompted a 1955 pamphlet entitled *Speak Truth to Power: A Quaker Search for an Alternative to Violence* that had a more explicit religious tone of radical nonviolence and that became far more influential.[54] The influence of these statements on the later direction of the AFSC, including its involvement in the Middle East conflict, will be discussed below.

During the postwar period Pickett himself was an increasingly controversial figure within the United States. In August 1945 he had signed a letter addressed to President Harry Truman with other clergymen condemning the atomic bomb as "an atrocity of a new magnitude" that "descended step by step to an equally low level of moral culpability" with the Japanese. In early 1950 he would sign a similar letter protesting the creation of the hydrogen bomb.[55] And in 1948 he had signed a letter complaining about inadequate safeguards for US government employees who were subjected to mandatory loyalty tests.[56] Within the AFSC and Quaker circles he derided the "pugnacious" attitude of the United States towards the Soviet Union.[57] More controversial still was Pickett's testimony in support of State Department official (and Quaker) Alger Hiss, who was accused in late 1949 of spying for the Soviet Union.[58]

Although some in the media associated Pickett with the "Reds" there is no indication that any of his views were taken into account by the American diplomats with whom Pickett consulted during the course of the AFSC mission in Gaza.[59] At the same time, these conventionally left-wing views, increasingly divorced from Quaker ideology, represented a growing radical streak within both Pickett and the AFSC as whole. Their significance for the direction of AFSC, its peace "renewal movement,"[60] and American pacifism during the 1950s and later is clear. Along with theology, this radical streak also comprised a series of contradictions that would be woven throughout the AFSC's short-lived Gaza relief operation.

In his 1947 speech presenting the Nobel Peace Prize to the AFSC and the Friends Service Council of Great Britain, Gunnar Jahr, chairman of the Nobel Committee, spelled out the rationale for the award:

> Through their work, the Quakers won the confidence of all, for both governments and people knew that their only purpose was to help. They did not thrust themselves upon people to win them to their faith. They drew no distinction between friend and foe. One expression of this confidence was the donation of considerable funds to the Quakers by others.[61]

# 3. The AFSC in the Middle East: The Official Origins of AFSC Involvement in the Middle East ∾

Official histories are deliberate and often instrumental. Experience, impartiality, and a reputation for not proselytizing were critical to AFSC's reputation and self-image, and it is these features that have been emphasized in accounts of how the organization became involved in Palestine Arab refugee relief. In his autobiography, Clarence Pickett, executive director of AFSC, described the circumstances of the organization being called to participate in Palestine refugee relief. The approach was made personally to him by a representative of the Secretary General, but Pickett knew that the mission would be fraught with problems:

> Our Committee's attitude toward the United Nations has from the beginning been one of the most cordial co-operation in all efforts looking toward peaceful settlements of disputes. On principle, therefore we were favorably disposed toward this invitation. However we knew how bitter was the struggle between Jews and Arabs and we were conscious of the fact that no quick and easy solution was likely to be found. We could not undertake a police operation, and we had enough experience to know that in large-scale displacement of populations the sheer problem of order has to be considered. Then there is the perennial problem of suitable personnel. Also, we were anxious about the implications of such a service. We understood all that lay behind the setting up of the Jewish state, the long period of suffering and persecution in Europe, the high hopes and idealism connected with the return to the home land. On the other side was the deep-seated bitterness not only of the Arab refugees but of all the Arab states surrounding the newly established state of Israel. It took little imagination to realize that this situation would test to the utmost both our administrative skill and our spiritual resources.[1]

Pickett and other AFSC personnel assumed that, given the AFSC's post-war European experience, the organization had insights that would be useful for working sympathetically with Israel. In return Jews, meaning Israelis, would have a high level of trust for the AFSC. Pickett explained that the Quaker religious orientation and aspiration to work at higher levels of religious peacemaking were also part of the decision to participate in refugee relief:

> Also throughout most of 1948 we had been involved in Palestine on the level of negotiation. Back in February, a proposal had come to us from concerned persons: could any slight step even be taken toward stopping the cruel, destructive war that was raging in Palestine? Since Jerusalem was historically a great religious center for both Jews and Moslems, as well as for Christians, it was suggested that an appeal from religious leaders for at least a "Peace of God" in Jerusalem might be effective. Would Quakers assume leadership in such an effort?[2]

A posthumous biography of Pickett suggested another detail regarding his personal reputation:

> The trust that men felt toward him opened many doors to him. One evidence of this trust was the invitation he received in May 1948 from the United Nations to serve as "Mayor of Jerusalem." Jews and Arabs united in approving this request. It was almost the only thing on which the two groups did agree in the troubled year. Many years later, Clarence summarized the circumstances in these words: During the period between cessation of the British control of Palestine and the establishment of the government of Israel, there was a period where there was no real government in Palestine. The United Nations asked me if I would be willing to go over and assume the title of Mayor of Jerusalem.[3]

In sharp contrast, Quaker field worker Marshall Sutton expressed the rationale for the Friends' involvement more laconically, reflecting a lack of self-consciousness regarding the politics of AFSC's involvement:

> In December 1948 the Director of United Nations Relief for Palestine Refugees signed agreements with three international agencies to handle the distribution and field operations of the relief project for Arab refugees. Those agencies were the international committee of the Red Cross, the League of the Red Cross Societies and the American Friends Service committee. The operating agencies are responsible for the reception, warehousing and transportation to the destination and distribution points of the supplies which include clothing, food and medical necessities. The League of the Red Cross Societies is responsible

for refugees in Lebanon, Syria and Transjordan and Israel and the American Friends Service Committee for the Gaza area.[4]

In fact, the AFSC's involvement was as political as it was humanitarian, and was born as much of the need to salvage the organization from its failures as it was to provide refugee relief.

## RELIGIOUS DIPLOMACY AND THE ORIGINS OF AFSC INVOLVEMENT IN THE MIDDLE EAST

The initial involvement of the AFSC in the Middle East was a matter of religious diplomacy, not refugee relief. Jerusalem had posed a central problem for the United Nations as it contemplated the Palestine question in 1947 and 1948. In August 1947 the United Nations Special Commission on Palestine (UNSCOP) had recommended partition of Palestine into Arab and Jewish states with an international zone consisting of Jerusalem and its environs. In contrast, the minority report proposed a federal state with Arab and Jewish components and recommended that Jerusalem be divided into two separate municipalities.[5] Jerusalem's holy places, however, had long been subject to separate legal regimes that complicated further relations between Jews, Muslims, and Christians, and the potential division of the city.[6]

Throughout the Fall of 1947 the United Nations focused additional attention on the problem of Jerusalem that culminated in complex recommendations for a *corpus separatum* to place it under a United Nations Trusteeship Council that would appoint a Governor. These were part of United Nations Resolution 181, adopted by the General Assembly on November 29, 1947.[7] Working out the details of this plan would prove difficult, particularly as civil war broke out between the Arab and Jewish communities. Despite intensive diplomatic efforts, the appointment of a governor could not be scheduled until April 1948, at which point the political and strategic situations had changed dramatically.[8] Most Protestant denominations with representatives and institutions in Jerusalem had strongly opposed partition but the AFSC had publicly endorsed the November 29 Partition resolution, a stance that had caused deep shock and alienation among Palestine Arab Quakers, in particular, Khalil Totah.[9,10]

Though Pickett later implied that he was the first choice for the position of Governor, by then entitled Special Municipal Commissioner, in fact the United Nations first asked Percy Clarke, general manager of the

Barclays Bank in Jerusalem, to take the post. When Clarke declined, Pickett and his biographers stated that the position was offered to him. When he too declined, the well-known Philadelphia lawyer and AFSC member Harold Evans accepted. Curiously, Pablo de Azcárate, secretary of the United Nations Consular Truce Commission in Jerusalem, and deputy Municipal Commissioner, mentioned only Evans in his account of the affair, suggesting that neither Clarke's nor Pickett's nominations were of much significance.[11] Evans' appointment lasted all of six weeks before the escalating conflict made it impossible for him to exercise any authority. He returned to the United States in June and the position of Special Municipal Commissioner lapsed.

Quaker religious diplomacy was also proceeding on several different tracks. Early in 1948 the elderly Rufus Jones had been approached by Francis B. Sayre, then president of the United Nations Trusteeship Council, and was asked to organize an appeal to religious leaders in the West to be addressed to religious leaders in Palestine.[12] Jones and AFSC Executive Director Clarence Pickett then initiated a petition addressed to both Arabs and Jews and calling for an immediate "Truce of God" that would halt the fighting and preserve the sanctity of Jerusalem. In March 1948 the appeal was signed by a number of American churchmen and sent to Rabbi Isaac Herzog, Ashkenazi Chief Rabbi of the British Mandate of Palestine, and Amin Bey Abdul Hadi, head of the Supreme Muslim Council.[13] No response was received. At the same time, a small mission was dispatched by the AFSC and the British Religious Society of Friends to further investigate the possibility of Quaker facilitation of direct negotiations and toward a truce that would preserve Jerusalem from destruction. James Vail, an American chemical engineer, and Edgar B. Castle, undertook the assignment.

While Castle had been to the Middle East before World War II, and had expressed hostility toward Zionism in the years since, neither he nor Vail had any particular familiarity with the region nor experience with diplomacy, religious, or otherwise. Nevertheless, they traveled to Cairo, Beirut, Damascus, Amman, and Jerusalem for an intensive series of meetings with representatives of various organizations. Their reports indicate a diffuse series of discussions.[14]

In Beirut, Vail and Castle were told that rich Jews had fled Aleppo due to anti-Jewish and anti-American rioting but they noted that they were awaiting another "objective report" on the situation. In Jerusalem, which was under siege, they met a variety of Jews, including Abraham Bergman, Assistant to the Mandatory District Commissioner, whose view they characterized as seeming "less extreme than those of other more prominent Jews we were soon to meet." Regarding their meeting with Chief Rabbi Isaac Herzog, they noted, "being obliged to report that we found little understanding of the feeling of the Arabs that Jews are invaders from the West." Their naiveté was unintentionally revealed in the report on their discussions with Leo Cohen of the Jewish Agency. Cohen indicated that Jews would support a truce but he sought clarification whether this meant the two sides would refrain from shooting into or out of the city, and how the 2,000 Jews in the Old City would receive food.

Vail and Castle had no answers for Cohen. But their report from Cairo was more effusive, particularly regarding their meeting with Abdul Rahman Azzam Pasha, Secretary General of the Arab League. They judged that Azzam receiving them at his home was a sign of the "serious concern and respect with which he viewed our mission." Azzam was also able to "appreciate the ultimate spiritual objectives of our concern because of his own wide comprehension of the spiritual values involved in the Palestinian conflict for the whole world and for the Middle East in particular." Azzam welcomed Quaker services and assured Vail and Castle that the Holy Places could be secured, were it not for the Irgun and Haganah, the Jewish paramilitary forces. He also assured them that in a binational Palestine, Jews would have "full cultural autonomy and full civic rights on a democratic basis of proportional representation." He even agreed to accept Jewish immigration "if there was also full freedom of emigration."

A variety of other meetings impressed Vail and Castle with the direness of the situation and the need for Quaker action, particularly on the issues of refugee relief and the internationalization of Jerusalem. But a small and revealing comment noted that, when addressing other Quakers in Beirut and Ramallah, "some apprehension was felt regarding the possible misinterpretation of our impartial distribution of relief between Arab and Jew. Any help given to the Jews would be interpreted by Arabs as a pro-Jewish action and might react adversely on local Quaker social and education activity." Vail and Castle recommended that the Quakers dispatch a small contingent to help the International Committee of the Red Cross, and proposed to Azzam that he support a truce, which would help bring about "a new understanding of the moral qualities of Islam" and help it achieve "a strong position of moral leadership."

The Vail-Castle mission was as doomed as it was naïve. Writing in *The Spectator* in mid-May, Castle bravely pushed truces and internationalization, and touted Azzam's proposal of April 28 regarding a truce. He noted, however, that "If, at this juncture, the Jews were to demand access to the

Wailing Wall, it would be a pity, much as one has to sympathise with their desire, for this would introduce avoidable complications."[15] But at the same time that Azzam had been reassuring Vail and Castle, he was negotiating with Arab leaders and attempting to overcome disputes prior to a united invasion of Palestine. Preparations for war were accelerating in all Arab states.[16] Azzam had also issued his threat to the Jews regarding a "war of extermination and momentous massacre" a full six months before meeting the Quakers.[17] Like Rufus Jones' wartime meeting with Reinhard Heydrich's associates, Vail and Castle appear to have heard what they came to hear.

Events on the ground fast outstripped the ability of any party, much less the Quakers, to control them. The second wave of Palestine Arab flight was well underway in advance of the British withdrawal and the creation of Israel. Israel declared independence on May 14 and was invaded by Arab armies the next day. A truce that had been arranged on May 2 collapsed on May 15, and it would not be until June 11 that United Nations mediator Folke Bernadotte was able to arrange another. Quaker intervention had failed utterly. But in June 1948, Rufus Jones died, leaving Clarence Pickett as the most famous American Quaker and fully in charge of the AFSC. This was to be a fateful turn.

The AFSC's religious diplomacy in 1948 and decision to participate in refugee relief must also be placed in the larger context of interdenominational Protestant politics in the aftermath of the Holocaust, and the broader influence of Protestant clergy, especially missionaries, on the course of American foreign policy. A few mainstream American Protestant leaders like Reinhold Niebuhr were favorable toward Zionism and the creation of Israel, in contrast to Roman Catholics who were vigorously opposed.[18] But as noted earlier, those liberal American Protestant denominations with connections and institutions in the Holy Land and Jerusalem were also opposed to Israel.[19]

For the Anglicans, the partition of Palestine was a theological and practical calamity. Their theology was firmly based on the idea that Judaism had been superseded and that Christians, particularly Anglicans and Episcopalians, comprised the "true Israelites" who would lead the redemption of the Holy Land in the name of Christianity. Anglican theology was rife with anti-Semitism, and regarded Judaism as a barbaric, antiquated, and inferior faith, while Zionism was seen as materialistic, hyper-nationalist, and vaguely Bolshevik. The Holy Land in general, and Jerusalem specifically, were regarded as unique spaces imbued with sanctity that should be dominated by no faith or denomination, although Anglicans, by virtue of their higher creed and universalist calling, were in the position to lead and guide others. Any division of Palestine was fundamentally unnatural, particularly if it benefited the Jews. This was a view shared by Western oil companies, the US State Department and the Central Intelligence Agency, many of whose personnel came from Protestant missionary backgrounds.[20]

Having been at the forefront of relief efforts for Armenian Christians before World War I and during the 1915 genocide and thereafter, Anglicans, as well as Congregationalists, who had built many of the American Protestant institutions in the Middle East, saw ominous parallels with the fate of Palestine Arab refugees. Anglicans also saw the church institutions and congregations they had carefully built in Palestine under British imperial control, and their nominal leadership of Palestinian Christianity, threatened by the political upheaval being forced on them, in their view, by the Jews.[21]

As an historic peace church, however, the Quakers and by extension the AFSC, were placed in a difficult situation by events in the Middle East. Quakers were fundamentally different from Anglicans, Episcopalians, and Congregationalists with respect to elements of Christian theology, such as the inerrant nature of Scripture, sacraments, and the need for clergy. But they shared theological assumptions regarding Jews and Judaism with other Protestant denominations, such as supersessionism and millenarianism. The fundamental Quaker notion of the "inner light," where the individual's conscience was guided by the presence of God within, also held collectivist and exclusionary ideologies such as nationalism in disdain.

At the same time, the AFSC's wartime experiences had indeed given them a unique relationship with American, and in a different way, European Jews and Jewish institutions. The organization had also endorsed the 1947 Partition of Palestine, a move that was well-received by most American Jewish organizations but one that put them at odds with other Protestants and with Quakers in Palestine. Squaring this circle would not be easy.

The AFSC had begun to assume a prominent voice in the American Protestant community, thanks both to their long work at refugee relief and rehabilitation and specific efforts during and after World War II to shape public and Protestant opinion. Among other things, the necessity to participate in the debate over the Middle East that was raging in American Protestant circles, and a quiet need for the leadership to try and compensate for the multiple failures of early 1948, appear to have driven the AFSC toward deeper involvement in Palestine Arab refugee relief.

## AFSC AND PALESTINE ARAB REFUGEE RELIEF, SUMMER 1948

After the AFSC's failures with the "Truce of God," the Evans' Municipal Commissionership of Jerusalem, and the Vail-Castle mission, the invitation in the late summer of 1948 to participate in Palestine Arab refugee relief came at an auspicious time. The AFSC's correspondence shows that the involvement grew from an informal response on the part of voluntary church-based groups to an international and multi-national effort.

Feelers regarding Quaker involvement in refugee relief began among church-based groups during the summer of 1948. On July 28, Paul Sturge of the British Friends Service Council in London wrote to Colin Bell, director of the AFSC's foreign section in the Philadelphia headquarters, and indicated that the Church World Service, an American cooperative group of denominations founded in 1946, had been in communication regarding refugee relief. Their funds, however, were only available to Christians "which is a limitation which we should find it very difficult to accept."[22] But Sturge added "if the efforts to begin a permanent settlement are successful and active hostilities are really over, there may be a considerable job in relation to Arab refugees in particular. Any work of this kind would still be open to the objection that it would be one-sided, and yet it would be a great pity it an opportunity to counteract some of the bitterness there is on the Arab side were missed."

Sturge believed that the opportunities for relief work would be among the Arabs, but on September 1, 1948 Colin Bell wrote to A. Willard Jones, former head of the Friends Boys' School in Ramallah, to relate that the Executive Committee of the AFSC's Foreign Service Section had received a suggestion from the United Nations, specifically Disaster Relief Program head Raphael Cilento, that it "might serve in the care of refugees within Israel or in the resettlement of expatriated persons in Israel."[23] Cilento had been dispatched by the United Nations in early August to survey the refugee situation and immediately pronounced the problem to be "a disaster comparable to an earthquake, flood or tidal wave." Cilento added that the Palestine Arab refugee problem had "reached the magnitude of the Jewish displaced persons problem in Europe."[24] He estimated the number of refugees at a minimum of 250,000 and possibly as high as 330,000.

Bell also welcomed Cilento's proposal that the AFSC send a small team to help with the resettlement "of some 25,000 destitute Arabs who may not leave Israeli territory and for whom all the help of friends is denied.

Working thus for Arabs and in close contact with Israelis we would hope at least to demonstrate an impartial concern for men as men." With typical Quaker understatement that mixed the spiritual with the practical, Bell added that the "Jews have their desperate needs also but they are of the spirit and as usual in such cases their poverty is not recognizable to themselves." Bell went on to ask Jones for help finding personnel, specifically, "a man who has drive, initiative, organizing ability, and also the infinite tact and gentleness of spirit to meet those who cannot look at any situation with objectivity, whose mental eyes are bloodshot."

Bell immediately set to work planning a relief operation in Israel. On August 24, he wrote to Paul Sturge of the British Friends Service Council in London regarding the project and proposed a joint team of six or seven members. Leadership, however, was a problem. The individuals Bell had in mind either possessed the Quakerly spirit but had no practical relief experience, or the reverse. He noted that one individual was a "full of vigor and relief '"no-how" [*sic*] but we feel he lacks something in sensitivity and an awareness of the necessity for a very delicate approach to Oriental minds which are aflame with prejudice and bitterness."[25]

Sturge's response to Bell is not preserved, but a letter of August 25 from Bernard Lawson, Acting Secretary of the Palestine Emergency Board of the British Friends Service Council, added a number of details. Much of his letter appears shaped by the ill-fated Vail-Castle mission and the "Truce of God" failure. He commented politely "We have noted with interest the tentative approach to Clarence Pickett from the United Nations, and I think that is just the kind of service many of us here are feeling after, rather a straight-forward piece of relief work to one side or the other. However, other Friends here feel strongly that we ought to take up the latter, and we have now called a committee for Wednesday afternoon of next week."[26] Lawson's letter plainly suggests British Friends were relieved at the prospect of returning to relief work and had been uncomfortable with Pickett's high profile religious diplomacy.

Bell's letters are significant in several ways. They show that the AFSC first became involved with refugee relief within Israel, not Gaza, and on a small scale only. Pickett's official history elides this completely. Bell also explicitly stated that the goals of the Israel operation would be the resettlement of Arab refugees and that the effort would in effect be a demonstration project in religious diplomacy but along the more familiar lines of refugee relief. The task would require exemplary leadership and Quakerly values, an issue that would come back repeatedly in the future. The Jews, though in need, would have to fend for themselves.[27] The AFSC's return to refugee relief was very much an effort to extend religious diplomacy, which had failed so badly earlier in 1948, but through the means of refugee relief on a manageable scale. British Friends were equally anxious to participate in traditional relief operations but were also looking ahead toward serving Arab refugees in an effort to reduce their "bitterness." Of all AFSC personnel, Bell appears to have been the one most concerned with conducting operations in Israel on their own merits and as a sign of even-handedness.

By late September, a draft proposal for AFSC relief work was ready. The document put the best possible face on matters and took the moral high ground by stating "It has been customary to expect that American and British Quakers would send relief teams, together with supplies, to areas of emergency need throughout the world. Accordingly, when the relief needs in Palestine became acute, there was heavy pressure upon the American Friends Service Committee to join in a coordinated relief campaign under the general aegis of the United Nations relief plan."[28] Raphael Cilento's polite suggestion to the Friends had now become "heavy pressure."

Hard-nosed qualifications emerged quickly. The AFSC lacked money and personnel to embark on its own relief project, and more importantly, "Quakers have always wished to combine with their relief operations the opportunity of creating a reconciliatory atmosphere; and in positions of great human tension, to work impartially for all." But impartiality notwithstanding, "it was patent that in the present Palestine situation physical needs were almost entirely upon the Arab side and that such needs as existed in Israel, the Israelis themselves would wish to take care of." Thus, in the space of only weeks, the original thrust of the program was changed, away from working in Israel with Arabs to working outside of Israel, albeit in unspecified locations.

The document went on to present the Vail-Castle mission and the Evans appointment as "High Commissioner" as "exploratory efforts," downplaying the failure of both and implying these were logically connected to the refugee relief effort. But the proposal then discussed Cilento's suggestion that a small Quaker team should address Arab needs within Israel in unenthusiastic terms, noting "Unless the Government of Israel is really convinced that a Quaker team would have some usefulness and unless they could issue a whole-hearted approval of the project, it would be quite impossible of fulfillment. The Quakers are not anxious to thrust themselves into places where they are not wanted."

The inconsistencies within the proposal are not easily explained except in terms of an emerging tension between what seemed the preferred way to participate and the concrete possibility that had thus far been suggested to them. The document reads more as a solicitation for a better proposal than a proposal in itself. It is also unclear to whom the AFSC proposal was circulated, although it may be suspected that the United Nations and the US State Department were likely targets.

The thrust of AFSC thinking in September and October of 1948 appears to have been to move away from the original Cilento suggestion and toward working with Palestine Arab refugees somewhere outside of Israel. Andrew Cordier's overture to Clarence Pickett in mid-October was thus likely as welcomed as it was passively prearranged.

The question of working in Israel would be a constant thorn in the side of the AFSC. Another letter from outside the organization pointed to the political attitudes toward Israel of Quakers already involved in Palestine. These would continue to haunt the AFSC's missions with Palestine Arab refugees and throughout the Arab world. Mildred E. White of the American Friends Board of Missions was active in Palestine from 1922 until 1954 and had been the supervisor of six village day schools in the Ramallah vicinity and then principal of the Friends Girl School. Speaking of this work, the 1920 Nebraska Yearly Meeting of Friends noted "These schools are a most efficient evangelizing agency" with the goal of making "the Palestine of tomorrow Christian by giving Christian education to the boys and girls of today."[29] But writing on December 2, 1948 to Colin Bell in her capacity as Education Secretary of the American Friends Board of Missions, she had pointed comments on the problems the AFSC was about to face:

> There is a <u>spiritual</u> danger involved—that of giving either side the mistaken impression that American Friends are trying to help grind some political axe or another. The mission [the Friends Girl School] has been close to this raw problem since its very beginning. During the Arab Rebellion in 1936–39, it was hard to make the Arabs understand why we pacifist Quakers could not contribute to their patriotic "cause" from school funds. At the same time the mission was under pressure from the English military to allow our buildings to be commandeered for use as barracks for English soldiers coming to Palestine to crush the Rebellion. This, too, was unthinkable for a Quaker mission.[30]

White also warned further that "Friends workers inside Israel are going into a more delicate and difficult situation. If they escape suspicion on the part of the Arabs that they are working for the Zionist state, they are likely to incur the fanatical enmity of the Jewish terrorists." As will be shown, the AFSC's Israel operation was to be a continual source of consternation for some AFSC personnel. White ended her letter on a note of condescension. Though she had strongly advocated for the devolution of control of Quaker educational efforts to Arab Quakers she commented "The small Christian minority in Palestine is in a dreadful situation, physically, and what is more dreadful, spiritually."

White's comments regarding Israel were significant. Her suspicions of Jewish "fanatical enmity" and Castle's outright anti-Zionism situate a considerable swath of American and British Quaker opinion decidedly against Israel, if not against Jews. This animus is rarely glimpsed in the AFSC's public statements. Still, in the interest of fairness and balance, Bell proceeded with a small program inside Israel. The bulk of the Quaker effort, however, would be devoted to the Palestine Arab refugees.

A rising sense of urgency, if not outright panic, over the fate of the refugees was beginning to grip Western governments in the Fall of 1948. On October 17, James McDonald, the Special Representative of the United States in Israel, and later Ambassador to Israel, wrote to President Harry Truman and claimed that the

> Arab refugee tragedy is rapidly reaching catastrophic proportions and should be treated as a disaster. Present and prospective relief are utterly inadequate. UN administrative machine is both inappropriate and inadequate and result in gross inefficient and wastefulness. (All adjective used above are realistically descriptive and are written out of fifteen years of personal contact with refugee problems.)
>
> Of approximately 400,000 refugees approaching winter with cold heavy rains will, it is estimated, kill more than 100,000 old men, women and children who are shelterless and have little or no food. Situation requires some comprehensive program and immediate action that dramatic and overwhelming calamities such as vast flood or earthquake would invoke. Nothing less with avert horrifying losses.[31]

McDonald went on to criticize the United Nations Disaster Relief Program, and the responses of United Nations mediator Folke Bernadotte as completely inadequate and proposed that all relief operations, including fundraising, be transferred to the International Red Cross. In a November 10 letter to the Acting Secretary of State, McDonald reiterated that Cilento's "scant refugee organization" was inadequate and that the rumored turnover of refugee relief to the Red Cross was good news. But he added prophetically, "I am completely skeptical UN blanket financial appear to member states whose responses would be slow and inadequate."[32] These fears would come to pass in the creation of UNRPR and UNRWA.

There was also rising distress and anger in American Protestant circles regarding the situation in Jerusalem, and about the plight of the Palestine Arab refugees. Anglicans and, as has been shown, Quakers, had many local institutions as well as personal connections and continued to signal about the impending refugee disaster. These were signals that the AFSC could not ignore, particularly as other religions and denominations began their own relief efforts.

In early October, twenty American organizations, Jewish and Christian, and a variety of major American corporations including oil companies, held a series of meetings to "consider acting together to provide food and other help for the estimated 360,000 Arabs and Jews who have been left homeless and in need by the fighting in Palestine."[33] The US State Department's Advisory Committee on Voluntary Foreign Aid, under the direction of acting chairman William L. Batt, had assembled the group in New York for discussions. The United Nations Children's Fund also offered aid,[34] and a papal encyclical at the end of October offered prayers for peace, and focused the attention of Catholics on the refugee situation.[35]

On October 28, 1948 the "Appeal for Holy Land Refugees" was launched by a group of five Christian voluntary organizations. A press release cited Count Folke Bernadotte's August plea for aid, saying "The choice is between saving the lives of many thousands of people now or permitting them to die."[36]

Also in October 1948, Rev. Dr. Walter C. Klein of St. George's Cathedral of Jerusalem, wrote an impassioned piece in *The Living Church*. With a unique blend of unselfconscious self-pity he warned:

> Worse than the weakened body are the disenchanted spirit and the baffled mind. The Middle East has lost its faith in us and does not know what to think of us. Try it yourself. Grow up believing in the generosity and good-will of the Occidental nations, especially Great Britain and the United States. Go to your village church every Sunday with the fortifying conviction that if your religion, the legacy of martyrs, is ever threatened the Christian powers will rush to your assistance. Then see your priests killed, your churches shelled, your house blown up or looted, and your family reduced to a ragged and hungry life in some refugee camp. Reflect all this is traceable to a decision made by your former protectors and preceptors. Or, if you are a Moslem, skip the religious aspect of it and see whether the spectacle of your country's misery increased your affection for the West. The American people must now reckon with the fact that their policy has brought the Palestinian Arabs to the brink of irreparable ruin.[37]

Klein added ominously "There are thousands of Arabs who cannot survive this winter without the aid that the United States alone can give." The "American Appeal for Holy Land Refugees" and other small-scale efforts coordinated by the Advisory Committee on Voluntary Foreign Aid appear to have begun relief work quickly but organized aid for the Palestine Arab refugees from the Anglican and Episcopal churches would take another year to materialize.

Given that overtures had been made to AFSC in August, it nevertheless took several months for the organization to commit itself, during which time cries regarding the plight of the refugees intensified, along with international diplomatic efforts. For one thing the internationalization of Jerusalem proposed under the 1947 Partition resolution was first discarded and then, after the assassination of Count Folke Bernadotte, reinstated and adopted by the United Nations.[38]

But the AFSC's decision to become involved in refugee relief was not up to Bell or Pickett alone. A decision of this magnitude would have to be taken by the organization's Foreign Service Executive Committee. The committee met in Philadelphia on November 17, 1948 and was chaired by James Vail. The minutes of the meeting noted that after a moment of silence, Colin Bell, who would become program manager for operations in Israel and Gaza, read a memo that expressed considerable trepidation about AFSC's participation:

> The United Nations enquiry whether Quakers would undertake a large-scale relief program in the Palestine area brings the AFSC face to face with a challenge larger and more fraught with political implications than it has yet had to face. Acceptance will strain our resources of personnel and administrative capacity to the utmost. We take the risk of failure which will be a public failure, and even if we have some success we shall certainly not satisfy everyone. We cannot avoid censure from some quarters in a scene where 'sweet reasonableness' is utterly lacking. We shall be in a world limelight, and we will have to face some compromises away from our traditional ways of working. On the other hand, refusal would be a grave decision. Success in Palestine is a vital necessity for the power of the UN. The opportunity to demonstrate the power of the non-violent approach is enormous. The political people have turned to us because they believe we have something more to offer than merely a politically neutral position.[39]

Bell's memo then listed a series of stipulations, the "Nineteen Points," which would condition AFSC's involvement:

1. Our identity and autonomy must be preserved. All concerned must understand that we are not acting as an agency of U.N., but as a private agency at the Invitation of U.N. and drawing upon U.N. monetary and other support. Such action does not identify us with any political decision taken by U.N. in respect of Palestine.

2. We understand that the U.N. Director of Relief will coordinate the total relief program throughout the several areas and will be concerned with over all allocations of money and supplies, It is essential that the U.N. Director be a person who is happy to entrust to us the direction of affairs in the field and who is sympathetic to our viewpoint.

3. While we realize that the invitation of U.N. has to be directed to an organization such as A.F.S.C. it should be made clear that A.F.S.C. may recruit Quakers or sympathetic non-Quakers who may not necessarily be Americans.

4. We would be prepared to administer the emergency relief program where the need seems greatest within the territorial limits of Palestine.

5. We would aim to organize an administration here and a force of 20 workers in the field by January 1, 1949. Future workers, if available, might be added later.

6. We would expect to operate in the field until August 1949 and thereabouts, depending upon the need and the availability of resources.

7. The nature of our activities would be that of emergency relief— attempting to preserve life and health and provide shelter for those whose destitution arises from the present troubles, without any discrimination except that of human need.

8. We would not be prepared to undertake this minimum service of relief unless we could be assured that a solution to the vital problem of resettlement is being vigorously sought by U.N., and all others vitally concerned.

9. We must be assured of a specific welcome, as opposed to mere toleration, by the authorities of Israel and Arab Palestine; and of preparedness to trust us absolutely so far as our non-political position is concerned—and we would ask the authorities to make appropriate publicity to this effect within the two territories.

10. We would require the authorities of both territories to recognize the necessity of giving complete freedom of movement and communication across frontiers and within the entire Palestine area to all Quaker representatives. Without this freedom the relief program would require far more personnel than we can produce. We would guarantee the neutrality of our representatives who would be in possession of a "Quaker passport."

11.    We would expect to employ or use the services of persons already in Palestine; we would not expect the same freedom of movement; or communication to be necessarily applicable to these persons as must be granted to workers sent out by us.

12.    We would be desirous of coordinating our efforts very closely with the body operating the relief program in surrounding areas and of arriving at a flexible and harmonious working agreement with that body.

13.    We would require to establish harmonious relations with and the active assistance of other indigenous and foreign agencies now in the field. In particular, we would consider it necessary to send at once a Quaker representative to meet with relief committees at Beirut and elsewhere, insofar as those committees are concerned with relief operations in the Palestine areas.

14.    We would not be prepared to depart from the traditional Quaker method of recruiting on a voluntary basis for our own representatives in the field, i.e. they will be maintained and if necessary granted dependency allowances but will not be paid salaries.

15.    It is our understanding that U.N. will handle all monetary appropriations for supplies, will purchase, insure, and ship all supplies and will hand shipping documents to us to enable us to take delivery at ports of discharge. We would require that U.N. arrange all clearances regarding freedom from import duty and removal of any barriers to movement from ports either inside or outside the Palestine area.

16.    We would hope that authorities on both side will allow freedom of entry and of movement of relief supplies through the entire Palestine area, regardless of the point of ultimate use.

17.    Adequate transport being vital to a bulk relief program we would need assurances from U.N. and from authorities—in any way connected with the Palestine areas that transport (particularly road) will be available, also fuel. We could not undertake at this time to begin the organization of a transport system. We shall not wish to use armed protection on for relief supply convoys or for personnel.

18.    We will use the accounting systems, controls, and methods of reporting which we have found effective in the past. We are unable to set up a complex administrative structure on an unfamiliar pattern. All accounts would be open to inspection at any time. Our ability to produce reports, statistics, etc. from the field will be very limited.

19.    We require to use U.N. funds for administrative expenses both inside and outside Palestine. We wish UN to agree to our presenting at appropriate periods a statement of expenses incurred for reimbursement by UN. We in turn will guarantee to hold such expenses down to a minimum consistent with efficiency; in our experience, this should not exceed 10% of total cost of program.[40]

The remainder of the minutes detail committee members' concerns about securing personnel for the mission and the possibility that they might have to be drawn from other AFSC projects, and the potential relationship with the United Nations and other relief agencies. As James Vail put it, the mission would require "in the individuals involved, an extraordinary degree of charity."

Bell's cautious statement to the AFSC and the Nineteen Points are critical elements for understanding the organization's motivations for becoming involved in Gaza, its methods of operation, and its self-image. At the outset it is strange to note that Bell regarded working in the Middle East as the most challenging situation yet faced by AFSC, as opposed to working under Nazi occupation during the early years of World War II. Bell clearly articulated the fact that the AFSC would be working in the "world limelight" and expressed a fear of failure, and a public one at that. The AFSC's abortive involvement in both the "Truce of God" and the Municipal Commissioner for Jerusalem are not mentioned but must have been on the minds of all participants, including James Vail. However, Bell judged it imperative to demonstrate "the power of the non-violent approach," as opposed to that of the "political people." A religious imperative appears to have been at work, which is ultimately indistinguishable from a political imperative.

Yet the Nineteen Points themselves were a political if not a frankly contractual document. They were designed to preserve maximum operational flexibility for AFSC, with minimal oversight by the United Nations, but at the same time demanded that the United Nations facilitate any and all funding and operational requirements. They display confidence in the AFSC's considerable operational experience and sophistication, detailing matters such as import duties, transportation, and accounting systems to the responsibility of United Nations'. But the Nineteen Points also demanded that a political settlement be "vigorously" sought, or as it puts it "a solution to the problem of resettlement." The Nineteen Points even demanded that AFSC operations be "welcomed rather than merely tolerated" by its hosts. These demands were remarkably specific and intrusive, and speak to the AFSC's high level of self-confidence not only in their own abilities but in their anticipated reception as well as the high level of risk they perceived for the operation as a whole. How AFSC would have responded had the United Nations not agreed to these points is unknown. Though a quorum of the Foreign Service Executive Committee was not present, it was recommended that the AFSC accept the United Nations' invitation saying "we are not able in clear conscience to decline to serve."

A letter from Elmore Jackson to Clarence Pickett reveals some of the complex negotiations behind AFSC's participation and includes details not represented in Pickett's own or other later accounts. In fact, United Nations' officials including Cordier were initially convinced that AFSC should take control over relief efforts in "all of Palestine," presumably meaning the West Bank, and there was discomfort regarding ICRC and LRCS involvement. The first director of UNRPR was US Ambassador to Egypt, Stanton Griffis, who had been detached from diplomatic duty for the project. He was especially uncomfortable about the likelihood that LRCS would have to work through local Red Crescent Societies.[41] The letter also reveals the involvement of Dr. Bayard Dodge, an Islamic scholar, recently retired as president of the American University of Beirut, in the negotiations. Dodge would become involved in the refugee relief issue again in quite different ways.

Nor was the ICRC held in especially high regard. When informed that the ICRC had accepted the invitation to participate in relief efforts, Brigadier Reginald H. Parminter, a retired British quartermaster previously employed by the United Nations Relief and Rehabilitation Administration, simply said "damn." The United Nations ultimately proposed that the AFSC take over responsibility for Arab refugees in the Gaza Strip, by then controlled by Egypt, and a much smaller number in Acre. Other organizations would be asked to provide relief elsewhere. In Jackson's view the Gaza Strip was ideal for the AFSC since it was "a small compact area or but one in which it will take, not numbers, but an integrity and obviously non-political group to get the work done."

The Nineteen Points were agreed to by the AFSC and by UNRPR Director Griffis. United Nations Secretary General Trygve Lie then issued the formal invitation to the AFSC on December 7. The creation of UNRPR and the agreement with AFSC, ICRC, and LRCS was noted only in passing by world media. The *Manchester Guardian* story ran on page six while the *New York Times* ran the story on page seven.[42]

In his memoir, Howard Wriggins, AFSC's Gaza liaison to UNRPR, added a telling detail regarding his own attitudes toward the conflict. Wriggins was an unusual figure, a conscientious objector who had worked with AFSC missions during World War II in Spain, Portugal, France, and North Africa. He later became Professor of International Relations

**Figure 3.1**  Signing the agreement to create UNRPR. From left Paul Rüegger, president of the International Committee of the Red Cross, Ambassador Stanton Griffis, Elmore Jackson of the AFSC, and M. B. de Rougé, Secretary General of the League of Red Cross Societies.
*Source*: Courtesy of the American Friends Service Committee.

at Columbia University, but also served as a staff member at the National Security Council in 1966 and 1967, through the Six Day War, and eventually was appointed US Ambassador to Sri Lanka and the Maldives. Wriggins had been invited to participate in the Gaza mission by Elmore Jackson and accepted, despite the fact that he had only recently returned to graduate school and was newly married:

> On the one hand, especially for one with some experience of the Middle East, the plight of the Palestinian refugees could well be imagined. The victory of Israeli armies could not conceal of the human cost to those who had fled the fighting. To many of Hitler's victims and those of us working with them in the early 1940s, Palestine seemed a place of refuge. Now the Palestinian refugees were, in one sense, the victims' victims and deserved our attention. The human need was so obvious, how could I deny the AFSC the Quaker humanitarian concern that had inspired me during World War II?[43]

It is difficult to ascertain how pervasive the idea that World War II's victims, the Jews, had turned into the victimizers, was among AFSC personnel. As will be suggested below, it was clearly evident among certain staff members, who complained that Jews were acting in a less than Quakerly manner, but a larger, historical sense of disappointment in Jews is more frequently expressed in documents relating to religious diplomacy. It is also difficult to ascertain how much their sense of disappointment was influenced by theological anti-Semitism and to what extent it shaped the larger AFSC mission and decision-making.

AFSC quickly found staffing for the Palestine relief mission in its usual ways, drawing on the international network of Quakers who had volunteered previously or who were actively engaged in other AFSC projects, including Poland and India-Pakistan, as well as various Friends committees throughout the United States. Jackson's December 5 letter to Pickett and Read had listed a number of names and indicated that contacts would be made with Friends committees in Great Britain, Scandinavia, South Africa, and Canada.[44] The main AFSC office in Philadelphia managed recruitment of American volunteers while doctors and nurses were recruited in Geneva by Howard Wriggins.[45]

Many volunteers were drawn to the work out of religious convictions and social and pacifist idealism. A smaller cadre of volunteers, however, had either some military experience or had participated in the Civilian Public Service (CPS) program during World War II. The CPS had been established to provide Conscientious Objectors with alternatives to military service. Participants were sent to work camps around the United States and built roads, irrigation projects, fought forest fires, and were engaged generally in building and maintaining infrastructure. Their skill levels, motivation, and problem-solving abilities appear to have been higher than those of other volunteers.

To judge from the AFSC's oral history of the Gaza Unit, as it became known, the attitudes of some of these somewhat older volunteers were more realistic, even cynical, than those who had lacked wartime experience.[46] As volunteer David Walker, a US military veteran and later an avowed pacifist, who went to Gaza with his wife Della, put it, "I don't think that many of the people who were on the team were prepared for this kind of chaos."[47] The leading role of CPS veterans in the Gaza operation was also consistent with Pickett's desire to professionalize AFSC personnel.

Colin Bell also approached Paul Sturge of the British Friends regarding personnel. After a discussion of possible participants Bell added, almost hopefully:

The American report of the refugee circumstances found in the New York Times mentioned that 500,000 Jewish refugees would have to be helped to immigrant [sic] from Arab nations. Though I should have thought this was a wild exaggeration it follows somewhat on my suggestion that may be there is some work for Quakers to do among Jews in Arab Lands. One begins to wonder whether a final solution to this tragic business might not be the exchange of Jewish population in North Africa with Arab refugees in Palestine.[48]

Bell's comment would come to pass, at least with regard to Jewish refugees, but the AFSC would not be involved. The possibility of the AFSC facilitating the resettlement of Palestine Arab refugees in North Africa, however, would resurface much later.

## INSTITUTIONALIZING PALESTINE ARAB RELIEF

In the summer of 1948 it became clear that the Palestine Arab refugee problem was growing rapidly and by the Fall it appeared to informed observers such as Raphael Cilento and James McDonald that the crisis was catastrophic and had potential for massive starvation, disease, and death. The initial proposal from the United Nations and the United States was for the International Committee of the Red Cross to take over all aspects of relief. By November, however, it had become apparent that the scale of the problem was such that a number of organizations, including the AFSC, would have to become involved. The other organizations involved in the relief effort highlight the approach and success of the AFSC, and point to the complex political situation and motives driving different parties.

The Geneva-based International Committee of the Red Cross (ICRC) was initially requested to take responsibility for Arab refugees in Israel and in the Jordanian-occupied areas, that is, the West Bank. Though the ICRC had long been involved in helping prisoners of war, tracing displaced persons and refugees, and providing medical aid, it had little experience in large-scale relief.[49] The practical and political implications of refugee relief were a challenge for an organization that has been described as "the cutting edge of impartiality...an expression of all that is finest among middle-aged, middle-class, middle-of-the-road Swiss males."[50]

The ICRC had originally become involved in Palestine in 1945 at the request of Zionist organizations protesting deportation of Palestinian Jews by the British Mandatory authorities to Eritrea. This was a far cry, however, from large-scale refugee relief operations. In her book on the ICRC, Junod argued that the ICRC's involvement in Palestine refugee relief was the product, in part, of the ICRC's political need for a mission at a time when the organization's failings in World War II were becoming well known and were imperiling its continued existence.[51] The Soviet Union, in particular, argued that the organization should be abolished and replaced by the League of Red Cross Societies (LRCS) that comprised national Red Cross groups. Junod also argued that the ongoing negotiations in Geneva on what would become the First through Fourth Geneva Conventions, signed in 1949, might also have prompted the ICRC's involvement. Beginning in early 1947, the ICRC sought a mediation role, but later that year was courted by the British to take over as provider of medical services for Palestinian Arabs, a role in which the ICRC was less interested. However, the outbreak of international war between Arab states and Israel made ICRC involvement unavoidable.[52]

The ICRC's involvement in field relief for Palestine refugees was a wholly new undertaking, one for which the organization was unprepared. The memoir of their field director attests to just how woefully unprepared they were, to the point of personnel being unfamiliar with either the languages or geography of the region.[53] Some of their difficulties with practical dimensions of relief operations will be discussed below and arguably had an influence on shaping the future of Palestine Arab refugee relief through UNRWA. Still, the Palestine experience helped ICRC survive in a difficult period, and emerge strengthened.

In contrast to the ICRC, the role of the LRCS in Palestine Arab refugee relief has not been well-studied. The LRCS was asked by the United Nations to take over responsibility for the widely dispersed refugees in Lebanon, Syria, Transjordan proper, Egypt and Iraq. By 1950 the League was a federation of 65 national Red Cross societies with some 100 million members worldwide.[54] The "relief bureaus" of the LRCS had experience in purchasing and shipping relief supplies to local societies, but not in actual field operations. The same was true of its nursing and health units that had previously acted in coordinating roles. Interestingly, the LRCS's experiences in Palestine are barely mentioned in its various histories.[55]

One of the ways in which the organization became involved was through W. de St. Aubin, a delegate of the League of Red Cross Societies. St. Aubin was attached to the United Nations in 1948 and 1949, first under UN mediators Count Folke Bernadotte and Ralph Bunche, and then as Director of the UN Disaster Relief Project in September 1948. St. Aubin had produced an important estimate of the number of refugees in August 1948, some 300,000, but revised it to one million in July of the next year.[56] The participation of Red Crescent societies in the LRSC effort might have been intended to facilitate the delivery of aid in Arab countries.

The ICRC and other organizations during World War II had faced a terrifying problem; speaking out regarding Nazi atrocities against Jews would have jeopardized access to other populations. The projection of neutrality and discretion were critical. Similar issues had arisen during earlier conflicts but never to the extent they did during World War II. The ICRC responded by maximizing confidentiality and issuing reports only to the host government rather than going public. This ethical issue of maintaining access in order to provide aid while simultaneously becoming effectively complicit in suppression of information remains a vexing one for NGOs, along with the problem of maintaining political neutrality.

In addition to the relief organizations, the United Nations' system was also expanding to address the political situation that had produced the refugee crisis. Shortly after the AFSC agreed to participate in the Gaza relief mission, the United Nations also established the Conciliation Commission for Palestine to continue the efforts of the Mediator, a position that had been established in May of 1948, and to carry out a variety of functions at the direction of the Security Council and the General Assembly, including the creation of subsidiary bodies.[57] The Conciliation Commission and its offshoot, the Economic Survey Mission, would become mechanisms for the UN to become ever more deeply enmeshed in facilitating peace between Israel and the Arab states, and for planning, if not executing, regional development and refugee relief. Most significant, however, was the clause in the Conciliation Commission's founding resolution 194 that stated:

> the refugees wishing to return to their homes and live at peace with their neighbours should be permitted to do so at the earliest practicable date, and that compensation should be paid for the property of those choosing not to return and for loss of or damage to property which, under principles of international law or in equity, should be made good by the Governments or authorities responsible; Instructs the Conciliation Commission to facilitate the repatriation, resettlement and economic and social rehabilitation of the refugees and the payment of compensation, and to maintain close relations with the Director of the United Nations Relief for Palestine Refugees and, through him, with the appropriate organs and agencies of the United Nations.[58]

The varying definitions of repatriation, resettlement, and in particular the vague term "rehabilitation" would become critical in the following years.

The structure of UNRPR was unique. In strong contrast to UNRWA only a year-and-a-half later, UNRPR was to be a nonoperational agency tasked only with securing funding and facilitating aid agencies' work on the ground with the host governments. UNPRP's staffing was extremely limited; a total of fifty staff members including eighteen locals.[59] United Nations Resolution 212 (III) of November 19, 1948 estimated that US $29,500,000 "will be required to provide relief for 500,000 refugees for a period of nine months from 1 December 1948 to 31 August 1949, and that an additional amount of approximately $2,500,000 will be required for administrative and local operational expenses."[60]

Five million dollars was advanced from the United Nations' "Working Capital Fund", reserve funds belonging to member states and still under their control, to start the project and all member states were urged to make voluntary contributions. On December 7, President Harry Truman announced that we would ask the US Congress to appropriate "up to $16,000,000 for aid to refugees from the Palestine fighting, the sum being about 50 percent of the total wanted from members of the United Nations."[61] This signaled the beginning of what would become UNRPR's perpetual financial crisis. Even with the British contribution of £900,000, equivalent to approximately $3,600,000, Stanton Griffis "emphasized that the small budget would permit only minimal care for refugees and that efforts would be concentrated on providing blankets and food."[62]

But the number of refugees to be provided for continued to grow. In December 1948, the three aid organizations, AFSC, ICRC, and LRCS, were each assigned approximately 200,000 refugees, and by the time all were in the field in January, the numbers of individuals applying for relief totaled 963,000. AFSC found itself with 260,000 applicants for aid.[63] The numbers of refugees, and the question of precisely who was to be provided with aid, were the most significant problems faced by UNRPR and then UNRWA. Defining refugees also remains one of the most intractable problems in the Arab-Israeli conflict today.

## HOW MANY REFUGEES?

The question of how many Palestine Arabs became refugees—and the very definition of refugee—continues to reverberate deeply today. Indeed, to use the term "refugee" at all in connection with Palestinians is to make a specific political statement regarding the unique status of a population that has been placed in legal stasis since 1948. The question of how Palestine Arabs became refugees has several dimensions; the historical and demographic details regarding their flight and dispersal, and the political and legal means by which they were defined and maintained as refugees by different parts of the international community. There is also the question of their numbers, which grew enormously in the months and years after 1948. All these are critical for understanding the early years of Palestine refugee relief and the role of the AFSC

The causes of flight have been among the most contentiously debated issues in the Arab-Israeli conflict, and have been more overburdened in subsequent decades by new data, revisionism, and fabrications. The question of numbers is critical to understanding the scale of events and for purposes here, the international response to the refugee crisis.

In 1948, as the result of the hostilities surrounding the Israeli declaration of statehood, approximately 650,000 Palestinian Arabs left their homes and fled into neighboring countries. According to both early and recent historical studies, there were at least three distinct phases of the exodus.[64] The first waves of abandonment began after the November 1947 ratification of United Nations General Assembly Resolution 181, known as the Partition Plan. At that point some 30,000 people, mostly from more affluent urban families in Jerusalem, Haifa, and Jaffa, began to leave. The second phase occurred in March 1948, when tens of thousands of Palestine Arabs from the Sharon coastal plains began to move to the Arab-controlled hill regions, outside the areas that had been designated to become part of Israel. During this phase, some 6,000 left their homes in Tiberias, 60,000 fled Haifa, and 65,000–70,000 left Jaffa.

The third and most dramatic phase began in May following Israel's declaration of independence and the subsequent military invasion by the Egyptian, Iraqi, Syrian, Lebanese, and Arab Legion (Transjordanian) armies.[65] During that period, the flight of Palestinian Arab civilians grew exponentially, and when the hostilities ended, the United Nations estimated that around 350,000 people had left after May. Estimates of refugee numbers varied widely and, in the view of the United Nations and other international organizations, began to grow rapidly, from 360,000 in September 1948 to 472,000 in October. The dispersal patterns of the refugees were more or less predictable. According to the United Nations, most refugees from the northern regions of the country (Haifa, the Galilee, Tiberias) fled further into Lebanon and Syria. Those from the coastal plain regions went east to Jordanian territory (including the West Bank). Those in the south went to the Gaza Strip, which was controlled by Egypt.

Throughout the Fall of 1948, as the new relief effort was being planned, estimates of the number of refugees varied widely. One news item in December noted estimates in August had been 330,000. An estimate in October by the United Nation's Acting Mediator, Ralph Bunche, saw this rise to 500,000, and by December State Department estimates ranged from 500,000 to 550,000.[66] Estimates from Palestine Arab and Arab League sources were consistently and dramatically higher, from 631,000 to 780,000. When UNRPR began operation on December 1, 1948, it found 962,643 persons registered on its relief rolls.[67]

Numbers were critical, for several reasons. Higher numbers of Palestine Arab refugees, real or imagined, were an obvious propaganda boon for Arab spokesmen. For the United Nations, however, the critical issue was money. The UNRPR had budgeted only for 500,000 refugees, based on estimates available from United Nations sources in October 1948. It was into this chaotic environment that the AFSC was drawn at the end of 1948.

A final issue regarding refugee numbers and AFSC's involvement should also be emphasized, namely, that the organization was entering into a wartime situation, with ongoing skirmishes and major operations. While AFSC had had some experience with such environments during the Spanish Civil War and the early part of World War II, the military situation around Gaza during 1948 and 1949 created shifting boundaries, near continual movements of refugees, and a dynamic and uncertain political situation.

AFSC took to the field in December 1948, precisely as the Israeli offensive known as Operation Horev was being launched. The offensive was designed to push the Egyptian Army out of the western Negev and it included raids into Gaza and the Sinai.[68] During the course of operations, Great Britain threatened to invoke the Anglo-Egyptian Treaty of 1936 and come to their ally's aid, particularly as fears grew that Israel intended to invade and annex portions of Transjordan and Egypt. British animosity towards Israel, already high in the acrimonious aftermath of Britain's withdrawal from the Mandate, was greatly intensified during early January when four Royal Air Force planes on a reconnaissance flight were shot down by Israeli aircraft. This temporarily brought Britain and Israel close to war.[69]

The military situation in the AFSC's territory stabilized in later January 1949, and the overall political situation was temporarily fixed by the February 1949 armistice, but the AFSC took up its mission in the midst of considerable turmoil. The subsequent swirl of international conferences and initiatives, and local contacts with low and high level officials of several combatant states, created an additional maze for both the refugees and aid organizations like AFSC.

# 4. AFSC in the Field: December 1948–December 1949 ∾

The AFSC deployed to Gaza quickly. Working in a region without any government, only a military occupation, created legal, conceptual, and moral problems for the organization. Egyptian authorities exercised partial sovereignty over Gaza, including military operations, border control, and provided limited relief for refugees, and attempted to control aspects of AFSC communications and transport. At the same time, the region was effectively stateless and Palestine Arab refugees, local Gaza residents, and Bedouin, were rapidly thrust into an increasingly complex social and legal setting.[1]

In his December 13, 1948 report to UNRPR, Director Griffis, John Devine of AFSC outlined the results of a survey trip to Gaza he had made earlier that month with another AFSC staffer. The report reflected some of the private concerns that AFSC felt as it became involved on the ground and the organization's emerging vision. Devine recounted his visit to the refugee centers, their general conditions, as well as the general situation, which was dire. The Egyptian military governor of Khan Yunis, for example, was described as having "very little interest in the problem, and no staff to help him."[2]

Some of Devine's suggestions reflected the AFSC's still low but rapidly growing level of political sophistication, juxtaposed against their core religious beliefs and self-image. He proposed, for example, that the Quakers (by which he meant the AFSC) "ought to try to get as many people as they can down to the Canal Zone." This would have been a practical approach to getting refugees closer to centers where supplies, economic opportunities, and locations for resettlement were available. Still, he went on to say, "I appreciate the fact that such a move would raise problems, particularly since the Quaker jurisdiction ends at the Palestinian border and the League of Red Cross Societies might have to take over in Egypt. That Quaker-League relationship is, incidentally, one which is full of potential headaches and should be clarified at the earliest possible date."[3] Devine seemed aware that neither the Egyptians nor the League of Red Cross Societies would have considered any efforts to move refugees closer toward Egypt, but believed it was still worth mentioning.[4]

Devine went on to make the practical suggestion that the AFSC work closely with the Arab Higher Refugee Council. He reasoned that since the Council "has just got its first taste of accomplishment with the flour that is now being distributed," the AFSC should let them operate in the "well-defined camps" while dealing itself with "floating populations." This way, he argued, "it would only be a short time until the Council realized it needed the Quakers' direct help, or until the refugees started to leave the camps to be nearer the Quakers' superior feeding centers." But Devine also displayed an amount of realism and added, "I do believe it would be better to go through this period of trial rather than to bludgeon the Council into completely minor role. The Quakers can't tackle the whole problem at once anyhow."[5]

The need to coax the refugees and other organizations along was part of the process. But Devine ended his report to Griffis on a less than characteristically Quakerly note, saying,

> I am very pleased to see the Quakers on the job and I shall be most interested to watch their work. I am sure that the Egyptians won't believe they are true since they are the antithesis of almost everything that has gone on in connection with this problem before. As long as the Quakers can acquire a completely hard-boiled attitude in dealing with Egyptian officialdom, I am sure that their simplicity, honesty, selflessness and naiveté will give them a better chance of success than all the high-pressure ideas available in the field.

The apparent contradiction of "hard-boiled" Quakers cut to the heart of the AFSC's subsequent experience.

Early in 1949 the US Department of State was also being counseled to take a hard-boiled approach with respect to UNRPR, only from the organization's new director. On January 11, 1949 the acting Secretary of State Robert Lovett, who had taken over for the recently retired General George C. Marshall, telegrammed the US representative at the United Nations and reported that UNRPR Director Griffis had expressed "strong hope Dept will incorporate safeguard clause giving Director UNRPR or Dept full discretionary power re expenditure US contribution."[6]

Griffis was already concerned that the relief effort might be "emasculated due lack govt cooperation in NE." Lovett added that the State Department was also studying ways to create legislative safeguards giving the Secretary of State discretionary powers over US payments. But he added that it was the UN Secretary General who had "unquestioned authority control all expenditures under terms UN resolution" and that this also included the US contribution. Three days later Lovett wrote to President Harry Truman recommending that the United States should back the UNRPR resolution with a special appropriation request to the US Congress.[7]

That Griffis reported confidentially to the State Department even though he was directing a UN program is remarkable. It is also noteworthy that his message was intended to protect American interests against those of the United Nations and conceivably those of the refugees. It is unknown whether AFSC personnel were aware of this sort of political collusion, into which they were soon to be drawn.

AFSC's public vision for the project was articulated in a press release entitled "United Nations Relief for Palestine—A New Pattern in International Welfare Administration," released by Elmore Jackson, associate secretary of the AFSC, in December 1948. The press release began by stating:

> A striking new experiment is being tried in the Middle East today in the handling of international relief problems. Behind the headlines coming from Palestine, and under the aegis of the United Nations, three non-governmental humanitarian agencies have undertaken a major administrative role in the world wide effort to meet the needs of the more than 700,000 persons who are now homeless as a result of the tensions and fighting in the Holy Land. Though in charge of field operations for the United Nations relief program, the three agencies are retaining their complete autonomy. Every precaution has been taken to preserve their individual traditions of impartiality, and to insure that their work is free of political pressure.[8]

That Jackson chose to begin the press release this way is remarkable. Without even naming the other organizations, the International Committee of the Red Cross and the LRCS, Jackson stressed their "complete autonomy" and "individual traditions of impartiality and freedom from political pressure." This again demonstrated how central concerns over practical and symbolic impartiality were to the AFSC and its self-image, and how readily the organization deployed that argument as part of its public relations strategy. The impartiality issue had not been emphasized in any American press coverage but had been made clear in one of the few articles on UNRPR in the *Manchester Guardian*.[9]

However, Jackson's press release went on to state "The experiment was, in large part, dictated by the necessity for speed." For the AFSC, the relief effort was precisely an experiment and not a long-term commitment. To reinforce the notion that refugee relief would be temporary, Jackson pointed out that the AFSC's involvement was predicated on UN Secretary General Trygve Lie's recommendation to the General Assembly that the organization "not set up an elaborate United Nations staff to handle the relief assistance. Instead, the Secretary General was permitted to seek the aid in distribution of non-political, non-governmental, voluntary organizations already experienced in field operations." AFSC thus announced at the outset that its efforts would be autonomous, nonpolitical, and temporary, with the implied belief that this contribution would be sufficient to address the refugee issue.

The nonpolitical and humanitarian orientation of relief operations had been articulated earlier by Count Folke Bernadotte, the United Nations Mediator on issues related to Palestine, in his last report to the Secretary-General:

> So long as large numbers of refugees remain in distress, I believe the responsibility for their relief should be assumed by the United Nations in conjunction with the neighboring Arab States, the Provisional Government of Israel, the specialized agencies and also all the voluntary bodies or organizations of a humanitarian and non-political nature [AFSC]. In concluding this part of the report, I must emphasize again the desperate urgency of this problem. The choice is between saving the lives of many thousands of people now or permitting them to die. The situation of the majority of these hapless refugees is already tragic, and to prevent them from being overwhelmed by further disaster and to make possible their ultimate rehabilitation, it is my warmest hope that the international community will give all the necessary support to make the measures I have outlined fully effective. I believe that for the international community to accept its share of responsibility for the refugees of Palestine is one of the minimum conditions for the success of its efforts to bring peace to the land.[10]

The ideal apolitical approach that Bernadotte desired was no doubt at least partially shaped by his own experience with the Swedish Red Cross in World War II. At AFSC there was also an understanding that the relief work would require on-going contacts with Israel and specifically Egypt.

As Elmore Jackson, a Quaker official who would later work with the US State Department in a secret diplomatic mission aimed at a political settlement between Egypt and Israel in 1955, wrote much later:

> Egyptian forces were in control in Gaza and it was understood that Quaker willingness to administer the program in that area was dependent on Egyptian approval. Dr. Mahmoud Fawzi, Egyptian Foreign Minister, in Paris in 1948 UN General Assembly, quickly gave that assent. As the former Egyptian Consul-General in Jerusalem he was intimately familiar with Palestine affairs. Since the American Friends Service Committee was already working with refugees in Israel, the UN invitation and the Egyptian response were explained to Ambassador Abba Eban, then a member of the Israeli General Assembly Delegation and later to become Israel's Foreign Minister. It was emphasized that Quakers might initially need Israeli cooperation in getting supplies into Gaza. He pledged that cooperation, and indeed, general Israeli assistance was soon enlisted, although in a somewhat different manner than had been anticipated.[11]

AFSC's field operations deployed quickly and with apparent efficiency. The Egyptian Army had already set up a number of stations in Gaza and had registered large numbers of refugees. Limited, ad hoc relief was also being provided by local groups with donations from the United Nations Children's Emergency Fund (UNICEF). Following the well-established AFSC script, technical teams made rapid assessments of infrastructure and transportation needs, while others began organizing supplies and distribution. Supplies for Gaza were offloaded in Port Said, cleared through Egyptian customs, and loaded onto rail cars for transport across the Sinai Peninsula.[12] They would then be offloaded in Gaza and trucked to distribution points.

But in order to distribute supplies, a system of ration cards had to be instituted. Initially central registration points were established and thousands of refugees joined in the crush to sign up. Later, AFSC personnel had to undertake their own registrations of refugees, often going tent by tent with an interpreter. This technique was to be repeated in later months, only with the intention of reducing the rolls of refugees. Field personnel quickly developed a series of detailed procedures for registration and distribution of relief based on the need to control the throng of refugees, maximize oversight, and verification of refugee claims, notably the ration card, and minimize the involvement of *mukhtars* (village headmen). Ration card facilities, for example, should have a single entrance and single exit, and inside "the ration card should be picked up at the line book and passed

**Figure 4.1**   Food distribution.
*Source*: Courtesy of the American Friends Service Committee.

from one punch clerk to the other and returned to the owner as they leave. In this way there is more control, less confusion, and less likelihood of substituting a false card."[13]

The reality that AFSC personnel encountered on the ground was different from that which they had been led to expect. AFSC volunteer and former Civilian Public Service member, Alwin Holtz, described in an oral history his first-hand experience with the matter of determining the nature and number of "refugees." AFSC personnel were not prepared for what they found:

> We had no idea what we were doing. We hadn't registered anybody and we had to set up a registration procedure; meanwhile, we had to alleviate the pain where people were dying in the streets, we were told. It wasn't true but we thought we had to get food in every little baby's mouth right now or they were all going to be dying in the street. All of those stories get exaggerated. It wasn't quite that bad. Certainly in the beginning it was confusion and utter chaos, and people were confused because they had just left their homes and wanted to go back and, you know, all this nonsense. That was the biggest problem in the

beginning…And it took us a little bit of time to figure out how we were going to do this so that it was orderly.[14]

Despite initial difficulties, feeding centers, public health operations, and even schools, were quickly established by AFSC volunteers. The schools were planned by the dean of the Cairo School of Social Work, Dr. Miko Zaki, and teachers found from among the refugees. But as Wriggins noted, "Books presented a problem, as some of the teachers balked at using Egyptian textbooks which were filled with praise for King Farouk."[15] By mid-April over 15,000 students were attending AFSC run schools and the total number of children was estimated at over 70,000.[16] Ultimately the AFSC operation employed between eight hundred and nine hundred refugees.[17]

Speaking from Beirut at the beginning of January, UNRPR Director Stanton Griffis announced that relief operations were underway in all regions but that the most serious problems were in Gaza where "no accurate count was possible because the refugees had fled in panic as the fighting broke out near them and thus they were in constant movement, but investigators have set the minimum at 150,000, with 200,000 more

**Figure 4.2**  Teachers at the AFSC sponsored school in Deir el-Balah.
*Source*: Courtesy of the American Friends Service Committee.

nearly accurate."[18] He added that the only funds available were the initial $5,000,000 lent by the United Nations.

## EARLY OPERATIONS AND GROWING CONCERNS

Learning to be "hard-boiled" with the Egyptian military was easier for some AFSC personnel than for others. Howard Wriggins, who periodically visited Gaza from his office in Geneva, described the Egyptian bureaucracy as merely "phlegmatic."[19] Field personnel had a quite different view. In an oral history, Alwin Holtz recounted how dealing with an obstreperous Egyptian lieutenant resulted in the temporary incarceration of the AFSC interpreter. Though the specific incident was resolved, Holtz was not above threatening the local commanding officer, whom he told "in no uncertain terms that if this ever happens again, we'll stop the distribution inall the centers, not just one. We'll just stop this until it gets settled. So, of course, he got frightened and issued orders to leave the Quakers alone and let them do what they want to do and don't bother with them. So we never had too much trouble after that."[20] The issue of using food as a weapon, however, would trouble some AFSC field personnel, particularly when it came to reducing the lists of refugees.

The AFSC also quickly set up medical facilities under the direction of Dr. Jerome Peterson, who had been temporarily transferred from the World Health Organization's mission in China. This was especially timely, since Stanton Griffis himself reported after his inspection tour that there was a measles epidemic and that "children are said to be dying of measles in considerable numbers."[21]

Despite these and other operational challenges, religious diplomacy went on unabated. In early February, after visiting the besieged Egyptian Army units at Fallujah, Cairo-based Deputy Chief of the AFSC mission, Delbert Replogle, met with a series of Israeli officials including Minister of Foreign Affairs Moshe Shertok (later Sharett). Among the questions Replogle put to Shertok on behalf of Pickett was whether the Israeli government would consider accepting the return of refugees as part of a "farm credit scheme" and after a period of "orientation and adjustment."[22] Replogle also offered AFSC assistance with the proposed return.

The offer is significant for at least two reasons. First, it illustrates the AFSC's traditional orientation toward rehabilitating agricultural communities and encouraging self-reliance, including through financing mechanisms. But even more importantly, this is one of the earliest proposals,

**Figure 4.3**   UNRPR director Ambassador Stanton Griffis visiting a refugee camp in Andjar, Lebanon.
*Source*: Courtesy of the American Friends Service Committee.

albeit informal, for a development solution to the refugee problem. This approach would grow enormously in the following months.

In his January 1949 inaugural address, President Harry Truman had proposed the Point IV program of technical assistance for developing countries. Designed specifically to demonstrate American commitment to raise standards of living in Asia, and to contradict Communist propaganda, the program was assigned to the State Department. A Technical Assistance Group was created in February 1949 to oversee development that evolved into the Technical Cooperation Administration in October 1950.[23] This program was the ancestor of the modern US Agency for International Development. As 1949 wore on, the development approach for the Middle East would be promoted on two tracks, from the State Department and through the United Nations, specifically the United Nations Conciliation Commission for Palestine's Beirut Conference of Arab States in late March 1949 and then the birth of the UN's Economic Survey Mission or Clapp Commission in August 1949.[24] Before long, development solutions would come to shape the international approach to the refugees.

After his inspection trip to Gaza in January, Stanton Griffis had reported that the refugees "were receiving about 2,000 calories of food a day" but that the "need for the $32,000,000 requested by the United Nations was desperate."[25] Back in Philadelphia the AFSC's focus was also on budgets. On February 23, Elmore Jackson, the AFSC's Associate Secretary and "Quaker Consultant to the United Nations Economic and Social Council" reported to AFSC's leaders regarding conversations he had held with the United Nations regarding the future of UNRPR and AFSC's participation. All expected the program to terminate on August 31, 1949, but decided that it was in AFSC's best interest to begin negotiations with the United Nations in late April or early May regarding a possible extension.[26] The terms and conditions of any extension were not discussed, but the letter reflects a growing awareness of what would become a looming August 31 deadline and increasing debate regarding AFSC's role thereafter.

The US Senate approved a $16,000,000 contribution in February.[27] But AFSC leadership appeared neither confident in a continued stream of funding, nor, more fundamentally, in the wisdom of the organization's continued involvement. Pickett himself raised the issue in a March 2 letter to Secretary General Trygve Lie in which he requested a meeting at the end of April "to discuss procedures leading to a tidy devolution or closure of the present operation." Suggesting a growing hesitation regarding the enterprise as a whole, Pickett added, "There is no doubt that needs will continue after August, but almost certainly they will be of a somewhat different character than those we are now trying to meet. The American Friends Service Committee would wish to wind up its operation under the present scheme in such a way as would most effectively dovetail with any further action which might be contemplated by the United Nations."[28]

Along with the nascent development solution, the interrelated problems of funding after August 31 and AFSC's unclear role, one other supremely important issue was beginning to come together in the minds of AFSC personnel the refugees' attitudes regarding the reasons for their flight and their hopes and fears for the future. In a lengthy memorandum to Mohamad Abbasay, the United Nations Food and Agriculture Organization's Nutrition Representative in the Near East, Delbert Replogle began to set out the contradictory results of interviews undertaken with refugees.

For one thing, Replogle reported that refugees held the "Dier Yaseen [*sic*] incident" "responsible for the running away of the greater percentage of the Arabs when the Mandate ended, and even before it did. They claim that had this not happened, most of the Arabs would have been now at their homes."[29] Flight notwithstanding, Replogle then asserted that "out of sheer misery the refugees are apt to accept any solution. They think that they cannot be more worse under any other circumstances."[30] But the concept of "any solution" is quickly and extensively qualified:

> Most if not all refugees wish to return back to their homes and land provided their security and safety are guranteed [sic] by the UN and Arab-League. We have to remember that farmers in this part of the world are very closely tied to their land where they were born. They do not like to move away even in the same country. They also in this particular case of Palestine that immigration is an act of tresion [sic] against their country which need every body to be present to defend it when the necessity arises; and that large scale immigration is a means of destruction to their country... When the question of partial return to their Jewish dominated homes was discussed, openions [sic] were conflicting. The vast majority stressed firmly that either all returns or none at all. Those who owned land were among this group. They do not want to part with their land for anything. When it was pointed out that this might be impossible, they remarked that true "democracy" which is claimed by every body does not allow such a thing. They stated that they must work to this end, and if they fail to achieve this, they cannot help it because it will not be their fault. A minority declined to express any opnion [sic] and said that is the duty of the Arab-League, and we are ready to do what they decide for us. This group is mostly formed of hired farmers.[31]

Replogle had, somewhat inarticulately, stumbled upon the most intractable problem, the attitudes of the refugees themselves. On the one hand, he reported that their situation was so dire that they were inclined to accept any solution. On the other hand, the landed—as opposed to the landless—refugees were sufficiently steadfast in their material and nationalist claims that they refused to consider resettlement, and would consider repatriation only if all refugees could somehow return, that is, if a status quo ante were somehow restored.

## PICKETT GOES TO THE MIDDLE EAST AND CHANGING PERCEPTIONS IN EARLY 1949

Clarence Pickett's two-and-a-half month trip to the Middle East in the first part of 1949, including a visit to Gaza in the company of Stanton Griffis, was a significant step toward the AFSC's understanding of the many dimensions of the refugee crisis. Pickett approached the problems

**Figure 4.4**   Clarence Pickett visiting the Middle East. From left, two unknown men, the Picketts, unknown woman, Stanton Griffis, and Emmett Gulley.
*Source*: Courtesy of the American Friends Service Committee.

and personalities with typical Quaker resolve and from the framework of his own experiences in previous situations.

The Quaker tradition of religious diplomacy and mediation, badly damaged by the failures of 1948, was again on full display when Pickett and Replogle met the Grand Mufti of Jerusalem, Haj Amin al-Husseini, in Cairo in early February. Though Pickett and Replogle were more knowledgeable and sophisticated than Vail and Castle, they appeared to have approached the Middle East with a similar level of naïveté, born of their Quaker belief in the underlying unity of all faiths and the goodwill of men. The memo of their meeting does not indicate whether Pickett and Replogle were aware of the Mufti's service to the Nazis during World War II, or his well-established and unmistakably bitter animus towards Jews, Zionists, and the West.[32] The goal of the meeting was "to explain to the Grand Mufti our aims and that the work which we were attempting to do for the Gaza refugees, 90 percent of whom were Moslems under his jurisdiction . . . to discover if he had any constructive ideas or could lend any assistance in that work… to see if there were some way we could solicit his aid in bringing religious instruction and encouragement to the 200,000 Moslems in the area where we were serving.[33] These goals echoed those of Vail and Castle's ill-fated mission of almost a year before.

The report initially suggests that, despite Pickett and Replogle's explanations, the two sides were poorly informed about one another. In response to the AFSC representatives, the Mufti presented "quite a long address" in which he suggested that "a place be made for Friday prayers in the various camps" since "spiritual relief as well as physical relief was needed." He then "pointed out that Islam is more a spiritual movement and not an organizational movement as are the Catholics." Pickett appears to have put the best face on this and "remarked that in lack of organization but emphasis on values Islam resembled Quakerism." The Mufti "was glad to know that the Catholics were feeding all Arabs alike" and "stated that he was very happy that the Quakers were not interfering with the spiritual life of the Moslems and would not take advantage of their misery to change their spiritual beliefs."[34]

Ecumenical understanding aside, the Mufti's political views were strident. He was "quite emphatic that from a practical point of view it was impossible for the refugees to return to their homes in Israel as the Jews would not permit them to do so, or if they would permit them to come back, the Arabs would so mistreat them that none would remain. He believed that it would be the natural thing to expect concerning any nationals that had been put out of the country by a conquering group."[35] The AFSC representatives appear to have been taken aback by his response: "We were disappointed in the amount of help that could be expected from the Grand Mufti and felt rather strongly that he had a lack of sympathy for the plight of his co-religionists."[36]

A press release dated March 20, 1949 reflected AFSC's thinking after Pickett's two and a half month visit to the region. The quick and effective AFSC field operation is touted, but mission creep is evident. In addition to feeding and housing, the press release notes, that "When the Palestine refugee program was undertaken late in 1948, the need of an educational program was not anticipated by either the United Nations or the Service Committee" and estimates that almost half of the 200,000 refugees being served by the AFSC are children. "Primers are being supplied by the Egyptian government, and a teaching staff has been secured from the refugees." Consistent with the spiritual orientation of the AFSC, "Quaker workers have set up prayer tents."[37]

**Figure 4.5**   Don Peretz.
*Source*: Courtesy of the American Friends Service Committee.

Consistent with the AFSC's desire to maintain an explicit non-political stance, and work on all sides of the conflict, the AFSC's Israel operation, the Acre Relief Unit, was also established in March 1949. This unit was designed to provide relief to Arabs who had remained within the walls of the Old City of Acre. Much smaller in scale, this project was undertaken in vastly different political circumstances than the Gaza operations. Though intended in part to facilitate Arab-Israeli reconciliation or at least cooperation, the project was exclusively aimed at providing relief to only a few thousand Arab refugees.

But the participation of Don Peretz, as one of the handful of AFSC volunteers in Israel, proved to be controversial when his Jewish background came under suspicion by members of the AFSC leadership, specifically Donald Stevenson, the AFSC's head in Beirut, under whose auspices the Acre unit fell. Interestingly, subsequent internal AFSC debates regarding Middle East operations mentioned the relief project in Acre or the later agricultural development project in the Arab village of Tur'an, primarily in terms of its small scale, apparent lack of efficiency and success, and the fact that it involved working with Jews. As noted earlier, the Israel project in particular was conceived in part as an exercise in religious diplomacy, one for which, as will be shown, Stevenson felt Jews were especially ill-suited. Peretz, a former Japanese translator in the US Army and foreign correspondent in Jerusalem for the National Broadcasting Company, had ironically been drawn to working for the AFSC through his studies at the Hebrew University in Jerusalem with Martin Buber and Judah Magnes, among the foremost Jewish proponents of a binational solution to the Arab-Jewish conflict.[38]

With the AFSC's expanding mission, however, came a widening view of certain root problems and solutions. The political situation was paralyzed, but improving the refugees themselves might open doors to larger political solutions and to rehabilitate and potentially resettle some refugees. In the March press release Pickett therefore further articulated a theme that was to become common for AFSC and the international community in 1949 and 1950:

> The Arab refugee wants nothing more than to go back to his own small farm, Pickett said. But he can never go back to his simple hand farming. He must face the fact that he is living in a modern world. Voluntary agencies like the Service Committee can help with this adjustment. If this can be done, a substantial repatriation is practicable. Also, resettlement in neighboring Arab States could take place.[39]

Pickett's development framework had been floated in part by Replogle's February meeting with Shertok, but another element was at play, Pickett's own personal experiences and those of the AFSC during the Depression with American farmers based on the Committee's debriefing. The analogy was strongly drawn:

> Mr. Pickett endorsed a long term resettlement plan policy, with irrigation development and similar projects in Syria, Trans-Jordan, and Iraq. "The experiences of our own Farm Security Administration should be made available to the Israeli and Arab Government," Mr. Pickett continued. "These states are changing over from hand agriculture to mechanized agriculture. It is important to give them technical advice and help. When that is done, I think we shall have grounds for insisting that Israel take back a substantial number of Arab refugees, and to hope for resettlement in Arab States also."[40]

Unfortunately, the backdrop to Pickett's confident statements regarding development was more complex, both inside the AFSC and with respect to other organizations. In an irritated March 11 memorandum to senior AFSC personnel, Howard Wriggins complained that "the idea of a new TVA in the Tigris-Euphratis [*sic*] valley, reorganization thereby of "backward" Arab agriculture, reclaiming of land, the establishing of photogenic subsistence homesteads...has apparently been advocated by the Zionists for many years, the idea being that all one has to do is move the Arabs out of Palestine and into Iraq and Transjordan, and thereby helping Transjordan and Iraq, and leaving room for Jewish immigrants into Palestine."[41]

Wriggins went on to complain that the "long-term Zionist program of public education in this regard has been so effective that resettlement is perhaps becoming the generally accepted "Solution"[42] He added that, on the basis of his "brief contact" with the refugees that "the only place where these people could really feel at home and labor with happiness would be the places from which they come. Their psychology and intellectual horizons are on the whole very limited indeed, and "home" therefore can only be within the familiar perimeter of their villages of origins."[43] Though this would obviously be an enormous burden for Israel, resettlement elsewhere as part of a regional development scheme would be even more expensive and thus doubly undesirable.

At the same time, like many contemporary outside observers, Wriggins confessed that he was confused by the Arab mindset as he perceived it:

> I was frankly unable properly to penetrate and fully understand the Arab attitude toward the Jews in Palestine. There was not the type of bitterness which one would expect if the actors in this drama were Europeans. There was a bitterness certainly against Jewish political leaders but, too, there was bitterness against Arab leaders who had so miserably betrayed their people's trust. Many still speak with appreciation of many of their Jewish friends and of how well both Jews and Arabs could have lived together, had it not been for the aspirations of the Jewish and Arab leadership. It seems to me that it is on the basis of this assumption of friendly relations between the non-political members of both communities that repatriation as a possible solution should not be forgotten.[44]

Wriggins' careful division of political and non-political members of both communities suggests that he was projecting his own distinctions onto those of Jews and Arabs. Similarly, the refugees' anger at their own leadership was not questioned. It was more likely that this anger was caused not by the Arab leaders' failure to compromise with the Jews, but rather their failure to win the war. Still, the need to cast the refugee crisis and the AFSC's relief work as non-political would remain deep and pervasive among some staff members in the field as well as in Geneva and Philadelphia even as the organization moved simultaneously toward explicit political stances on other issues.

In general, the AFSC made few efforts to publicize or promote the good work they were doing with the refugees. This is in contrast with a series of quiet efforts made to publicize other AFSC projects, such as a small series of documentary films made during the late 1930s in association with the Harmon Foundation that featured AFSC work camps.[45] But Pickett himself appears to have been determined to remain publicly involved with the refugee issue. In addition to the press release issued by the AFSC after Clarence Pickett's study trip to the Middle East, Pickett also published his findings in an opinion piece in the *Philadelphia Inquirer*. In it, he restated the goals of his mission: to help launch the Quaker refugee program, negotiate with the neighboring governments ways where they can bolster relief efforts and discuss long term plans for the Palestinian refugees. He then appealed to the governments of the Middle East, the United Nations and individuals to come together to work toward a long lasting solution for the refugee problem, laying out six major points:

1. The refugees would have to realize that if they returned home, their lives would not be the same. Most had been farmers who farmed their land as they did in the days of Jesus. But they would live in a different country– a new state, a modern state, and would have to make the adjustment;
2. Arab refugees left behind valuable property. For those who do not return, there should be a prompt and full indemnity for property loss. For those who wished to return, early agreements should provide repatriation;
3. A public works program should be developed, pending longer range projects, financed by the United Nations;
4. Technical assistance in modern agricultural methods should be given to train the refugees for repatriation in Israel or resettlement elsewhere;
5. If the above steps were followed, there was every reason to urge a substantial repatriation of Arabs into the State of Israel;
6. Resettlement programs in Syria, Jordan, and Iraq would require outside funding and great technical skill, planning, and time but could become productive enough to support the refugees who did not return to their homes.[46]

Pickett's analysis was logical and proceeded on the assumption that all participants in the refugee drama wanted to resolve the issue and maximize not simply their own but the collective gain, in productivity and security. Resettlement appeared to be the final option. But within the State Department and the Foreign Office, the idea was being explored carefully.

# 5. AFSC and the Politics of Regional Development ✍

The pushback within the AFSC articulated by Wriggins against resettlement as part of regional development was being felt elsewhere. On March 18, AFSC staffer George Mathues reported to James Read, secretary in the Foreign Service Section at AFSC, about a meeting of the American Volunteer Relief Agencies in the Middle East, an informal group organized by the US Department of State led by Special Assistant to the Secretary of State for the Middle East, Coordinator for Palestine Refugee Matters—and wealthy petroleum geologist—George McGhee. This group was comprised of a number of organizations including the National Catholic Welfare Conference (NCWC), the Near East Foundation, the Church World Service, and representatives from Gulf Oil, the Arab-American Oil Company, and the US Department of State. Mathues reported that Monsignor Thomas McMahon of the NCWC was adamant that UNRPR was not giving credit or financial support to other relief organizations, including his own. McMahon also decried the lack of coordination between UNRPR and private aid groups. Above all, McMahon stressed that "repatriation is the only answer to the refugee problem. It should be our "party" line, although we should not go into politics."[1]

Mathues also paraphrased McMahon as stating, "The President and State Department are completely pro-Israel at the expense of justice and their American reputation in the Middle East. America is 'public enemy number 1 in the Middle East.'" The State Department representative "took issue with the Father on the State Department's and President's position re Israel, but was soon silenced by the impressive reciting of detailed facts by Father McMahon of the United States' statements and actions in this regard."[2] Interestingly, many personnel within the State Department held the same viewpoint as McMahon.[3]

The sort of competition for public awareness and limited funding about which NCWC complained in 1949 remains a contentious issue in the political economics of modern NGOs today. Still, the attitude expressed by NCWC and other organizations at that meeting toward the AFSC and other relief agencies is telling: feeding the refugees is properly the responsibility of United Nations. Mathues expressed concern over the apparent show of jealousy, but the fact is that in the year before UNRWA was created, other aid organizations felt that the refugees were the UN responsibility. This cannot have helped but shape the creation of UNRWA.

McGhee's motives for mobilizing voluntary support had been made clear in a memorandum to new Secretary of State Dean Acheson only days before the meeting with aid organizations. On March 15, McGhee had recommended that US policy should recognize that that it was "in the interest of the United States that an early and effective solution be found to the problem of the Palestine refugees. Such solution should make possible their repatriation or resettlement in such a manner as to minimize present and potential political and economic tensions prejudicial to United States interests."[4] The memorandum indicated the US should offer technical and financial assistance, but refuse "to accept sole responsibility for solution for the problem."

A policy paper that accompanied McGhee's memorandum estimated the number of "destitute, idle" refugees at 725,000, and estimated that some 600,000 of those would be permanently resettled in Arab states.[5] It also cited a 1948 statement by the US Joint Chiefs of Staff which "characterized the Near Eastern area as an area of critical strategic importance, and emphasized the necessity, from a military standpoint, of maintaining the Arab world oriented towards the United States and Great Britain. They therefore recommended that, as a measure to strengthen our military position, the United States, should make provision for generous assistance to the Arab refugees from Palestine."[6] The memorandum assumed that cooperation from Arab states could be obtained with "substantial material assistance from outside sources" that would benefit the host countries as well as the refugees.

Another series of secret State Department analyses on resettlement, declassified only in 2010, were undertaken from March through May 1949. These studies, which included a series of technical British analyses executed by the Middle East Secretariat of the Foreign Office, explored various aspects of resettlement, including agricultural and other opportunities in Jordan, Lebanon, Syria and Iraq, financing, development, leadership and compensation, and explored both the history of the Palestine refugee issue and historical precedents such as Greek refugees from Turkey.[7]

The AFSC could not have been aware of secret State Department and US military policy papers which cast the refugee issue exclusively within the context of American national interests. But the larger contexts, including the variety of development and security initiatives taken after the Marshall Plan in these earliest years of the Cold War also cannot have escaped their view. As Howard Wriggins put it many years later, "it was hard for us on the spot to realize that our concern for the refugees was a small matter to the major powers beginning to be embroiled in the Cold War."[8] Wriggins, however, wrote from the perspective of a former professor of international affairs, National Security Council staffer, and American ambassador.

The United States' vision for the development of the Middle East was shaped by the growing Cold War, including new security architectures, decolonization, and the need to expand commercial opportunities and to keep Middle Eastern oil flowing. This entailed ensuring the stability of Arab regimes, a situation that was jeopardized by the Palestine refugee problem. Even before the end of World War II the United States had been considering postwar possibilities for American business in the Middle East and North Africa, a prospect that was not well-received by Great Britain.[9] By the end of World War II development and security were explicitly linked in American policy through the Marshall Plan and the Truman Doctrine. But Egypt had been excluded from these programs and in early 1949 appealed to the State Department for support under the newly announced Point IV program. Negotiations over an American-Egyptian commercial treaty also proceeded slowly thanks to the Arab-Israeli situation generally and the specific issue of American cotton tariffs.[10]

Throughout late 1948 and early 1949 the issue of Palestine refugees complicated American policy. Military planners insisted on the British retaining bases in the Canal Zone but the State Department demanded that Britain adhere to the arms embargo on the region, at least until Israel and the Arab states signed formal armistices. Less concerned than their British counterparts about Israeli "expansionism," American diplomats also regarded the existence of Israel as an unavoidable, if not entirely palatable, fact. Building on the experience of the Marshall Plan, the scale of development programs proposed by American planners, like the centerpiece, Point IV, were appropriately large for the new geostrategic goals. The emphasis on economic aid was also in keeping with emerging concepts that became known as modernization theory during the 1960s.

These held that economic prosperity was a necessary condition to promote and sustain democracy, and that traditional social structures were impediments to modernization.[11] Development became an article of faith on the assumption, as one academic put it, "What America is... the modernizing Middle East seeks to become."[12] Various military cooperation plans, discussed below, also envisioned large-scale social and economic development directed at local militaries and national infrastructures.

Great Britain had a different vision of "development diplomacy." The postwar Labour government of Prime Minister Clement Atlee and Foreign Secretary Ernest Bevin sought to maintain Britain's global influence by reconfiguring the empire into a commonwealth at whose center would be Britain. This entailed balancing a number of national interests, including the need to stand at the center of an export-driven global commonwealth and the ideological devotion to decolonization and centralized economic planning. The question of retaining overseas bases was problematic, particularly after the partition of India when securing the route to India was no longer as critical an issue.

Rising Cold War tensions in Asia provided an additional rationale for keeping bases in Egypt and Iraq, as did the series of treaties with those countries and Transjordan. These were also defense assets that the United States did not possess and which appeared necessary in the postwar period as the states of the "Northern Tier," Greece, Turkey, and Iran, went through upheavals and faced the Soviet bloc. Playing a global role with respect to the United States, which was committed to the end of colonialism, was another part of the complex equation facing British officials during this period.[13]

The Labour government and Bevin personally viewed Middle Eastern development as highly desirable. Bevin's "peasants not pashas" policy was a strategy designed to retain as much British influence in order to circumvent their previous alliances with rulers and "palace go-betweens." In Bevin's view, rising standards of living would subvert local nationalist sentiments and would also have the effect of developing new markets, as well as thwart both American capitalism and Soviet communism.[14] At first glance Britain appeared well positioned to accomplish this goal of "informal empire." The wartime Middle East Supply Centre had initially been aimed at addressing critical wartime transportation needs but then swiftly grew into a general economic development apparatus.[15] The British Middle East Office was then founded in September 1945 to further development aims.[16] This organization accomplished small but significant work in technical fields such as land use and conservation[17] but after 1947 its work was shifted more toward providing regional intelligence and as a base for traditional diplomacy.[18]

Palestine, however, was an enormous complication and burden, made even more so by the refugee crisis and the reaction of Arab states, already approaching the boiling point under nationalist pressures. These pressures were greatest precisely in two of the states, Egypt and Iraq, where Britain had treaties and bases, and where development opportunities appeared greatest. Closest to Gaza were the continued perceived requirement for retaining defense facilities in Egypt. A January 1949 memorandum by the Secretary of State for Foreign Affairs to the Cabinet articulated British policy in terms of supporting American and United Nations efforts to bring about negotiations but added "we cannot neglect taking the necessary precautions to safeguard vital British interests in the Middle East should fighting break out again."[19] The terms refugee and development did not appear in the memorandum.

At an immediate level those interests could be defined in terms of the British relationship with three countries directly involved in the war against Israel, Transjordan, Egypt, and Iraq. In early January 1949 Jordan had invoked the Anglo-Transjordan Treaty of March 1948 and Britain had sent a battalion to Aqaba but evidently did not desire to become involved in a direct military confrontation with Israel or in a political confrontation with the United States.[20] The difficult realities of reconciling itself to the unhappy outcome after the withdrawal from the Palestine mandate, which meant a loss of regional influence and the emergence of Israel, and being relegated to a secondary role to the United States, all drove British policy in the early months of 1949.

On March 22, Secretary of State for War Emmanuel Shinwell also issued a lengthy memorandum to the Cabinet Defense Committee regarding long-term policy in Egypt, focusing on the retention of facilities. In it he complained that the enormous wartime expenditures on facilities would be lost if these were turned over to Egypt or abandoned, and that a proposed East African storage facility should be reduced in scale to save money.[21] At the same time, there was growing awareness that the Anglo-Egyptian Treaty of 1936 could be, "disowned," as another memorandum put it.[22] The Defense Committee of the British Cabinet was also being pushed by the Chiefs of Staff about resuming arms sales to Egypt. This would have the effect of securing Britain's defense relationship with Egypt, as well as its basing rights, and improving its economic position.[23] The memoranda are reminders that British considerations regarding defense and colonial postures took precedence over refugee policy. It is significant to note that throughout 1949 the issue of refugees did not enter into British defense considerations, nor did it even receive more than passing attention from the Cabinet itself. Development would reappear as a British goal later in 1949, but national self-interest did not wane.

For France, however, another of the creators of the Conciliation Commission, a wholly different set of geopolitical concerns were at work. These did not affect the AFSC in Gaza directly, but had an impact on UNRPR and then on the shape and direction of UNRWA. French policy toward the Palestinians must be seen largely in the context of the last phase of Anglo-French rivalry in the Levant. France was as interested in maintaining its influence in Lebanon and Syria as Great Britain was with Egypt and Transjordan. For Syria, however, the matter was greatly complicated by the continual series of military coups, in 1949 and 1954.[24] Another vast complication were the French colonies in North Africa. One result was French support for Israel, intended in part to thwart or at least tweak Great Britain. But with regard to UNRPR and then UNRWA, France was cautious. It appears as though these efforts, with their development components, were regarded as Anglo-Saxon interventions that were "part of a plot to keep France out of the Middle East."[25]

Whatever the AFSC's internal debates there were regarding regional development schemes, one issue appears to have been agreed upon, the temporary nature of the mission in Gaza. If anything, in a draft document for submission to the United Nations written in March 1949, AFSC's tone was becoming even more insistent:

> Following a review of the refugee situation in Palestine generally and more particularly in the Gaza strip, the AFSC wishes to state its position regarding the continuance of the refugee relief program. The AFSC wishes to withdraw from direct refugee relief in the Gaza strip at the earliest possible moment compatible with the fulfillment of its moral obligation to the refugee population. It is obvious that prolonged direct relief contributes to the moral degeneration of the refugees and that it may also, by its palliative effects, militate against a swift political settlement of the problem.[26]

The statement is highly significant for a number of reasons. For one thing, AFSC saw itself as having a moral obligation to the refugees. This would appear to be in contrast to their contractual obligation to the United Nations. The sense of having established, after only some two months in the field, a moral relationship with the refugees, is palpable. At the same time, AFSC was adamant that its commitment to relief operations in Gaza is strictly limited. The rationale expressed, "that prolonged direct relief contributes to the moral degeneration of the refugees and that it may also, by its palliative effects, militate against a swift political settlement of the problem," is perhaps the single most perceptive statement made with respect to Palestine refugee relief across some six decades. It reflected the Quakers' growing unhappiness with the condition of the refugees, and their prescient concerns regarding their role in possibly perpetuating the refugee problem as a whole.

There is no description in AFSC documentation of rising tensions between Egypt and Israel in March 1949. Egypt's closure of the Suez Canal to Israeli shipping even after the armistice between the two states impelled the Israeli takeover of the southern Negev that month. Egypt's Canal restrictions were also interfering with international trade. But these factors may be reflected at the end of March and the beginning of April 1949 in hardening perceptions at AFSC regarding the refugee situation and the organization's role. Pickett expressed his unhappiness at the strident insistence on repatriation in a letter to Wriggins in which he posited that "If there was full-scale repatriation, I am sure there would be serious overpopulation of Israel with the early cry of 'lebensraum' and the probable attempt to expand into one of the neighboring countries, probably Syria."[27] Pickett continued to insist that any repatriation be "moderate" and be accompanied by both agricultural education and regional development.

Despite internal objections from AFSC staff members, and the opposition of the American Volunteer Relief Agencies in the Middle East and its member organizations, the development option was swiftly coming to the forefront. This was taking place on several fronts simultaneously. On April 9, the United Nations Conciliation Commission for Palestine created the Technical Mission on Refugees, based on the repatriation, resettlement, and rehabilitation formula. The Technical Mission was charged with determining the number, origins, and livelihoods of refugees, and was asked to recommend both means of determining which refugees might want to return to their former homes in the future, and "practicable" projects in terms of "immediate work relief."[28] In practical terms, this was another United Nations operation with which the AFSC and other aid agencies would now have to contend. In the summer of 1949 it would be joined by two other programs.

The Beirut Conference from March 21 to April 5 had seen the Arab states push repatriation as the only possible solution to the refugee problem, and the Israeli government, though obviously not present, rejected it with equal determination. Without any agreement from Arab states to consider even accepting resettlement of refugees who might seek it, Israeli officials did not feel compelled to make any conciliatory gestures.[29] The first Lausanne conference at the very end of April saw some progress, with the Israeli side agreeing to consider limited repatriation in exchange for Arab willingness to discuss boundary issues. In effect, however, postponing any large-scale decisions regarding refugees made the situation more difficult for AFSC and other aid organizations. The glimmer of political hope meant that at the very least, the refugees would have to be maintained still further.

The Syrian coup of March 30, 1949, when the Syrian army led by Chief of Staff Husni Za'im overthrew President Shukri al-Quwwatli, introduced still more uncertainty, as did the two subsequent coups of 1949, that of Colonel Sami al-Hinnawi in August and Colonel 'Adib al-Shishakli in December. All three regimes would toy inconclusively with the idea of resettling substantial numbers of Palestine Arab refugees, in exchange for substantial American economic and military aid, into 1952.[30]

AFSC's relationship to the regional development concept, though, was unclear. Nonetheless, the central role that AFSC played in the growing American and United Nations efforts to study and propose solutions to the refugee crisis is well documented. An April 7 letter from Replogle to Pickett, for example, related how a representative of US Secretary of State Dean Acheson approached AFSC field representatives for counsel regarding what would become the Economic Survey Mission. Replogle was adamant that "the word 'refugee' is to be avoided and a flavor or broader economic rehabilitation in the titled [*sic*],"[31] but Replogle could not answer for the AFSC leadership when asked whether the organization could participate, either in administration or specific projects having to do with resettlement and repatriation. Nor can it be said whether this type of political consultation behind the scenes was discomforting to the AFSC's self-image as a nonpolitical body.

The larger answer to the refugee problem, however, was now as clear to Replogle as it had been to Pickett a month earlier: "The problem of such administration would be not only to resettlement the refugees but in so doing raise the whole economic level of the common people in the Middle East on a long-range basis through the development of roads, communications, irrigation projects, improved methods of agriculture and economic business stimulus."[32]

Replogle's implicit skepticism regarding AFSC's role in this emerged in his note to Pickett on another issue, the matter of personnel. "The question of personnel for the remaining period of our commitment in southern Palestine and if we decide to continue on for further service has been a very great concern on the minds of us all," Replogle wrote. He then requested that a staff member in Gaza, Eldon Mills, be allowed to return to the United States to report in person regarding personnel matters, and states that "our best wishes and our prayers are with you and we only wish we had more specific information to help you make these difficult [personnel] decisions."[33]

But Replogle also let slip a curious comment regarding Israel and his interlocutors, and the presumed power of "world Jewry." Speaking about his meetings with various Israeli civilian officials, including those in the Public Heath, Agriculture, Social Welfare, and Foreign Ministries, Replogle stated:

> These people feel handicapped by the military I gathered and it is to be hoped and probably expected that with the signing of the armistice the power of the military can be decreased. I was told military civilian rule would end shortly after the signing of the armistice. I hope this is true for all concerned. What happed [sic] at Falluja and what happened in the villages in northern Galilee that we have witnessed and many other things that we have only heard of is due in my mind to the irresponsibility of this military clique. I feel sure that the Government in Tel Aviv would not sanction it and is highly annoyed by these things. If the force of world Jewry could be brought to bear to strengthen the hand of the liberal minded Jewish people at the expense of military, a great service could be done.[34]

Replogle refers here to the agreement to allow the escape of Egyptian forces and Arab civilians from the "Fallujah pocket" under the terms of the February 4, 1949 Armistice Agreement, and the subsequent abuses by Israeli forces that were observed by AFSC personnel.[35] His remarks regarding the Israeli military clique were not clarified elsewhere, nor were his personal feelings regarding Jews,[36] but the Quaker image of "world Jewry" as being predominantly (and properly) liberal was clear. It should be recalled that the AFSC's experience with Jewish aid organizations and Jewish refugees in Europe was one of the factors that impelled the group to become involved in the Middle East in the first place. Perhaps this is a reflection of Replogle's mirror imaging, as he expected the Jews' fighting to create a nation-state to be as liberal as those he knew in European refugee relief work.

## AFSC, UNRPR, AND LOCAL ECONOMIES, SPRING AND SUMMER 1949

During the spring of 1949 the scale and nature of the refugee problem was becoming increasingly evident to UNRPR. In a meeting of the American Appeal for Holy Land Refugees on April 22, which was attended by representatives of the major aid organizations and American oil companies, Ambassador Stanton Griffis, Director of UNRPR, noted that the total number of refugees was now between 700,000 and one million but that "this total, whatever it might be had little relation to the actual number of bona fide refugees. These probably do not exceed 500,000." Griffis interpreted the rest as being from "Nomadic tribes. They filter in and out of the camps and it is exceedingly difficult, if not impossible to separate them from the real refugees."[37] He encouraged private aid organizations to preserve and expand their operations to supplement UNRPR, and the gathered representatives voted to draft an agreement to increase cooperation with the program.

By now the problem of "who is a refugee" was becoming clear to all participants, and the number of refugees was becoming overwhelming. UNRPR had begun its work in December 1948 with an improbable 962,643 refugees on its lists. In fact, the problem that refugee numbers were being inflated by Bedouin, local residents, double counting and fraud was well-understood already in the Fall of 1948. Sir Raphael Cilento, director of the United Nations Disaster Relief Project, had reported this to the Foreign Office in October. By July 1949, St. Aubin, also of the Disaster Relief Project, estimated the number of "refugees" at one million.[38] In June 1949, however, the United Nations Conciliation Commission for Palestine in Geneva as being told by UNRPR Deputy Director Parminter that only some 650,000 of the figure of 940,000 were true refugees.[39]

The head of the British Middle East Office in Cairo, Sir John Troutbeck, also commented specifically on the AFSC's problem in a report to the Foreign Office after a June 1949 fact-finding trip to Gaza:

> They admit however that the figures are unreliable, as it is impossible to stop all fraud in the making of returns. Deaths for example are never registered nor are the names struck off the books of those who leave the district clandestinely. Some names too are probably registered more than once for the extra rations. But the Quakers assured me that they have made serious attempts to carry out a census and believe they have more information in that respect than the Red Cross organizations which are working in other areas. Their figures include

Bedouin whom they feed and care for just like other refugees. They seemed a little doubtful whether this was a right decision, but once it had been taken it could not be reversed, and in any case the Bedouin, though less destitute than most of the refugees proper, are thought to have lost a great part of their possessions. They and the other refugees live in separate camps and in a state of mutual antipathy.[40]

AFSC employee Alwin Holtz described the situation more bluntly: "The people of Gaza, maybe 20,000 or 25,000 people, were worse off than the refugees. They were starving. This again, of course, the Quakers can say was sensible to do this kind of thing, but to us it made sense."[41] Holtz also described an important aspect of the overstated refugee lists that was not understood by those outside Gaza:

> [W]e were very organized. There wasn't an aspect of the Gaza village refugee life that we hadn't tried to attend to. We went into education and everything. By that time we had a huge and very, very good [medical program]. We set up health clinics. We went into education; we put up huge tents and had schools and appointed teachers and had people supervising it with the local Gaza officials, the education people. We were into the middle of everything. You can't think of anything we didn't do. We did special prenatal [care] for pregnant women. Then it turned out that their habit is when somebody dies they have to have a shroud, a wrapping. We began to furnish those; the mukhtar would come and say so and so died and they need a shroud. Then we would replace newborns; if somebody died, we would let them put another one on [rations]. Because it finally evolved that 200,000 rations in the Gaza Strip was a running economy, and, of course, that became an important thing.[42]

Quaker pastor Lorton Heusel, biographer of Delbert and Ruth Replogle, noted the cat and mouse game the AFSC's personnel played with the refugees:

> In setting up a feeding program, one of the priority tasks was to compile an accurate census of the refugees around Gaza. Their first approach was to count each man and all members of his family. The Arabs, realizing that the amount of food they received depended on the number of children they had in their family devised a clever plan to inflate their numbers. To help their families "grow", the children, after being counted as members of one family, were routed around the building to become members of a "new" family. Thus, a family which normally had six children would "adopt" three of the neighbor's children for the purpose of census taking. When the Service Committee became aware of the situation, the census procedure was interrupted until

another more accurate method could be devised. The solution was to count the refugees at night when everyone was asleep. Although it took days, the committee was able to establish the exact number of refugees in the area at 225, 000, plus another 25,000 citizens of Gaza.[43]

In effect, AFSC had created an entire economy in Gaza, in which rations were a central form of currency. As AFSC staffer Paul Johnson described in an Oral History "Simple and innocent...for instance, when milk was given out to everybody a lot of people didn't like milk and didn't want it and they sold it to the local market. A couple of eager beavers set up yogurt making systems and cheese too. They made yogurt and sold it on the market...Wasn't underground! It was sold on the street all over the place. Somebody was eating the product, it wasn't a waste. It was a little around the corner, or under the table you might say, but somebody was getting the benefit. It's like the weaving project or the sale of ration boxes and bags."[44] But Johnson also noted some of the means that were necessary for AFSC personnel to do their jobs, "All the active men on the staff were concerned with this and considered what they could do. They offered bribes, they tricked, they did all kinds of things. Don't say I said that, but they did. They found out things they weren't supposed to know and they really had to do this because there simply would not be enough food. It was a risk."[45]

The friendly personal relationships that the AFSC had built with the refugees permitted them to cut the ration lists, although not without drama. This became particularly acute when AFSC conducted a survey of the refugees on behalf of the Conciliation Commission:

> When we figured we had 280,000 people—but we knew we didn't, and all our friends told us we didn't and told us why it was. As a matter of fact, by that time we had invented a friendly underground that believed in us and knew that we were trying to help and knew that it was not fair that some mukhtars had six or seven cards, that it was time to do something. I told them at the time, "The U.N. is not going to furnish that much stuff. They're screaming now that they think they have too many. We're going to start a project of cutting down, camp by camp. We'll work with the mukhtars, and when we get information and we know something, we'll do the investigation."[46]

The means by which the survey was done were simple enough, but Holtz and other field workers approached the problem both with considerable shrewdness and an overall awareness that they were, in effect, shaping the entire economy of Gaza:

We literally closed off the village—they knew what we were doing—and we went in and in each tent counted the people. We were smart enough by then to know, we watched them because the kids would transfer back. So we would count the kids, and a kid would sneak in and go out the back of the tent to the next one. We'd grab him and put him back, like that. (chuckling) So the count was still inflated, but it was reasonable and everybody accepted it. And then, when they started to get worried about the whole thing, I went to a meeting when we got down to the bottom. They knew that we had less than 200,000—actually, we got down to about 180,000—and Keene started talking to me about that and I said, "James Keene, you can't cut [the rations]. That's the economy. Of course we're giving out too much, but they sell it to one another and then they barter and they trade. The ones who have too many people on their cards, they use it. Their economy is built on our flour and rice and oil and the things that we're doing. And we're furnishing education, we're furnishing clinics for every conceivable thing anybody ever had, we are doing a milk distribution for the kids, we're doing all of this, and it's working. There isn't any question. But we've got to have 200,000 rations or there'll be riots in the streets."[47]

Other means of cutting ration lists entailed simple detective work. AFSC volunteer Paul John noted "If somebody died it would never be reported, of course, because with his name already on the ration list, after he died they still could collect rations from him. At one point some brilliant character discovered that when someone died if you offered his family a winding sheet, a shroud, when he came in to collect the shroud you could work one number quickly."[48] Requiring midwives at births, and offering swaddling cloths to infants, also provided more accurate counts.

Holtz and Johnson also noted that the cuts were not undertaken without additional manufactured drama, including preplanned "riots," often instigated by the Egyptian authorities. More problematic, however, was the fact that the surveys and ration list cuts were being done by the AFSC but not by the other relief organizations: "We began cutting lists, and this startled the hell out of them [the United Nations], because they couldn't make any cuts in the International Red Cross and the League of Red Cross Societies, and the administration in Beirut didn't know what was going on here. Although they were supposed to be doing this in every section, and we were the ones who [did it]."[49]

Emmett Gulley, the head of the Gaza mission, described the AFSC's census achievement in greater detail. At a Beirut conference in the summer of 1949 both the LRSC and ICRC were pessimistic about the task, with a

**Figure 5.1**    Original AFSC caption, "Dealing with a riot!"
*Source*: Courtesy of the American Friends Service Committee.

representative of the latter organization stating it would take eighty statisticians and three months. Gully stated that

> I saw no necessity, or possibility of hiring so many statisticians, nor any need for extra help, time, or funds. I reminded them that they had requested this statistical information about a month before and we had gone ahead and secured it and had it ready to turn over to them. The silence which ensued was intense. You could have heard a pin drop. Then everybody wanted to know how we did it. It was really very simple. We simply placed a native worker in each distribution line. As the refugees passed down the line, this worked filled out a form giving the needed information. No extra time or money was needed.[50]

Some AFSC expressed qualms regarding the issues of cutting ration lists and refugee dishonesty but the problem of "who is a refugee" was largely addressed in a Quaker-like manner, while the problem of inflated ration lists were dealt with in a sensitive but ultimately hard-boiled fashion.[51]

The problem of identifying the actual number of refugees in Gaza was different than in the rest of the Arab world because of the region's small and constrained dimensions and the Quakers' forthright approach to counting them. This experience could not be duplicated elsewhere by LRCS or ICRC, which though aware of the problem, do not appear to have tried hard to address it.[52] As Gabbay noted, these organizations had to deal with refugees dispersed across large areas, which frequently forced them to turn relief distribution over to local "Mukhtars, or to groups representing the villages, for distribution to the families. Very frequently, these supplies disappeared and did not reach the refugees."[53] In effect, the aid organizations and the UNRPR were already undertaking a haphazard regional development project using international funding, at least partially at the expense of the refugees. The project also ensured that the population estimates, including those executed over the summer of 1949 for the Economic Survey Mission, would be inflated.

But in May, even before any surveys were attempted, AFSC's Howard Wriggins in Geneva had already provided the Conciliation Commission with a statistical analysis that showed the maximum possible number of refugees ranged between 670,000 and 700,000. Using statistics provided to the Anglo-American Committee of Inquiry in 1946 by the Mandatory government, Wriggins also showed that some 200,000 of those refugees came from areas that were outside of Israel, although he was careful not to "exclude fear of Israeli's extremists as the chief motivation for their flight."[54] He added that "future increases in the numbers of refugees should be viewed with skepticism, since they are probably composed of destitute local inhabitants rather than of refugees from Israel." Wriggins' results went unmentioned in subsequent AFSC and UNRPR deliberations and have disappeared from historical analyses.

Other AFSC employees in the field had similar experiences that pushed them toward initiatives to stimulate the local Gaza economy and the larger regional development paradigm. Emmett Gulley, the overall director of AFSC operations in Gaza, continued to articulate a resettlement scheme for refugees in the Jordan Valley, but also noted that in addition to the weaving industry AFSC was developing in Gaza, a fishing industry was being contemplated. But personnel issues, particularly after the looming August 31 deadline, continued to be his primary concern.[55]

The issue of UNRPR being a source of economic support for local economies played out in other ways as well. In June, UNRPR Director Griffis was faced with a crisis when a report in the *New York Times* indicated that UNRPR had been buying low quality flour at above market prices, and that more than $1,000,000 had been "wasted in excess profits for middlemen."[56] The LRCS operating in Lebanon had uncovered the scandal that involved secret contracts between UNRPR and suppliers. The United Nations had barred LRCS representatives from even seeing the contracts until protests were lodged directly with Secretary

General Trygve Lie, who ordered Griffis to investigate the procurement system.

The embarrassment for UNRPR and Griffis personally was considerable. At first Griffis denied that the food stuffs were unfit, conceding that "our food is not from the Ritz and the refugees have definitely complained to high heaven," but blamed "rumors started by disgruntled Lebanese merchants.[57] Griffis pointed out that it was unlikely that the unspecified middlemen would have made $1,000,000 profit on contracts worth only $2,625,000, and representatives of ICRC, LRCS, and Howard Wriggins of the AFSC all denied the reports.

Regardless of the report's accuracy, the scandal quickly prompted a major, fateful chance in UNRPR procurement policy. It was announced that henceforth, UNRPR would purchase as much of the food supplies as possible, an estimated 75 percent, from local Middle Eastern governments. Under the new program UNRPR did not expect to pay lower prices for food, but expected that there would be "less chance" for middlemen.[58] A Syrian proposal for UNRPR to pay it directly for refugee aid was rejected, but the obvious observations that "local merchants" had manufactured the scandal and that as a result, Arab governments had abruptly been given a major economic stake in maintaining the refugee status quo was not made.

Though the United Nations General Assembly had approved an extension of the UNRPR mission through October, funding was still absent. The August deadline, coupled with the vague discussions regarding limited repatriation that were circulating as part of the Lausanne conferences, were frustrating to AFSC leadership in Philadelphia. Colin Bell, the program director for the Gaza and Israel programs, warned Pickett in June that the AFSC's "Foreign Service Executive and the Board were both emphatic at the time we went into Palestine that we must not continue beyond a short-term operation if by doing so any existing program of the Committee be hampered for personnel or money."[59] These warnings notwithstanding, a new phase of the international effort to cope with the refugee problem was about to be launched with the Economic Survey Mission, in effect, the development initiative that Pickett had been calling for since the winter, but about which AFSC personnel were deeply divided.

# 6. AFSC, the Economic Survey Mission, and Regional Development ✑

As the momentum increased for ever-larger international solutions to the refugee problem, the AFSC became more anxious. Other UNRPR aid organizations were expressing similar concerns about funding, and swift withdrawal, directly to the Secretary General.[1] One new approach was proposed in a May 18 letter from Elmore Jackson to Clarence Pickett. Jackson noted that he had heard that former US President Herbert Hoover had at last become interested in the Palestine Arab refugee problem. Building on this, he then asked Pickett "Would it be feasible for thee to take the lead in setting up a committee in the United States composed of people who have been or are relatively neutral with regard to the Arab-Jewish conflict, but who feel a deep obligation to try to help and find a satisfactory overall approach in which each country in the Middle East could play its part."[2] Jackson went on to suggest that such a committee should come out in support of the Conciliation Commission's proposals, whatever they may be.

The unusual use of the formal "thee" suited the unusual request to the nation's most prominent Quaker. Jackson's letter was copied to James Read, Colin Bell and Howard Wriggins and should be construed as a call for a new religious diplomatic initiative but one where the Pickett, not the AFSC, would take the lead. It should be recalled that Pickett had been involved with similar committees for several decades, using his AFSC title for identification only. The letter suggests the impasse that was perceived during the long spring of 1949 and the search for means to achieve breakthroughs. It is not clear why Pickett did not follow up on this proposal. But Jackson's mention of an "overall approach in which each country in the Middle East could play its part" carried the strong implication of resettlement of Palestine Arab refugees in other Arab countries.

On June 15, Colin Bell and Clarence Pickett attended a meeting of aid and relief organizations at the State Department organized by Assistant Secretary of State for the Middle East George McGhee, along with corporate representatives from the oil, construction, and shipping industries. No "top level" representative from any Jewish organization attended. The meeting was chaired by Arthur Ringland, the Director of the State Department's Advisory Committee on Voluntary Foreign Aid, who indicated that the goal would be to set up a "body to coordinate fund raising in this country, also publicity, and also to synchronize in the field the activities of voluntary agencies and others."[3] Bell reported that the contradictions were immediately evident between goals of various organizations engaged, for example, in religious missions and their relief activities. He also expressed the hope that a "simple liaison committee such as we had in the India/Pakistan crisis, would suffice."

Bell's comments are more revealing, however, of other issues. He noted the AFSC's "general closeness" to the thinking of the State Department and, more importantly, "the obvious anxiety of the U.S. Government that the refugee problem be tackled quickly and on a broad scale."[4] By now the regional development paradigm was firmly entrenched in the State Department. Bell noted that a State Department representative had confidently announced that "Development of the Middle East and its general prosperity can actually be accelerated by the settlement of the refugee problem."

To accomplish this, an "economic survey group" headed by a prominent American such as former President Herbert Hoover was being proposed by the US to work with the Conciliation Commission. It would survey the refugees and provide a series of recommendations to the Conciliation Commission before September.[5] Another representative at the meeting surveyed resettlement possibilities. Lebanon and Egypt were deemed impossible, but Syria and Iraq were viewed positively, although with regard to the latter, there was the "problem of importing Sunni Arabs from Palestine into a population composed of Shiia [*sic*] Arabs. Normally they don't mix well!"[6]

As Bell laconically reported, the American representative to the Lausanne conference stated the process was "completely bogged down." An intriguing Israeli offer to take over Gaza, with some 200,000 refugees and 70,000 local inhabitants, provided there was international aid, had been made early in the conference, but was seen by Arab states as a ploy for Israel to increase its territory.[7] Elmore Jackson had warned Colin Bell earlier in May that such a proposal had been mentioned in his and Pickett's discussions with Israel's UN ambassador, Abba Eban, the implications of which for the AFSC were that "We may yet find ourselves working entirely within the State of Israel."[8] This plan would resurface in later 1950 after the completion of AFSC's field operations.

On the same day that Pickett and Bell met Ringland's group in Washington, June 15, the American Ambassador to Israel, James McDonald, wrote to George McGhee with a revealing suggestion: "Could not Griffis's office have its mandate so broadened as to constitute a requisite base for the projected resettlement operations?"[9] This would have entailed a significant reorientation of UNRPR and American backing, something that McDonald conceded could be "embarrassing." But in response McGhee replied two weeks later saying that the State Department "have viewed the PCC as a body which could initiate studies and pave the way for the development of a resettlement program."[10] Though McGhee expressed concern that neither Israel nor the Arab states had presented any firm commitments regarding numbers of refugees "they would undertake to repatriate or resettle," he noted that "We have had in mind for some time the establishment by the PCC of an Economic Survey Group to be composed of outstanding individuals whose personal authority would carry great weight." Thus, while State Department representatives were attesting to Ringland's guests regarding the difficulties of resettlement, McGhee was intent to push ahead with studies to facilitate that end.

In June, Elmore Jackson was able to report that the UNRPR funding situation appeared to be improving and that adequate resources would likely permit the extension of AFSC operations until October 1. How to resolve the issue of long-term funding, however, was still unclear.[11] Also unresolved were larger political issues being negotiated at Lausanne and feelers being circulated elsewhere. For example, Jackson mentioned the problem of an Egyptian proposal that was withdrawn once it became known to other Arab states, and a Syrian proposal to Israel to accept 300,000 refugees.[12] None of these came to fruition, but they complicated long-term planning by AFSC and other relief groups and heightened the tension in the short-term.

Over the summer of 1949 the funding situation generally appeared grim, and in July the AFSC was warned by the office of the United Nations Secretary General that "funds and supplies now available will be exhausted by 31 August 1949."[13] The political crisis produced by stalemate of the Lausanne conference had triggered a series of proposals and messages regarding refugees in late July and early August that culminated in another near-crisis of relations between the United States and Israel.[14]

As diplomacy lagged, other forces were pushing development approaches. British interest in development planning was also again on the rise, and in July Foreign Secretary Bevin convened a meeting of Middle East representatives in London to optimistically review the opportunities. Participants were severely divided over many points, including the desirability of using development to push for greater Arab unity, as an end in itself and to thwart Israeli "expansionism." Bevin himself continued to push for the annexation of the West Bank to Jordan, and to define the overriding British concern in the Palestine problem as the retention of military bases in the Middle East, especially Egypt.[15]

Bevin's August memorandum on the meeting stated matters cited the primary Middle Eastern problems in terms of "the danger of disintegration due to the backwardness of many Middle East countries and the instability of their relations with one another," the Arab Israel situation, and communist penetration and Soviet aggression.[16] It added that "our general task must be to help Middle East Governments and peoples to develop in such a way as to avoid the above dangers and to maintain and increase our influence." The memorandum then set out a variety of reforms that were needed in the region, including large-scale irrigation and flood control projects. These were not specifically cited as means to address the Palestine refugee crisis but rather as means to raise standards of living generally. The memorandum stated British intentions to work with the Conciliation Commission to resolve the outstanding Arab-Israeli issues, including refugees, as well as territorial matters and Jerusalem. It then moved on to more substantial questions, namely defense, including the possibility of regional organizations, arms supplies, and Anglo-American cooperation. In all this, however, the memorandum noted that Great Britain had "very limited resources."

Yet even as international diplomacy stalled, and the UNRPR termination date loomed, AFSC personnel continued to undertake their own high level, if inconclusive, religious diplomacy, including meetings with Eban and with the new Israeli ambassador to the US, Eliahu Elath. Donald Stevenson, who would become involved in AFSC's Israel operations as head of the Beirut office, asked Elath "how Israel has room for more Jews but not for Arabs. He got a little stirred up by the question and said that Israel would not turn Jews away." Stevenson added that "Mr. Elath loses sight of the need for justice for the Arab in stressing justice for the Jew. He has something of a case, however, in pointing out that there are large areas of the Tigris and Euphrates Valley which could support the Arab refugees."[17] It is interesting to note in this respect that while AFSC officials did occasionally report Jewish immigration into Israel, at no time did they comment on the circumstances, namely disenfranchisement and dispossession of Jews in Arab countries. As will be noted below, Stevenson in particular regarded accounts of Jews being persecuted in Iraq as questionable if not false.

Nonetheless, Stevenson was able to report to Clark the very next day on a meeting at the United Nations in which Undersecretary in Charge of General Assembly and Related Affairs Andrew Cordier reported to him and James Read, Secretary in the AFSC Foreign Service Section, that financial pledges had come in and the relief operation therefore seemed secure through the winter. Importantly, Cordier also asked Stevenson and Read whether AFSC would be willing to take over all relief work. Stevenson reported that "Read pointed out that A.F.S.C. was much more interested in resettlement and reconstruction than in administering relief."[18] The prospect of the relief operation becoming long-term, much less open-ended, cannot have been received well in Philadelphia. Nor is it likely that the AFSC was pleased that the United Nations Security Council had lifted its arms embargo on Israel and the Arab states on August 11.

Read, later who served as the United Nations Deputy High Commissioner (1951–1960) and later became president of Wilmington College (1960–1969) highlighted the AFSC's skepticism:

> Under the AFSC-UN agreement, the relief program in southern Palestine comes to an end…the question has been raised as to whether or not the AFSC is prepared to accept the UN request should one be sent, to stay beyond this date, and perhaps eventually assist in resettlement and repatriation.[19]

The Friends were not confident that they could work under a United Nations agency, but still felt strongly about their ability to provide services. This was one source of their pessimism when discussions with the United Nations began about extending their work. Their strong self-perception, which was shared by the State Department, was that AFSC knowledge and abilities were valuable and should not be lost in the process of transition. Colin Bell had described these issues to Clarence Pickett in May of 1949:

> In my memo regarding alternatives for further service in Palestine the suggestion of working under the League was merely one of a set of alternatives which I was trying to examine. Of course, I would share your reluctance to work under an agency [UN] like this unless it meant that during an

interim period we should thereby be reducing our obligations to undertake direct relief. I believe (in fact UN sources have unofficially stated) that the AFSC could become bogged down in hard core refugee relief for a very long time and to such an extent that our limited personnel and resources would be flowing into relief operation rather than into much more difficult but more significant efforts to settle and integrate the Arabs. At our talk at Lake Success ten days ago I threw out the idea to Cordier that it might be very much to UN's interest not to resist our getting free of emergency relief commitments, if thereby we could make a contribution which was more significant in terms of conciliation. I spoke of the possibility that we might be used in settling Arabs back into Israel and he said, 'of course, there would be nobody more capable of doing this than the Quakers, if anyone can.' Hence, my anxiety to limit our relief commitments so that when the time comes for us to move away from the Gaza area with the refugees we are in a position to do so.[20]

However, long-term solutions were becoming the preferred vehicles for dealing with the refugees. The establishment of the Economic Survey Mission by the Conciliation Commission for Palestine at the end of August in effect created a more robust Technical Mission on Refugees. Its mission was described in these terms:

1. to promote the establishment in the Middle East of economic conditions favorable to the establishment of peace and stability in that area;
2. to facilitate the repatriation, resettlement, and economic and social rehabilitation of the refugees in order to integrate them into the economic life of the areas in which they will reside. The refugees will be settled under conditions which will permit them to become self-sustaining within a minimum period of time;
3. to aid the interested Governments to further such measures and development programs as are required to overcome economic dislocations created by the hostilities.[21]

The Economic Survey Mission was thus the culmination of the American-led regional development concept that had emerged in the winter of 1949, and to which Clarence Pickett had made a number of early contributions. But, with the participation of British, French, and Turkish representatives, it was also a de facto political process that appeared to offer both a horizon and a reason to delay hard decisions among the various parties engaged in negotiations. The orientation of the Commission, particularly under Director Gordon Clapp, formerly the chairman of the

Tennessee Valley Authority, signaled to all parties that the US would back a large-scale regional development orientation that would benefit the major states, and possibly even the refugees.[22]

The Tennessee Valley Authority (TVA) had been created by an act of the United States Congress in 1933. It was designed as a regional economic development agency with responsibilities for flood control, electrification, reforestation, fertilizer production, agricultural education, and river navigation throughout the Tennessee Valley, an area that includes the state of Tennessee, parts of Kentucky, Mississippi and Alabama, and smaller portions of Georgia, North Carolina, and Virginia.

The TVA was the first regional economic development project in American history and was by almost any measure a dramatic success. The region's endemic malaria was eliminated, and health and life expectancy were improved through education on "rural hygiene" and improved medical access. Educational efforts improved agricultural output through the introduction of modern techniques such as crop rotation, chemical fertilizers, and soil conservation. Rural electrification attracted a variety of industries to the region, increasing employment and raising standards of living. The TVA itself employed large numbers of local unskilled workers, as well as skilled workers in various management roles, mostly from other regions. Hydroelectric projects on the region's rivers during World War II made it a center for vital aluminum production and for the Manhattan Project.[23]

The TVA was supervised by a large Federal bureaucracy empowered to cross state boundaries in order to execute massive projects that included the relocation of tens of thousands of people from areas slated to be flooded for reservoirs. Along with centralized, top-down planning, strong cooperation with industrial corporations was also a hallmark of the TVA. Despite the resistance that was encountered from American rural populations in the first decades of the TVA, it became a paradigmatic symbol of what could be accomplished with large-scale, top-down, but decentralized regional development schemes. In the aftermath of World War II, where the TVA and other such efforts had been vital for lifting America out of the Great Depression and winning the war, similar projects around the world became an article of faith with American diplomats and economic planners.[24] Proper American technical assistance, however, would be required for multipurpose TVA style projects to succeed in areas as different as India and Pakistan, Iran, Egypt, Vietnam, or the Middle East.

George McGhee, the US Assistant Secretary of State for the Middle East, had proposed the selection of Clapp

> because he symbolized dams and water which were the key to the Middle East development. I got Clapp to Washington. He spent the evening with me at my farm and he went over to see the President. The President urged him to take the job, which he did without hesitation. We hoped that by pointing out the advantages of accepting capital to develop their countries (particularly the building of dams and the irrigating of land) the Arab states would see the advantages of using the refugees as resources and would welcome them. Israel could take some back; the Arabs could keep some. We wanted to remove the political aura which surrounded the problem.[25]

This strategy, with its implicit resettlement component, did not succeed. Despite initial positive responses from Arab states, the Clapp mission was quickly perceived as an official American undertaking. Secretary of State Dean Acheson instructed American representatives in Lebanon to stress to Arab authorities that "ESM was activated by PCC as UN organ" and that they should make "special effort to dissipate FonMin [Foreign Minister] fears that establishment of ESM implies abandonment by UN or US of political or other functions of PCC."[26] Even American relations with Great Britain were being affected by the launch of the ESM. On September 10, Acheson wrote the American Embassy in London instructing representatives there to request more public British support.[27] The British response conveyed back to Acheson was that Arab states were complaining now that "political objectives being subordinated to economic objectives and that their case consequently prejudiced."[28]

But the British position itself on Clapp was lukewarm at best. Their own development activities through the British Middle East Office were well advanced but still small-scale,[29] and there was no desire to be upstaged by the United States or the United Nations. In a meeting in Washington, Foreign Secretary Ernest Bevin complained to Acheson and George McGhee that "the United Nations appoint commissions which get nowhere and which lead to more and more *fait accompli* which cannot be changed."[30] Arab attitudes were rapidly hardening as well, as Acheson indicated in a telegram to the US embassy in London that word from the embassy in Baghdad was that the Iraqis were signaling they would in fact not be meeting Clapp. This would lead to the possibility that the Arab League would reject meeting Clapp that would "of course spell deathblow to ESM."[31]

This quickly prompted a change in the ESM's tone as well as mission. By the next day, September 14, Stuart W. Rockwell, Officer-in-charge for Palestine-Israel-Jordan Affairs, reported from Lausanne that the Palestine Conciliation Commission was indicating to both Arab and Israeli delegations that it "did not believe would be useful at present offer detailed suggestions re refugee."[32] More American pressure on Arab governments accompanied the ESM's rapid redefinition of its goals and by September 19, Clapp himself was reporting to Acheson from Beirut via the American Legation that "I am convinced that early discussions Arab states should be along lines works projects instead relief, with less talk of resettlement during first stages."[33]

Talk of resettlement and even regional development was already proving disruptive. In the minds of some, the two were entangled in ways that likely appeared counterintuitive to Clapp and his colleagues. In early September it was reported from Beirut that Emir Fawaz Shaalam, described as the paramount chief of the Ruwalla tribal federation in Syria, had come out against resettling Palestine Arab refugees in Syria "in newly developed lands, particularly lands that might be brought under irrigation."[34] The report stated further that all 125,000 tribesmen wanted to settle into agricultural life and that the tribes' "open opposition" "could frustrate equally the economic survey group of the United Nations coming to the Near East this month to seek an economic basis for settlement of the refugee problem, which now amounts to a program for resettlement in the Arab states."[35]

The British representative to the Economic Survey Mission, Sir Desmond Morton, made it clear in a telegram to the Foreign Office in late September that the Clapp Mission only received invitations to visit Arab countries when it unilaterally proposed that the "problem of permanent resettlement of Arab refugees will be set aside for the present in favour of attempting to find, in collaboration with governments, temporary employment for refugees in place of direct relief."[36] The political dimension of the Clapp Mission was thus cast aside in favor of renewed emphasis on economic development, and pointedly, without mention of resettlement. That remained, however, implicit.

Despite the Clapp Mission's limited two month mandate, frustration was increasing elsewhere. Writing from Geneva in mid-September, UNRPR Field Director James Keen, who would become Deputy Director of UNRWA, pessimistically wrote to Colin Bell, saying, "I should be very sorry if procedural difficulties should blunt the fine edge of our attack on the illusory idea that the world owes the Arab Refugees a living. Apart from the effect on morale I believe relief work is an essential first step toward any long term economic development project, but fear that the publicity given the Clapp Mission may have thrown the whole issue back into the political melting pot."[37]

Keen's misfortunes were compounded by the September resignation of Stanton Griffis from UNRPR, who was appointed US Ambassador to Argentina, and the failure of the United Nations to appoint a new director for UNRPR.[38] But Keen's comments regarding the "morale" of the refugees, and the apparently already inculcated idea that the "world owed them a living" are significant, since these are two criticisms that had been made six months earlier by AFSC. In fact, the prospect of that situation occurring had improved on August 10, when at the recommendation of the State Department, President Harry Truman issued a finding that released another $1.3 million for UNRPR.[39]

The refugees' entitlement mindset was fully on display to the Clapp Mission as well. Don Stevenson reported on a visit of the ESM to Gaza, where "In one of the camps, the refugees staged quite a demonstration. A large sign had been printed in English on which were the following, numbered as indicated: 1. Send us back home. 2. Compensate us. 3. Maintain us until we are refreshed. Just what they had in mind by 'refreshed' I leave to your imagination."[40]

An important corollary to the refugee mindset revealed itself as well in an impassioned letter from the AFSC Gaza Unit as a whole to Clarence Pickett, written in mid-October. The letter set out to describe the "current attitudes and thinking of the refugees in the Gaza area" but not other groups of refugees:

> Since it is very difficult for refugees here to communicate with the outside world, we feel we have an obligation to convey what we can of their opinions and thinking at the present time. They feel strongly that the United Nations is responsible for their plight, and therefore has the total responsibility to feed, house, clothe, and repatriate them. This is in addition to the feeling of many of them that the Arab governments have also let them down; some even feel that left alone they could have, and even now might reach a solution with the Jews. According the relief we bring them appears to them to be their right and in no way an act of humanitarian charity on the part of the United Nations.[41]

The letter made it clear that the refugees' only wish is to go home, regardless of the "changed culture which is growing in Israel." To compound things, the letter reported that:

They know that their skills are deteriorating. They recognize the erosion of the soul which their situation is fostering. No daily run of reports or statistics can adequately convey the harm and injury done to family life, to young people with no hope of work or school. A culture just on the verge of progress—by western standards—has been set back a generation. Violence and criminality, always close to the surface here, move closer. One of us was told the other day upon leaving, "Remember us in your heart"—the implication being that no concrete help would be forthcoming.[42]

The letter concluded with a recitation of the worsening conditions in the camps, and Pickett is urged to make use of the letter in any way he sees fit. The document is remarkable, not only for its pathos, but for a number of reasons. For one thing, the letter stated explicitly that it is giving voice to refugees who are otherwise unable to communicate. Thus, in the guise of a report, the AFSC Gaza Unit here explicitly had become an advocate for the refugees. In fact, the dramatic words of the Gaza Unit would resurface later in another context. For another thing, the letter offered validation of the "moral degeneration" argument that had been made much earlier. Here, however, the argument was used to implicitly demand a political solution on the refugees' terms, as opposed to indicating that the situation was in effect insoluble and that the AFSC's involvement should be terminated.

Finally, the letter illustrated that the refugees' narrative, which would become an integral part of the Palestinian national narrative as a whole, was completely crystallized less than a year and a half after their "exile." They bore no responsibility whatsoever for their unfortunate fate; their own political processes and decisions, and those of their leaders, go unmentioned. The Arab states bear some responsibility, but it is not made clear whether that means in their failure to defeat Israel in war or in encouraging or facilitating the refugees' flight. The United Nations bears ultimate responsibility for the situation, presumably by considering partition in 1947, and thus must maintain the refugees until the situation is resolved in their favor, by complete and total repatriation and compensation. The solutions demanded are clear and absolute, and arguably have not changed until this day.

## INTERNAL TENSIONS AND INTERNATIONAL SOLUTIONS, FALL 1949

In the Fall of 1949 the various contradictions were being played out, both with respect to the Quakers' relationship with the refugees and to the larger political situation, not least of all the growing commitment of the US to development solutions. Some contradictions were inherent in the UNRPR mission of facilitating repatriation, resettlement, and the vague middle ground of rehabilitation. While short-term rehabilitation, such as the Gaza weaving industry created by AFSC, was intended to raise skills, morale, and cash, contributed to the local economy and raised living standards, it was also seen as a harbinger of resettlement. Efforts at paring the refugee lists, called for by the Technical Mission and meaningfully accomplished only by AFSC, were also regarded as efforts to reduce the international commitment to the refugees and minimize the Arab states' burden of resettlement.

All indications were that the AFSC would be ending field operations in Gaza but efforts were being made to continue and even expand operations in Israel. The conflicted rationale for this was displayed in a lengthy October 17 memorandum from Colin Bell. Bell, the most philo-semitic AFSC staffer, initially waxed poetically about his weeklong visit to Israel and the Israeli achievement:

> The achievements are very great. Two safe, clean, modern cities, Tel Aviv and Haifa, have developed at a fantastic pace during the past two or three decades. The people in them are proud, suntanned, healthy specimens, and the children are radiant. But it is in the countryside to which the original idealists of Zionism originally came, that the real revolution has taken place ... I visited six of these rural settlements and saw there the moracle of people who, spring from the urbanized, opportunist life which for centuries has been the enforced lot of Jewry, now live without personal property of any sort and are engaged in the most primary production known to man.[43]

But Bell tempered his praise for Israel by pointing to several problems within the "tiny melting-pot working at white heat to produce a homogenous community," namely "the human factor within Israel and the monetary support from without." The struggle between the secular and the religious elements of the Israeli population, and the military, "idols of the nation, continue to be a political thorn in the flesh of the civilian government." Support from world Jewry, particularly American Jews, was necessary, for economic survival would require contributions of "enormous sums to the unromantic business of balancing the Israel national budget." More dangerous, in Bell's view, was "the very understandable development of a nationalistic spirit should Israel fail to find a national soul. History suggests that other nations in similar circumstances would exhibit a similar intense preoccupation with themselves—but one's hope for the new state is that it might transcend rather than follow historical precedent."

Bell then proceeded to review the small-scale relief efforts that had already been undertaken within Israel, aimed at Arab refugees, and to construct an argument for expanding operations based on traditional AFSC values:

> The AFSC is accustomed to going into areas of primitive social development or among people who are for the time being physically and spiritually below par. The situation in Israel is quite otherwise. The ruling majority is at a peak in mental and bodily vigor. It is self-reliant, hypersensitive, and in some directions perhaps the most able national community in the world. It feels it has all the blueprints and the know-how for a properly planed society. Its main conscious need is money. The Arab minority, on the other hand, is depressed, bewildered, and in a state of suspension between medievalism and modernity.[44]

Bell's description of his meeting with Yehoshua Palmon, Israeli Prime Minister David Ben-Gurion's advisor on Arab affairs, indicated to Bell that the AFSC was "not regarded merely as busybodies who have to be tolerated for the sake of good public relations." Though Palmon made clear that the Israeli government's objections to projects that would segregate rather than integrate Israel's new Arab citizens, as well as the "personnel of the adventurer type" ("little Lawrences," in Palmon's words), he and Bell agreed on two specific and limited AFSC initiatives. The first would be a community center in the Old City of Acre that would be aimed at joint welfare, cultural, and sporting programs for both Arabs and Jews but that would "start with the Arab community and work gradually toward joint activities with both groups, when the time seems ripe."[45] The second was for a small project in the Lower Galilee teaching Arab villagers about mechanized agriculture.[46]

As he had for over a year, Bell continued to seek out opportunities in Israel to demonstrate fairness, serve populations "in a state of suspension between medievalism and modernity," and in effect, to further the AFSC's religious diplomatic goals. But as the pressures increased on the AFSC, more internal complaints regarding the existing Gaza operation were surfacing. The impersonal nature of field workers' relationships with the refugees, necessitated by the scale of the operation and the need for efficiency, was evidently troubling. An October 15 letter from Charles

Read to AFSC headquarters complained that "AFSC must recognize that we can not conduct a mass distribution, in which we are acting virtually as a semi-governmental body, as we would conduct a normal Quaker operation."[47] Read's comments regarding the AFSC's "semi-governmental" suggest both a troubling internal perception at variance with the traditional self-image of the AFSC as wholly independent and non-political, and a vague harbinger of the future necessity to warehouse the refugees ad infinitum.

More revealing comments about Israel and Jews also made their way into internal correspondence. Donald Stevenson's distrust of Israel, already evident in his dealings with Eban and Elath, was also now expressing itself in opposition to the small AFSC program in Israel. It also appears to have extended to a dislike of Jews. On November 7, Don Peretz, by now back in the United States, sent a letter to Stevenson commenting on what Stevenson had evidently called "present injustices toward the Arabs" in Israel.[48] Peretz noted that he too had been "shocked to find a nightly curfew placed upon the Arab areas." But he went on to try to present a balanced explanation of "the environmental context from which these injustices were first singled out."

"Matters were so complex that it was impossible to determine the whys and wherefores of any single incident or group of incidents by uprooting them and examining them as sterile test-tube cases." The situation in Israel was so chaotic as to be overwhelming, particularly for Yemenite and North Africa Jews, but no less so for Jews from behind the Iron Curtain who were nearly trapped there. These circumstances did not, for Peretz justify Arabs "being moved off their land without compensation." Indeed, Peretz recounted one episode where his intervention prevented such an occurrence. He went on to discuss Deir Yassin, a "treasonable act of barbarism," "a moral stab in the back of the Jewish community," and a host of other issues. Nevertheless, "Israel has more political freedom than any other Middle East country." Peretz concluded by stating "I think it is possible to be both pro-Israel without being pro-Arab, and pro-Arab without being anti-Israel. I consider myself both" and argued strongly that if "AFSC abandons Israel, then the original motivation for work in the Middle East is also abandoned."

In a letter to Bronson Clark on November 25, Stevenson commented on the report from Peretz and the general situation of the Acre project. He indirectly criticized Colin Bell, the main AFSC leader who had supported the project in Israel, and who had articulated over a year earlier the need for the project's leadership to exhibit exemplary Quaker values. But

Stevenson reserved most of his criticism for Peretz. These were sufficiently pointed, even hostile, that Stevenson requested that Clark restrict distribution of his comments within AFSC. Stevenson responded to Peretz's introductory remarks regarding Israeli treatment of Arab and Jewish refugees with some scorn and suggested, "Because the Jews in Europe have been robbed has nothing to do with the justice or lack of justice of robbing the Arabs of their living. Two wrongs do not make a right."[49]

In the space of a few paragraphs, Stevenson went on to criticize Peretz's performance in the field, expressed doubt that "the Jewish Agency with its private army, the Haganah, could not have suppressed the Stern Gang and Irgun if it so desired," and mocked the inability of the Israeli government to locate the killer of Count Folke Bernadotte. Responding to Peretz's claim that the legal status of the Israeli Communist Party demonstrated the country's political freedom, Stevenson acidly stated, "Communism is so strong in Israel that some say (this was told me by several members of the Clapp Commission) that an actual count in Israel today would give a victory to the Communist Party. The Israel government, however, could not dare to allow this because Israel would then lose her chief supporter, the United States, and the financial support of American Jewry."[50]

Stevenson's animus against Israel was becoming unmistakable. He could not, for example, find any corroborating evidence to the Israeli claim that the Arab governments had advised the Arabs to leave Palestine. In an October letter to Bell, he claimed that according to the eyewitnesses he had spoken to, Zionist forces would bomb the cities by night and then leave an open road by day so people could leave. His impression was also that what had happened in Deir Yassin also took place in cities like Haifa, Jaffa, Lud and others. All this validated to Stevenson the idea that there was a deliberate plan by the Zionists to drive the Arabs out of Palestine and that Israel therefore had to own up to its responsibility for taking in the refugees. Further, he went on to say that he found Israel to be more of what he called a police state rather than a democracy:

> Spies are everywhere, and I don't doubt but that the Quakers are under very close surveillance, nationalism is the god, based on a religious myth, which seems to me, has no more basis than the American 'Manifest Destiny' slogan...One can sympathize profoundly with the Jewish immigrants who are being brought to Israel, and at the same time be quite out of sympathy with the type of government that is welcoming them to the shores of Palestine.[51]

As Stevenson wrote to Clark in November, what was needed in Acre

> are some Quakers who are not pro either side but believe in extending the spirit of good will and understanding to all men. I do not believe we should have those on the Acre Team who are glowing enthusiasts for the State of Israel and tend to gloss over the imperfections because of their belief in the Zionist cause. We must have a staff in Acre composed of people with the Quaker spirit who can maintain, along with friendships for Jews and Arabs, a certain amount of detachment from the current political and international scene.[52]

Yet Stevenson's deepest criticism was reserved for Peretz himself, of whom he said, "I don't want to be too hard on Don Peretz. I am sure he meant well and I do not question his motives. I doubt if he is able as a Jew and a Zionist, however, to take an independent position toward Israel."[53] Even at this late date, the Quaker ideals of detachment were being espoused, coincidentally in the context of criticizing one of the only Jewish volunteers in the field. But it may also be suspected that Stevenson reacted so strongly in part because Peretz, a non-Quaker journalist, had high public visibility while Quakers did not.

As the Quakers argued among themselves, the US commitment to the yet to be issued Clapp recommendations was already growing, as a September 9 State Department memorandum made clear. This memorandum, by John Halderman, Assistant Chief of the Division of International Organization Affairs, also shows how deeply rooted the Palestine refugee problem was becoming with the State Department itself. The "Palestine case" was now to be divided up among the many committees of his division, but decisions would be deferred until the Clapp report since "consideration of most aspects of the Palestine case must necessarily be based on the Reports of the Conciliation Commission and the Economic Survey Mission."[54]

The rising prominence of the Economic Survey Mission was also serving to postpone direct action to address the needs of UNRPR. The AFSC and other organizations were reacting to this with growing frustration. In testimony before the United Nations' Ad Hoc Advisory Committee on Relief to Palestine Refugees, one individual after another spoke about the uncertainty that pervaded the program and the transition to a future arrangement. Clarence Pickett cautioned that the AFSC would "under certain conditions we would be willing to continue, setting 30 April 1950 as the date, not with finality...If that sounds a little arbitrary, it is not because we do not understand the very great difficulty in which the Secretary-General finds himself. We are not unaccustomed to launching out on faith that apology will support those things which decency and good would require. But it is not emiss [*sic*] to have a clear statement of which will be required if we are going to be able to go on. I think the Secretary-General understands that we know he cannot give assurances in terms of dollars in the bank, but that he can give assurances in terms of what he proposes to submit to the General Assembly."[55]

In his remarks on the same day to the Ad Hoc Advisory Committee, Stanton Griffis commented on the relief agencies which "cried aloud to all and sundry that they could not go on because it was all a matter of uncertainty, they had no way to plan their operations, they had no way to know how long their people were going to stay out there, or whether we would ever get them back. But in the last analysis, they have done a sensation job."[56] Griffis praised the United Nations, the Secretary General, and the Arab states, but in a folksy aside he noted "I have had strong disagreements with practically every government in the Near East, with all of the different agencies, with the United Nations, with UNICEF and with everyone else, but when they found that the disposition of the cow was good, if it had any milk, they all co-operated, and it has been a very very pleasant experience, both in the Near East and here." Funding was the milk that made the operation go, and which fostered sweetness and cooperation from all parties. Continuing this seemed almost separate from the relief mission itself.

The Clapp Mission's primary task, to investigate and make recommendations for regional economic development, had also raised the specter of large-scale resettlement. Though the Clapp Mission's terms used the same repatriation, resettlement, and rehabilitation formula, the implicit resettlement implications of regional economic development were clear. This appeared to divide both the members of the Clapp Mission and the AFSC.

A letter from Donald Stevenson to Bronson Clark on October 27 described some of the growing rifts. In it he reported on a meeting he and Charles Read had with Dillon Myer of the Clapp Mission's Refugee Section. Like Clapp, Myer had no prior relief experience as such. However, Myer had directed the controversial War Relocation Authority that had relocated and housed Japanese-Americans during World War II, and then had been the commissioner of two public housing authorities. Like Clapp, large-scale resettlement and development were his specialty. Myer's participation in the Clapp Mission had been personally encouraged by both Clarence Pickett and by Assistant Secretary of State for the Middle East George McGhee.[57]

Stevenson reported that Myer had made it clear that "it is useless to send Arabs back to Israel even if Israel will accept them under UN pressure, for the UN could not enforce fair treatment and many of the Arabs would soon drift out of Israel back into Arab states. For this reason the refugees must be settled elsewhere."[58] The AFSC's specific problem in Gaza would then have to be resolved by moving refugees by "convoy across Israel to long term settlements in Syria and possibly Iraq." At the same time, it was Myer's view that the "Egyptians are completely unrealistic in holding on to the Gaza strip. On the one hand they will not take any refugees in, on the other hand they will not relinquish the strip either to the Jews or to Hashemite Jordan."[59] As had been the case in the past with other United Nations officials, Myer concluded by inquiring whether the AFSC would consider a "continuing relationship with a UN agency along the lines of social services." Stevenson was pleased at the prospect of working with Myer in the future.

Stevenson's comments were ironic, given Myer's role with Japanese-American relocation during the war, and subsequent service as the Commissioner of the Bureau of Indian Affairs, two enterprises of dubious morality. Moreover, as Myer made clear much later in an oral history, his "services were apparently not needed or generally accepted" by Clapp, and so most of Myer's time in the field was spent visiting refugee centers. Myer's minority report contesting Clapp's conclusions was not included in the published version, and Myer described the entire experience as "one of the worst fiascos [*sic*] that I think I have ever been involved in."[60] Clarence Pickett and George McGhee at the State Department, however, were provided with copies of the minority report.

When asked decades later about the Clapp Mission, which he had so strongly supported, and whether the prospect of an economic development solution had any real chance of success, McGee stated simply, "No. Later this same idea was tried again by Eric Johnston, the movie czar, but without success. The political aspect of it loomed much more importantly in the minds of both the Arab leaders and Israel."[61] Why this conclusion, so obvious in retrospect, was not apparent at the time is unknown. In a piece published a few years before undertaking his mission, Clapp had reflected that "What is going on in the Tennessee Valley is in essence an adventure in faith-faith in man's ability voluntarily to achieve harmony between human pursuits in making a living and nature's fruitful habits of growth and production."[62] Such faith in the ability to achieve harmony through science, technology, and development, so characteristic of the early "Atomic Age," now seems exaggerated.

The Clapp Mission's preliminary report of November 6 stated its goal as making recommendations for "the finding of temporary work for Palestinian Arab refugees" "since the matter is extremely urgent and cannot await long-term decisions, attention has been concentrated on short-term projects."[63] This did not please the AFSC. The choice between repatriation and resettlement was becoming ever more stark, even as the AFSC's own efforts at rehabilitation were making progress in Gaza. The development paradigm and the deferral of making hard choices that had been necessary merely to launch the mission were running afoul of the AFSC's growing impatience. Cordelia Trimble of the Gaza Unit reported to Bronson Clark on November 29 that "the field feels the report is hopelessly inadequate in that it does not immediately propose either the repatriation and/or resettlement of the Gaza refugees."[64]

Most importantly, however, the Clapp report recommended a new—and temporary—relief scheme for the refugees to "direct the programmes of relief and public works on or after April 1, 1950."[65] Direct relief would cease at the end of 1950 and the new program would "halt the demoralizing process of pauperization" that the refugees were undergoing. The report estimated a total of 627,000 refugees, and the inclusion of 25,000 additional destitute Arabs, for a total of 652,000. In contrast, in its draft version of the final report, UNRPR simply noted that it had fed 940,000 "refugees."[66]

The response of the State Department to the Clapp report was positive, except for the idea of a "Near Eastern Development Institute" that would have administrative responsibilities. Secretary of State Dean Acheson stated bluntly to the American representative in Lebanon, and apparently to Clapp himself, that "UNRPR shld [sic] continue function through present operating agencies. We believe operating agencies can be persuaded continue participate in view gravity situation involved. In fact we see no other satisfactory answer to adm problem since any change from present system wld [sic] require organization and recruitment large staff for relatively short period. Experts tell us such staff is simply not available because of many international organizations operating in other areas of world."[67] The growing commitment of the United States to long-term development would therefore force prolonging the interim solutions, in which AFSC played a central role.

Despite its earlier differences with the United States, the focus on the Clapp recommendations was also the agreed upon position with Great Britain. A mid-November meeting between representatives of the United States and the United Kingdom noted that "it is important that the Clapp report lay the basis for longer range development programs."[68] The document, classified secret, also stated that "the Arabs must take the major responsibility for carrying out development work" but added that "private capital was not attracted by the type of project envisaged for the Middle East countries." Nor would the Point IV program involve direct financial assistance.[69] How all this was to be reconciled with efforts to involve relief organizations like AFSC, on the one hand, and oil companies, on the other, is not immediately apparent.

Curiously, there are indications that Gordon Clapp himself may not have supported his own report as wholeheartedly as it may have seemed. In an unsigned memorandum from the State Department to President Harry Truman it is noted that "Mr. Clapp has indicated to the Department, but not in the report, that it is premature to embark on a more ambitious program because: (1) the Arab Governments are not yet prepared to discuss resettlement on a large scale; (2) Israel has been unwilling to undertake repatriation of a substantial number; and (3) sufficient engineering has not yet been done to warrant the initiation of large expenditures."[70]

Regardless, a wide-ranging reorganization of US aid was also underway. In November 1949, the American group Church World Service launched its "Bethlehem appeal" for refugees, and the British Council of Churches finally organized a number of separate relief efforts into the "Christian Relief in The Holy Land."[71] Also in November 1949, Arthur Ringland's Advisory Committee on Voluntary Foreign Aid, which had previously been an interdepartmental liaison group straddling the State Department and the Department of Agriculture, was relocated into the State Department under the Office of the Assistant Secretary for Economic Affairs.[72]

Concurrently, the US State Department convened a meeting of Chiefs of Mission in Istanbul to discuss the Clapp report and the Point IV proposals (and to which Clapp himself was invited by George McGhee).[73] Regarding the former, the conference commented that the "interim report displays excellent workmanship and grasp of the situation and is heartily endorsed" but cautioned that implementation of the report, particularly with respect to carrying out of the pilot projects, may be handicapped at the start in certain states because of the ESM's connection with the PCC and the Palestine problem."[74]

Similarly effusive language was used regarding Point IV, which was "admirably adapted to the furtherance of U.S. policy in the N.E. and the development of the resources of that area for the benefit of its peoples", as well as similar cautions regarding the need for the program to be "flexible and adapted to the particular needs of each country."[75] Assistant Secretary of State George McGhee's public statement echoed these conclusions but the confidential recapitulation of the conference's conclusions noted that particular attention had been devoted to the ESM and Point IV and the "development of mutually profitable trade and investment relations in the area."[76] The economic dimension of regional development, and increasingly, the military aspect of Anglo-American cooperation that would culminate, with French participation, in the Tripartite Declaration of May 1950 and the resumption of arms sales for "legitimate self-defense" to the region under the guise of arms control[77] could not have escaped the attention of the AFSC.

Another major issue that was emerging was the issue of organizing and funding the new United Nations agency. The mid-November meeting between British and American representatives outlined a number of areas of agreement that turned out to be momentous for what would become UNRWA. The new agency should begin work as soon as possible, that "any new agency set up should not be administered or controlled by the secretariat of the United Nations," nor should it "include Slav or other undesirable membership," and that "the proposed arrangement should not involve any government directly in the responsibility of handling relief funds raised under U.N. auspices."[78]

By making the new agency autonomous, the American and British designers hoped to maintain as much administrative and financial control as possible. Keeping "Slavs" out would presumably ensure that the new organization would not fall under control of the Soviet Union or its satellites. Finally, the financial arrangements excluded all governmental controls, presumably to ensure that donors other than the United States and Great Britain could not dictate organizational policy. This structure failed to take heed of Ambassador James McDonald's doubts of November 1948 regarding member contributions to an international relief effort. These precautions also failed to conceive that the relief organization would survive over sixty years and along the way, fall into the hands of its charges. The financial and administrative independence given to UNRWA as means of maintaining Western control backfired badly.

Apparently confident that control could be maintained, United States, Britain, France, and Turkey introduced a resolution to establish a UN refugee agency on November 30. On December 1, Bronson Clark reported negatively to Donald Stevenson and Charles Read, the heads of AFSC's Beirut and Cairo offices, respectively, about the proposal. His comments captured once and for all the contradictions among repatriation, resettlement, and rehabilitation:

From our point of view the resolution does not satisfy us. The concern of those of you in the field to have the Gaza refugees moved has been uppermost in the minds of Elmore and Cordelia, as they talk with various members of the delegations. It is quite clear that the U.S. Resolution, like the Clapp Report, may be a beginning of rehabilitation for the refugees in Arab Palestine and in the nearby Arab States, but that it is inadequate for the Gaza refugees. The problem briefly is this. If a specific point is made in a resolution that the Gaza refugees be moved, it immediately raises the question, "Moved to where?" This question will provoke in the Ad Hoc Committee the precise deadlock on the precise issues that exist within the Conciliation Commission. This deadlock will jeopardize even the continuance of relief.[79]

Any conceivable approach to the refugees was by definition a political one and would in turn trigger a political response from another party and potentially jeopardize that solution and potentially the provision of aid. The AFSC was trapped, and was in clear violation of its own "Nineteen Points", specifically point number eight that stated "We would not be prepared to undertake this minimum service of relief unless we could be assured that a solution to the vital problem of resettlement is being vigorously sought by U.N., & all others vitally concerned." Clark went on to note that he and Elmore Jackson had discussed whether to ask Clarence Pickett to make a statement pointing out the problems with the resolution, but this too was judged as having the potential to paralyze the process.

However, if the leadership of AFSC was reluctant to become involved in fundamentally political as opposed to relief debates, the Gaza Unit's October letter to Pickett had already been put to political use. Clark noted that "the Gaza unit should know that the letter which they wrote to Clarence Pickett on October 12, expressing the unit's concern over conditions among the refugees, and which was forwarded by Clarence to Tryvge Lie in substantially the same form,[80] was quoted practically verbatim by the Egyptian delegate, and that through his voice the unit's concern was expressed in dramatic fashion before all the delegates who were present."[81]

Although not cited by Clark, Lie's quotations from the Gaza Unit's letter had immediately made their way into the newspapers, where their comments were characterized as "urgent pleas" made by the "Quaker organization."[82] In fact, it appears that Pickett and Henry J. Cadbury, AFSC's executive board chairman, had not merely forwarded excerpts of the Gaza Unit letter, but had drafted their own that they signed in the name of AFSC. Gaza refugees were thus given voice directly under the imprimatur of the AFSC's highest leadership.

The AFSC's statement to the Ad Hoc Committee on December 2 was, by comparison, subdued, but subtly in harmony with the position staked out by the Gaza Unit:

> The situation will require, we believe, a special adaptation of the new United Nations program in Southern Palestine which will put the emphasis on rehabilitation and self-help activities in preparation for the refugees' being re-integrated into the economic and social life like the Middle Eastern communities. Such self-help projects, however, contribute to morale of the refugees only if they lead to an early absorption of the refugees into the economic life of the surrounding area. We trust that the special circumstances surrounding the problem in Southern Palestine will be recognized by the Committee and by the new United Nations administration that is proposed. On behalf of the refugees, we would like to urge all parties to re-double their efforts to find a long-range humanitarian solution of this difficult problem.[83]

With the novel phrase "re-integrated" the AFSC sidestepped the question of whether it supported repatriation or resettlement, for refugees whom it vaguely hoped would be "absorbed" into the economic life of the surrounding area." The term "reintegration" had been used only once by the United Nations, in September 1948, in connection to the refugees.[84] In the coming years it would become one of the linchpins for the United Nations and, at least temporarily, for the AFSC.

# 7. The AFSC and UNRWA: The End of UNRPR ❧

On December 8, 1949, the United Nations General Assembly passed Resolution 302 (IV). It expressed the organization's "gratitude to the International Committee of the Red Cross, to the League of Red Cross Societies and to the American Friends Service Committee for the contribution they have made to this humanitarian cause by discharging, in the face of great difficulties, the responsibility they voluntarily assumed for the distribution of relief supplies and the general care of the refugees; and welcomes the assurance they have given the Secretary-General that they will continue their co-operation with the United Nations until the end of March 1950 on a mutually acceptable basis."[1]

After commending, thanking, and expressing gratitude to other organizations involved in refugee aid and relief, the resolution got down to the heart of the matter of solving the refugee problem:

> [The resolution] *Establishes* the United Nations Relief and Works Agency for Palestine Refugees in the Near East: (a) To carry out in collaboration with local governments the direct relief and works programmes as recommended by the Economic Survey Mission;
>
> (b) To consult with the interested Near Eastern Governments concerning measures to be taken by them preparatory to the time when international assistance for relief and works projects is no longer available.[2]

The resolution stipulated further that the UNRPR program would extended until April 1, 1950, established various staff and financial arrangements, and also that financial contributions to the new relief and works agency would, as with UNRPR, be voluntary. Thus UNRWA was born.

The Department of State was by now reluctantly reconciled to the lack of progress toward a political solution. In a memorandum summarizing the situation to date, American representatives at the United Nations noted that the Conciliation Commission's most recent work had consisted mostly of facilitating the transmission of proposals from the Arab and Israeli sides regarding refugees and boundaries, since the Arab states were not prepared to enter into direct negotiations as desired by Israel. At the same time, the Arab states were requesting that the Commission submit its own proposals.[3] These dynamics remain familiar to this day. But in a sign of how askance the Conciliation Commission itself had become in the eyes of the Arab states and the refugees, precisely over the issue of resettlement, "it is not desirable to give unnecessary publicity to contacts between the Conciliation Commission and the Advisory Commission of the Refugee Agency." In general, since "Developments may occur which will lead the parties to seek the Commission's assistance. The Commission should avoid doing anything which might make more difficult the parties turning to the Commission under such circumstances."[4] The State Department thus staked its hopes on the Economic Survey Mission's recommendations and the new refugee agency.

Growing doubts over the prospects of the new agency receiving funding from Congress, and any meaningful contribution from British and French allies, also contributed to the State Department's distress.[5] So too did meetings with Arab diplomats, who interjected refugee issues into bilateral relations with the United States, and their own negotiations with Israel. For example, on January 11, George McGhee met Yusuf Haikal, the Jordanian ambassador. Though Jordan was actively pursuing contacts with Israel, Haikal repeatedly raised the refugee issue, even as McGhee cautioned that doing so jeopardized negotiations. Haikal responded with a statement that lies somewhere between extortion and a request for a bribe, saying

> it was very difficult for any of the Arab States to be reasonable vis-à-vis Israel when their leaders thought of the homeless refugees and the vast amount of Arab property taken over by the Israelis. If the refugees were not to return, what was to become of their property? Dr. Haikal estimated the total value of this property at twelve billion dollars, and said that it was obvious that Israel could not afford to pay this sum, despite the vague promises the Israelis may have made about compensation. Mr. McGhee said the twelve billion dollars seemed to be a very large sum.[6]

Such meetings, which included vague threats from Arab states of renewed war,[7] and unfavorable comments in Arab newspapers, may have prompted the State Department to press on with economic development and the new relief agency as the only ways to demonstrate American and international good faith.

The growing numbers of refugees and the potential threat they posed to Middle Eastern states continually vexed the State Department. In February 1950, George McGhee testified before the US Congress and stated:

> The presence of three quarter of a million idle, destitute people—a number greater than the combined strength of all the standing armies of the Near East—whose discontent increases with the passage of time, is the greatest threat to the security of the area which now exists.[8]

McGhee added, with considerable candor:

> Against this background, our solicitude for the Palestine refugees, partly based on humanitarian considerations, has additional justification. As long as the refugee problem remains unresolved, the delicate equilibrium affected by the armistices is endangered. As long as this problem remains unresolved, attainment of a political settlement in Palestine is delayed, and a major source of friction between Israel and the Arab states is perpetuated to the detriment of peace in the entire Near East. Finally, as long as this problem remains unresolved, the refugees themselves will continue to serve as a natural focal point for exploitation by Communist and disruptive elements which neither we nor the Near Eastern governments can ignore.

Though the AFSC had been internally opposed to the Economic Survey Mission's proposals for a new agency, the December 8 UNRWA resolution appeared to promise to at least some field workers that the duration of their involvement would not be expanded significantly, but also that they would have the opportunity to reemphasize the types of works programs that they had traditionally undertaken, and that had been executed on a limited scale already in Gaza. In mid-January Delbert Replogle testified before the US House Foreign Affairs Committee in favor of the Point IV program, saying that the United States had a "moral and selfish duty" to help what reports of his remarks described as "backward areas and peoples."[9] Replogle qualified his recommendations by stating that the United States could reduce suspicions of its motives if Point IV aid were delivered through the United Nations.

A January 26 AFSC memorandum intended for the State Department also put the best face on the changing circumstances. It stated that while work opportunities in Gaza were "peculiar," "developing skills and knowledge in the refugees themselves in fact makes them more likely for resettlement." At the same time, these efforts should not "prejudice the chances of resettlement." As the Committee asserted in their memorandum for the possibility of future work in Gaza:

> All activities indicated in this memorandum, while more extensive than those usually included in a works program, are of a self-help and morale-building nature, and calculated to arrest the worsening of the refugees' situation while resettlement is worked out.[10]

Though the term resettlement was used repeatedly, from the context it may be that the AFSC's writer was already substituting the term resettlement for repatriation.

This uncertainty was not reflected in a draft copy of press release regarding the work of the Gaza Unit. In particular, it touted the need for schools since:

> If they can be nurtured and encouraged by international educational organizations until local states free themselves from the bitterness of the present difficulties in the Middle East the Arab peoples will in the long run run their own public works projects and not be dependent upon tax payers of member states of the United Nations who are providing money in public works projects. The importance of the schools is stressed for three reasons: (1) that it is not only for boys, but for girls also, (2) that it is education and not just propaganda for adolescent nationalism, and (3) it is free and open to all classes. Each of these points represents a revolutionary concept in the area.[11]

The draft was insightful regarding the need for coeducational schools, the problem of "adolescent" nationalism being fed to young people, and the class-based nature of Arab refugee society. Taken as a whole, along with its early more laconic comments regarding the limited nature of the existing education that consisted primarily of Koran recitation, the draft reflected a deep appreciation and negative assessment of the state of refugee and Arab society. Moreover, the draft noted, "If it is true that young people are conditioned mainly by their environments, then these young boys and girls are being conditioned to grow up asocial or even anti-social. Many of them will probably fail to adapt at all to the demands of normal living. We cannot afford to let idleness be the devil's plough."[12]

This positive attitude, however, was not shared by the entire organization. In December 1949 Charles W. Bronson of the AFSC had already expressed doubt over remaining in the region, since the position of being caught between Arabs and Israelis and their irreconcilable differences would only damage the organization's reputation.[13] Withdrawing from Gaza, though, in particular, would not prove easy.

The United Nations Secretary General Trygve Lie formally requested at the beginning of February that the AFSC remain in Gaza until May 1950. This prompted a meeting of the AFSC's Foreign Service Executive Committee. Bronson Clark's memorandum to the Foreign Service Executive Committee on February 9 summarized matters. Julia Branson, the new head of that committee, had visited the Gaza operation in January and had floated a plan to the field workers for a "holding operation for the U.N." Speaking for the field workers, Paul Johnson, the new Gaza director, had felt compelled to respond, "on one basic point we are absolutely clear. We forcefully and vigorously feel that the AFSC must not renew its responsibility for the present type of operation after March 31. We feel we can take this viewpoint vigorously at this time because we are approaching the working out of a practical alternative which perhaps we did not have at the time of previous renewals of responsibility."[14]

At a subsequent meeting Branson also reported "complete unanimity" from the Gaza Unit, and after discussions in Beirut with Stevenson and Read, she reported on the difficulties that the newborn UNRWA was having finding staff. She stated, "Certainly nothing has happened that we know of here to give us much faith that the new agency is going to come into being and be able to carry on."[15] The AFSC proposal that UNRWA would simply pay AFSC staffers to continue on an interim basis was rejected by UNRWA's new deputy director James Keen, who had moved from UNRPR to UNRWA, and by Acting Director Brigadier General Reginald H. Parminter. Every sign still pointed to the AFSC's getting out on schedule.

By now, however, the question of Quaker religious diplomacy had also expanded far beyond the confines of the Eastern Mediterranean. The status of Jerusalem had been a question into which the AFSC had been drawn a number of times. The AFSC's earlier involvement in the abortive "Truce of Jerusalem," Municipal Commissionership, and Vail-Castle mission had evidently cooled the organization's enthusiasm to become involved on the issue, even though United Nations General Assembly Resolution 303 in December 1949 reiterated the body's commitment to the concept.[16] In the weeks before the resolution passed, Clarence Pickett had been asked by the pro-Israel group, "The Nation Associates" to sign a petition on the question of Jerusalem. In a memorandum to Pickett, Colin Bell commented "the compilers of the memorandum had quite strong pro-Jewish leanings." While he privately endorsed the concept of internationalizing Jerusalem, Bell recommended strongly against the AFSC, Pickett, or Harold Evans signing on to The Nation Associates' plan since it "could be interpreted as having a political slant rather than a purely humanitarian one."[17]

The AFSC's reputation was also drawing it into matters far from Gaza. In January 1950, Don Stevenson was contemplating a visit to Iraq at Israel's request, and in a letter to Bronson Clark debated its merits and implications. Stevenson suspected that "Israel and the World Zionist Organization would not be unhappy over a report from me that the condition of the Jews in Iraq is worsening."[18] He expressed doubt regarding the "supposed Jewish pogrom" in Iraq, but feared that "the worse conditions are in the Arab States the more likely it is that the flow of immigration to Israel will continue, and the better propaganda there is available to swell the coffers of the United Jewish Appeal."

That worry notwithstanding, Stevenson's main concern was the AFSC appearing to be "an agent of the government of Israel on a concern which the Iraq Government is not a party." Moreover, "if the report is an unfavorable one as far as the Iraq government is concerned, how does that leave us in our relationships with the Arab States? If the report more or less whitewashes the Iraq government, our Jewish friends will say we are not presenting the true picture."[19] He then worried about obtaining an Iraqi visa, since his passport was filled with Israeli stamps, and stated that in discussions with members of the Lebanese Jewish community, he was assured that "the situation has certainly not worsened in Iraq, or the Jewish community here in Beirut would know about it." His dismissive approach preserved AFSC's access to Arab countries, but did little to help either Arab refugees or Jewish Iraqis.[20]

A little more than a month later, Stevenson again wrote to Clark, only this time to consider more deeply the implications of the Clapp Mission's December 28 report. Now the number of refugees was stated to be 750,000, eighty percent of whom were judged to be farmers, and the question of how much resettlement would cost was raised. Stevenson's primary issue was responsibility for resettlement. He expressed frustration with Israeli officials who "have told me that Israel has moral responsibility to help take care of the Arab refugees but 'has her own refugee problems so can actually do nothing for the Arabs.'"[21] Interestingly, he notes that Israeli officials had suggested an international loan for resettlement "along the lines of the League of Nations funds for Greek resettlement," an intriguing suggestion that was never pursued.[22]

Some of Stevenson's concerns appear to have been situated at the level of religious diplomacy. He suggested, for example, that the AFSC undertake a report summarizing its experiences and making proposals in order that matters be "lifted up onto a different level" and that this should be done in "spite of the dangers of 'politiking.'" On a more practical level, he also noted that any resettlement arrangement would have to consider the Gaza refugees. It is difficult to escape the impression that Stevenson was frustrated with the entire situation and was looking for a means to disentangle AFSC in a manner that was consistent with whatever sense of his religious or moral obligations that remained.

Stevenson had one more outburst regarding Israel, this time in a letter to Bronson Clark regarding efforts to put pressure on Israel to take in Arab refugees. He commented sarcastically, for example, whether it was because of its democratic nature that "Israel wished to assume the position of the Russian Communists and Poles in driving out thousands of people without a penny of compensation? I think not. Whether the Israeli psychological warfare methods or the Arab States' propaganda drove the refugees out is beside the point."[23]

Stevenson also reported on Israel's treatment of the Arab community and its conduct during Israel's War of Independence. Even in 1950 Stevenson was quick to remind his constituents that the war is "not yet officially over" and we should not forget that "only an Armistice exists between Israel and the Arab States,"[24] reporting that Arabs are denied use or access to "their properties" and are not integrated into Israel's economy. Moreover, he raised the legal status of the Arab land and property he did not believe was "abandoned" and argued that the "so-called abandoned" property be held in a trust by the council for Custody of Absentees Property.

Repositioning the AFSC to leave Gaza, both psychologically, and publicly, appears to have occupied a number of staff members. In a letter to an American newspaper editor, for example, Charles Read touted the many accomplishments of the AFSC, along with its sister aid organizations, in providing for what are described as 800,000 refugees. He also praised the staff of UNRPR and its high caliber.[25] But it was only after great difficulty that UNRWA finally appointed its first Director on March 7, 1950, retired Canadian Major-General Howard Kennedy. An engineer and former Quartermaster-General of the Canadian Army during World War II, Kennedy's background symbolized the new organization's aspirations to short-term relief operations.

## THE LAST GASP OF AMERICAN VOLUNTARY ORGANIZATIONS

At the same time as the AFSC was preparing itself to disengage from Gaza, and in the absence of any significant development of UNRWA, the US Department of State was scrambling to patch together a temporary solution. In January, the Advisory Committee on Voluntary Foreign Aid requested and received the proposal from AFSC regarding continued operations in Gaza. This proposal emphasized schools, medical care, retraining, and limited public works.[26] In February, Arthur Ringland, the director of the committee, began circulating the proposal, and in March invited Pickett to a meeting at the State Department to discuss it alongside other aid organizations. He also proposed that AFSC should begin investigating the interests and capabilities of other aid organizations in Gaza, with the clear implication that AFSC would be assuming at least the temporary lead in the region.[27]

There is no report from Pickett regarding his meeting with Ringland. The next day, however, Charles Read and Bronson Clark also met in New York with Ringland, the representatives to the new UNRWA Advisory Committee, the American head of the committee John Blandford (and future UNRWA director), the British delegate Sir Henry Knight, and the Near East Committee of the American Council of Voluntary Agencies. Clark's report was especially discouraging. He noted that Ringland had circulated AFSC's proposal to the other organizations "asking them if they were doing any work in the Strip and what they thought of our proposals. This was a strange move on Ringland's part because, obviously, none of the other Agencies are doing anything in the Strip. I think, personally, that Ringland is laying the groundwork for a formal proposal that we carry on as a private agency some of the social service projects outlined in our memo doing so with financial support from private sources."[28]

Clark was also unimpressed by Blandford's "Hopeless innocuous speech about how the Advisory Committee needed the wisdom and judgment of the Voluntary Agencies, etc. etc., much the same speech that Clapp made prior to his departure." Knight's understated assurances that the British government would contribute to the initial $27,450,000 appropriation for UNRWA were also not reassuring.

In a follow-up letter to Johnson after a meeting of the AFSC's Foreign Service Executive Committee, Clark stressed a number of these depressing points. He believed that the AFSC would indeed be asked to undertake a project in Gaza, but that full funding for UNRWA would not be forthcoming. Finances aside, he expressed deeper misgivings about remaining in Gaza. He and Read had told Ringland that if AFSC and other organizations were to undertake such projects, it would be "a pity to in any way remove what pressure we had on the UN to undertake social welfare service."[29] Still, the Foreign Service Executive Committee had decided to put the matter back to Ringland with five points for consideration, that there be sufficient funding, that the new projects "be identified in some way as coming under the program of the new UN agency," that they be of limited duration, and that "in the event that the oil companies provided substantial sums, they could in no way expect the Service Committee to publicize the fact that they were donors."[30] Clark's sensitivity to the potential public relations effects on oil company funding coming to light are especially intriguing, given the contacts that had already been taking place for a year through Ringland.

With proposals that the AFSC undertake projects in Greece, China, Germany, and Japan, the Gaza commitment was no longer paramount. The financial and personnel commitments of Gaza had been such that other large-scale operations could not be considered. Now, though, AFSC was looking for a way to get out of Gaza and get on with their work elsewhere. Clark was "considerably bothered by the implication in all this that the UN won't do anything but feed the Gaza refugees and private funds will have to take care of the auxiliary projects,"[31] but his tone suggests that he was ready to move on. Clarence Pickett's retrospective view on the matter was similarly despairing. He commented that the State Department's initiative was a "clear admission of the fact that the refugees' basic problem would remain unsolved for a long time to come. And it has proved to be so." After the April 30 termination of the UNRPR program, only twenty-five AFSC volunteers remained as UNRWA employees.

The AFSC's final report to the United Nations put the best face on the entire experience and laconically noted that the "refugee problem was still far from being solved."[32] The statement noting how the ration lists had been cut from 260,000 to less than 200,000, using British Mandate records, particularly sugar ration lists, and actually doing a tent by tent survey,[33] were mentioned with similar brevity, as were the achievements of the public health and other projects. The report summarized all of AFSC's advice and warnings. Organizing and delivering relief was not the problem, but rather the lack of a political solution, and "reducing the ration lists to what was believed to be a realistic figure and one that would meet with the ration budget allotted to the area."[34] Aid had been regularly delivered on time every two weeks to groups of refugees, nearly at the same hour. Medical

**Figure 7.1**    AFSC sponsored carpentry shop.
*Source*: Courtesy of the American Friends Service Committee.

aid was also delivered with great efficiency, including health clinics, eye clinics, fly control, and neo-natal care. The report proudly noted that "in this period there were no widespread epidemics, very little gross malnutrition, the birth-death rate remained at what appeared to be a normal rate," but added that "while there was surprisingly little tuberculosis, there was an increase in venereal disease."[35] Some 200,000 meters of cloth were produced by local weavers and a garment project was planned, along with a cooperative enterprise for carpenters.

Despite these advances, several problems were noted, as they had been in the past. The report stated that "the visit of the Clapp Mission raised hopes and the subsequent visit of the Palestine Conciliation Commission gave the refugees respite from the humdrum of an uncomfortable existence." Still, the key issue remained who was and who was not a refugee. The report continued:

> There was a growing realization on the part of the occupation authorities, of the refugees and of the distributing agency that an unsolved problem remained in the form of the local residents who are not by definition refugees (and therefore are not entitled to rations) but who are in many cases worse condition than

the refugees. This, too, has been the subject of much planning and discussion without, it must be said, much to show for the effort.[36]

Yet the report ended oddly with the statement that the "general outlook and attitude of the refugees has been subject to the persistent wearing of time."[37] This was a far cry from the Gaza Unit's description of the general environment of pathos that had been sent by Clarence Pickett to Trygve Lie the previous Fall that was then incorporated into an Egyptian delegate's speech. It is, moreover, an even further cry from the internal communications dating to the outset of the AFSC's involvement that lamented the refugees' "moral degeneration." It is unclear whether the writers were concerned that negative comments regarding the refugees would have been interpreted as excessively political, or even would have led to reduced AFSC access to Arab countries, such as was feared by Stevenson with regard to Iraq. If there were such concerns, they were not founded.

The AFSC emerged from Gaza, and its flirtations with the US Government and oil companies, with its reputation fully intact. The Israel program continued at low levels, and periodic efforts continued to entice the organization back into the field and otherwise utilize their resources. In June, James Keen wrote to Clarence Pickett asking that Pickett persuade Paul Johnson, the AFSC's Gaza head, to remain and work for UNRWA in order to "see if it is possible to make something out of a seemingly hopeless situation which exists in Gaza."[38] Interestingly, Keen, by now Deputy Director of UNRWA, repeated his earlier comments regarding the refugees' attitude of "the belief that the world owes them a living."

Another emerging problem in Gaza was the integration of local Arab refugee employees into the new relief efforts, since their participation tended to reflect and increase the preexisting stratification of society. As UNRWA Deputy Director James Keen wrote to Clarence Pickett:

> The Quaker operation was entirely based upon the individual efforts made by the international members and a nucleus of Palestinian local employees. Organizational establishments such as the distribution of work, clearly defined departments, Manning Table and the like, were instruments seldom used by this Group. There was a tendency to tackle a problem by the individual staff member to whom the problem was presented rather than by an established procedure. There was also a marked tendency in the Quaker group to rely very much upon the nucleus of Palestinian employees mentioned previously, and unconsciously the situation arose where it was difficult to discern who was actually in charge, the international UN members or the privileged group of

refugee employees among the higher graded ones A certain decentralization seems justified and has already tentatively been effected to a small extent. One of the peculiar administrative hang-overs from the old days is that the strip is divided into several camps where there is no camp leader. The establishment of such a position is envisaged, and when properly implemented would certainly relieve Hqs of much unnecessary and time consuming work and the same time furnish Hqs with sound comments concerning the inevitable complaints from the refugees.[39]

Keen's comments were remarkable given that he was already employed by the newborn UNRWA. And given that his observation regarding the employment of local Arabs by the AFSC, it is ironic that UNRWA eventually transformed itself into the largest employer of the Palestinian refugees in Gaza, precisely the trap Keen described in 1950.

AFSC's assessment of its own relative successes and failures in Gaza was fixed at an early date. In a June 1950 letter from Bronson Clark to former AFSC Gaza volunteer and writer Ernest Morgan, the former made clear that "it would be correct to say that the AFSC has been deeply concerned that there has been no political progress made so that the refugee question could be solved. At times we did examine our program, wondering whether we were making the [word unclear in original] of a political solution more palliative. We did finally decide that in the absence of any programs on the question the UN should assume responsibility, and this conclusion co-incided with the creation of the new agency referred to above. We were happy, indeed, to hand over our responsibility, but we by no means withdrew in protest."[40]

A tension, however, remained between field personnel and AFSC headquarters staff that reflected the dissatisfaction of both sides regarding the outcome of the Gaza program. A June 1950 letter from Paul Johnson to Clarence Picket, written from Cairo, noted for example, that James Keen had requested a Quaker be sent to Gaza to take over the position of Chief District Officer. Johnson had forwarded the request to Charles Read, who had failed to respond, and that had elicited "only a most inadequate letter from Bronson Clark, which one day I will take to him in a spirit of great affection but sharp difference. Its essence was that executive personnel was too hard to locate for AFSC to send any to Gaza. You may feel that way in Philadelphia, but as to the propriety of sensitiveness of saying so I am not so sure."[41] Johnson added that "Keen's reaction to the reception of his proposal, which in the absence of a direct answer I felt obliged to transmit to him, was exceedingly sharp."

AFSC's role in designing UNRWA was minimal, but other efforts were still being made to involve AFSC again in aid operations. For example, in November 1950 Bronson Clark and Delbert Replogle responded to a letter from British Quaker Hugh Jenkins, who inquired about the AFSC resuming work in Gaza. Clark thought that it would only be possible if the Egyptian government relaxed border and import controls, while Replogle pondered whether a small team, similar to that working in Israel, might be able to continue.[42]

More substantive efforts to draw AFSC back into the Middle East came from other organizations in 1950. In June, Bronson Clark reported to Lewis Hoskins, the AFSC's National Executive Secretary, regarding a lunch with Bayard Dodge that he and Julia Branson attended, along with a number of American pro-Arab advocates. Dodge had become involved with a newly formed group called "Holyland Emergency Liaison Program" (HELP), along with Kermit Roosevelt, Jr. As Clark noted, "This meeting represents another move in a series of moves which, like the iceberg, show only one-quarter on the surface what goes on, while three-quarters of the maneuverings are hidden."[43] If anything, Clark underestimated how much of the iceberg was visible.

Roosevelt, still an officer of the newly formed Central Intelligence Agency (CIA), and Virginia Gildersleeve, former dean of Barnard College and a trustee of American University of Beirut, were among the leading anti-Zionist activists of the day. Dodge's father, Cleveland H. Dodge, had been deeply involved with both American University in Beirut and Roberts College in Istanbul. He had also been the founder of the American Committee for Armenian and Syrian Relief in 1915 (later renamed the American Committee for Relief in the Near East, or "Near East Relief" and eventually the Near East Foundation), formed to help Christian victims of the Turks. As a close friend of President Woodrow Wilson, Cleveland Dodge had been ideally situated to influence American policy. His son, however, found a very different political and cultural landscape.

Roosevelt had been a member of the "Institute for Arab American Affairs," directed by Quaker educator Khalil Totah,[44] during the late 1940s, and had published an influential attack on Zionism.[45] Gildersleeve and Dodge had also publicly opposed the partition of Palestine since at least 1947, threatening that "massacres of Jews will occur in outlying districts of Palestine and possibly also in Iraq," and that the "collapse of American prestige is sure to have an unwholesome reaction in America and to stimulate anti-Semitism within the United States."[46] In an influential article in *Reader's Digest* Bayard Dodge warned that "All the work done by our philanthropic nonprofit American agencies in the Arab world—our Near East Foundation, our missions, our YMCA and YWCA, our Boston Jesuit college in Baghdad, our colleges in Cairo, Beirut, Damascus—would be threatened with complete frustration and collapse."[47] For Dodge and other missionaries, American prestige and "our" progressive institutions were in effect one and the same.

In 1948 Roosevelt and Gildersleeve had formed the short-lived "Committee for Justice and Peace in the Holy Land." This group brought together a number of academics opposed to Zionism and included Henry Sloan Coffin, president emeritus of the Union Theological Seminary, and American Reform rabbi Morris Lazaron, as well as William Phillips, former Under Secretary of State and a member of the Anglo-American Committee of Inquiry of Palestine. This group, too, warned that "extreme Zionist pressure" was in "danger of disruption of our national unity and encouraging anti-Semitism."[48] It also worked in close cooperation with the Jewish anti-Zionist group the American Council for Judaism and with State Department officials, notably Loy Henderson, head of the Bureau of Near Eastern Affairs.[49]

In 1949 the "Holy Land Christian Committee" was also formed to help Christians in Israel.[50] "HELP" was another iteration but the officers of this group included Lessing J. Rosenwald, former chairman of the board of Sears and Roebuck and one-time president of the American Council for Judaism, and Allen Dulles, former State Department and Office of Strategic Services official and future director of the Central Intelligence Agency (CIA). Dulles was already serving with the Office of Policy Coordination, a strategic intelligence unit that had been made part of the CIA that year. HELP was directed by another serving CIA employee, William A. Eddy, former US Minister Plenipotentiary to the Kingdom of Saudi Arabia. Eddy was also employed as a consultant to the Arabian American Oil Company (ARAMCO).[51] In its press releases HELP warned that "lasting piece is not possible until relief, rehabilitation, and reconstruction are effected" and that the "hundreds of thousands of starving, sick, shelterless, create a fertile field for Communist intrigue."[52]

In 1949, Roosevelt's efforts had been cited by George McGhee in his secret policy statement of Secretary of State Dean Acheson, with the implication that money had been committed to relief efforts by an unnamed oil company.[53] In 1951, Roosevelt, together with two dozen pro-Arab,

American educators, theologians, and writers, including Gildersleeve and Harry Emerson Fosdick—who had been deeply opposed to Zionism since at least 1927—founded the "American Friends of the Middle East." This group was partially funded by the Central Intelligence Agency and ARAMCO.[54]

Although Clark could not be aware of it, HELP was a short-lived transition between the equally brief "Committee for Justice and Peace in the Holy Land" and longer-lived "American Friends of the Middle East." He and AFSC had also been drawn into the discussion regarding HELP as a bridge between two entirely different organizations, the American Appeal for Holy Land Refugees and the Near East Committee of the American Council of Voluntary Agencies that was administered by Arthur Ringland of the US State Department. As Clark put it, "This body, composed entirely of pro-Arab, anti-Zionist elements, was not to be an operating agency but was to serve as a publicity front for the operating agencies."[55]

Clark may not have been aware of Roosevelt's CIA connections and possibly those of HELP, which he believed only came into existence, thanks to money from the ARAMCO oil company. However, he was astute enough to realize the political dead end that Ringland had created:

> As things now stand HELP is running out of money and probably will have to shut down, as it seems to have incurred the enmity of all factions. We, of course, know that Arthur Ringland has been attempting to create some sort of new coordinating group, and, with an incredible lack of astuteness, he backed HELP and now finds himself in a buggy behind a dead horse. His efforts to get AFSC to take the lead in a new coordinating group in an effort to give the present situation an air of respectability, which could rise above the political entanglements and hopefully shake some money out of large donors, stems from the failure of HELP. I think it is clear that his handling of this latter matter will not produce results.[56]

Clark added that for the moment, AFSC "should keep clear from any entangling alliances." For its part, HELP did not last. In May 1950 it gave an award to the anti-Zionist journalist Dorothy Thompson, which was presented by Stanton Griffis, the US Ambassador to Argentina.[57] Thompson would go on to co-found "American Friends of the Middle East" in early 1951. The organization still exists today as "AMIDEAST," and is "a leading American non-profit organization engaged in international education, training and development activities in the Middle East and North Africa."[58]

## AFSC AS AN UNRWA CONTRACTOR

AFSC's role as an UNRWA contractor was neither smooth nor happy. A September 1950 letter from Bronson Clark to Corrine Hardesty and Cassius Fenton, an AFSC finance officer, described the situation. He noted, for example, that "the trend from May 1st has been to tie the program up in bureaucratic red-tape and headquarters control. It is demonstrated by making policy without reference to the field or even a survey of the field, and results in stupidity and muddling that beats everything I have ever seen."[59] Nor was Clark impressed with James Keen, who "has surrounded himself with a bunch of jug-heads and he admits it, yet he does nothing to rectify the situation."[60] As for UNRWA as a whole, "Concern for the refugee is at a minimum and most concern seems to be for the type of car you drive and to hold on to your job. In short, the whole program lacks guts, integrity and administrative good-sense." These somewhat un-Quakerly comments were followed up by an equally frank assessment of AFSC's work: "I think it is safe to say that our suspicion that we were doing a better job than all other areas is a gross understatement. I think I can say in all modesty that we are terrific."[61]

Field worker Al Holtz was even less Quakerly in a letter to Corrine Hardesty. He noted that the Egyptians had taken over instruction in Gaza schools and "the kids are learning reading, writing and bombing tactics."[62] He also detailed a minor conspiracy between an UNRWA official and a local notable that resulted in a false accusation of homosexual behavior against another AFSC volunteer, Vernon Pings: "Kennedy [the new UNRA Director] wanted to fire him without a hearing. When we went out and got the proof that it was false they refused to back Vern and transferred him to Lebanon."[63] Even so, Holtz observed that "Believe me, the Arab that was in Gaza ain't going to forget the Quakers so quick—startling but true."[64]

The UNRWA assessment of AFSC's contribution, however, was mixed. In November, James Keen sent Clarence Pickett an analysis by an unnamed Norwegian UNRWA officer the previous month of AFSC personnel who remained in the Gaza operations. Although mindful of the unique circumstances in Gaza, the report had difficulty comprehending the AFSC's approach and the Quaker spirit. Speaking of the AFSC's relationship with the locals, the report observed that "they held that all men are 'friends' and it was with this firm conviction that they approached the problem of administration of the program in the Gaza Strip."[65] However, "their enthusiasm was easily matched with exaggerated self-confidence which did not always have an open mind to outside criticism. Hence the tendency of this group to consider itself self-sufficient and look upon Hqs. as an institution disseminating more 'red tape' than guidance."[66]

Moreover, the AFSC's former success and resulting popularity with the refugees had become an obstacle for UNRWA: "When U.N.R.P.R. was replaced by U.N.R.W.A. no effort was made to transfer this Quaker Group popularity to the new organization. Today, the UN office is continually confronted with statements such as: 'it is not like in the old days of the Quakers.' Consequently U.N.R.W.A. must not only overcome the physical problems of the Strip, but must also combat this mental block of disapproval on the part of the local staff and the refugees themselves."[67] Blaming UNRWA's shortcomings on the inability to recreate the efficiency and popularity of UNRPR was remarkable. Whether Keen's bitterness at having been rejected in his request to Paul Johnson in June contributed to this negative assessment is unknown. Pickett, however, responded in a perhaps less than Quakerly fashion, saying he was "sorry that we had rather more poorly chosen members of that staff than we ordinarily have."[68]

Regardless of the negative assessment solicited by Keen, UNRWA Director Howard Kennedy continued to try to entice AFSC to resume some sort of formal role in Gaza, as did Arthur Ringland of the State Department. Ringland had for months been once again attempting to get voluntary agencies involved in relief, now under the aegis of the newly implemented Point IV program.[69] In early February 1951, James Keen, UNRWA Deputy Director, also wrote to Clarence Pickett and walked back from his earlier assessment of AFSC's role in Gaza saying, "I know that many of my friends have by no means lost their interest now that they have left the Middle East. I believe the report indicates reasonably satisfactory conditions but that you will find special pleasure in that the confidence of the refugees in the integrity and goodwill of the Agency appears to have been maintained, this was I think one of the happiest features of the Quaker program."[70] Later in February, Pickett responded to Keen that, with regard to Kennedy's request, the AFSC would "take the matter under advisement." He also commented to Keen that Ringland's request did not seem to be a "wise policy."[71] Refusing to becoming involved in Gaza on any formal level, beyond providing personnel to participate in UNRWA operations as contractors, was now the policy of AFSC.

At the end of 1951, however, there was another brief period of intense discussions between UNRWA and AFSC, and within AFSC itself, regarding possible future involvement in refugee affairs. On October 22, Paul

Johnson of AFSC met the new Director John Blandford and other UNRWA personnel in Beirut. As the UNRWA minutes of the meeting described it, Johnson had come to the Middle East on an extended study tour. He "expressed his pleasure at being back in the area" and asked whether AFSC could "play a role in reintegration."[72] The minutes recorded that Johnson related AFSC's interest in four areas of work for UNRWA, social welfare and clothing, training and education, assistance to economic refugees that had been suggested by the British Foreign Office, and reintegration. It added, "The latter was clearly the AFSC's major interest. Syria was the most obvious place for this but he has also talked with the Agency's Liaison Officer in Tripolitania which might also prove a suitable area for such schemes if Agency policy allowed." The understanding of reintegration as resettlement was clear.

But the minutes also provided an insight into the AFSC field representative's thinking about a renewed role as a United Nations contractor: "The AFSC did not propose to come in under the UN flag but would prefer to remain an independent unofficial agency that might for that very reason be able to accomplish things that were impossible for the Agency for political reasons; the committee would this maintain its protective coloring which might prove useful for back door approaches."[73] Such a *sub rosa* arrangement shows how far the AFSC had come in two years with regard to a contradictory "hard-boiled" yet non-political approach to the refugee problem.

As was the case a year earlier, there was a contrast between the attitudes of the AFSC's field personnel and the senior staff in Philadelphia. The minutes of the AFSC's Sub-committee on Social and Technical Assistance meeting of November 1 show an uncertain reception of Johnson's discussions with UNRWA and implied he was exceeding his mandate. It stated that Johnson believed there was "a great deal of enthusiasm among the various people has advised with and he finds himself in the unusual position of having to hold back. He has inquired for further information. He is aware of the limitations of his mandate, i.e. to merely make a preliminary survey and analysis for purposes of report, and he feels he is approaching those limitations here."[74]

Writing to Pickett a few days later, Johnson enthused about "most intriguing possibility for Quaker service seems to be refugee resettlement in Libya. Syria, where I am sure major resettlement will take place some day, is for the present quite impossible. Other ideas are exceedingly tentative."[75] Knowingly or not, Johnson was reviving Colin Bell's November 1948 musings about an AFSC role in an Arab-Jewish population exchange. Johnson also discussed various schemes for control of the Gaza Strip, including Jordanian rule and international trusteeship. Any possibility of refugee resettlement, however, was hampered however by the Egyptian policy of refusing

> all requests for refugee transfer out of the Strip, even for individuals called to a specific employment opportunity. This policy is superficially justified by the current investigations of refugee-resettlement in the Sinai, in order, say the Egyptians, not to draw off those people most capable and with the most initiative, and leave for the Sinai project only the hard core of unemployables. But I believe the policy is in fact rather a reflection of some obscure notion that 'possession' of 200,000 Gaza refugees is some sort of lever in international bargaining. Thus removal of the Strip from Egyptian control seems one of the basic requirements for resettlement of the refugees, evan [*sic*] at the one-at-a-time pace, to say nothing of anything genuinely meriting the name of a program.[76]

The next day Johnson wrote again to Pickett and expressed additional frustration after his meeting with UNRWA Deputy Director James Keen. Johnson described a vague back and forth with Keen, where each side sounded out the other regarding possible interests and conditions, but in the end he could not pin Keen down; "this answer is clearly not the information we sought. It is not a decision for or against Libyan resettlement; it is not a decision for or against voluntary group participation, much less a comment on financing. And these decisions have plainly not been taken."[77] Johnson believed strongly that the American and British members of the UNRWA Advisory Committee supported the resettlement idea, but he added that it was unknown whether UNRWA itself would as well. At that point, though, Johnson complained bitterly that "I have been unable to penetrate the bureaucratic Paper Curtain within these hallowed precincts to see Blandford, who has been 'leaving Paris' for four days. I hope he may be brought to bay in Paris!"

By November 20, Johnson was losing hope in any renewed AFSC participation. With regard to whether AFSC should become involved in resettlement or remain focused on training, Johnson commented, "A case could be made for the belief that both ends might be served in a single project, or in each of several projects. Investigations are partially complete only. For the time being I can clear see resettlement outlines, while possibilities for training work are yet very foggy."[78] But three paragraphs, later Johnson admits regarding resettlement "UN is stuck, and getting nowhere. No single scheme, of any size and character, is in operation anywhere, whatever you may hear to the contrary." Though Johnson was supportive "to deny the problems in the way, either of conceiving the scheme or of carry it out, would be singularly foolish."

Two weeks earlier, however, Johnson had recognized that the refugees were being used as a tool by Egypt. By November 20, however, he had rethought the question. His explanation of the matter shows how relief and religious diplomacy had become finally and thoroughly blended. His comments are a remarkable *Cri de Coeur*. In supporting the inchoate, indeed, nonexistent, Libyan resettlement idea, Johnson prefaced his comments by saying:

> This next paragraph I hesitate to transcribe from my draft, for obvious reasons, yet I mean it with utter solemnity. I have not wish to be unduly melodramatic, but if Friends are unable to find a way to help bring about a move toward voluntary resettlement, in however small a way, I see no power whatever that can do it under present political circumstances. I have toyed with the idea of laying it so heavily upon you to send out here not a single person of small stature, but the broadest-gauge and most influential international Quaker delegation you can contrive, with power not only to investigate but to commit our organizations to assumption of responsibility for accepting any opportunities that can be brought into existence. I will happily carry their suitcases.[79]

Johnson's call was similar to Elmore Jackson's request to Clarence Pickett in May 1949 that he convened prominent Americans to publicly support the Conciliation Commission's efforts. But Johnson quickly related the truth of the matter regarding Libyan resettlement, "we brought it out of the limbo of forgotten things, and insisted talking about it" despite the fact that the proposals were "according to UNRWA higher staff as dead as herrings." Johnson admitted again that "it bears repetition: The Arab Governments do not want the refugee problem solved on its merits, and will willingly accept solution only if their political price is met." Still, Johnson believed, if AFSC took the lead "we may open the way for a broader solution by public authority." The situation was essentially futile, but AFSC must nevertheless take the lead.

At the December 3rd meeting of the Sub-committee on Social and Technical Assistance, the matter of resettling refugees in Libya was finally put in proper context. The minutes explained laconically, that "the question of the transfer of refugees to Libya had come up as far back as last February in the UNRWA. Recommendations were made over this period and then the subject was dropped in September. The fact that Paul Johnson has been raising the issue has reopened it."[80] Johnson's veritable call to arms, evoking an unparalleled crisis that required nothing less than mobilization of AFSC's full array of political power, ultimately fell on deaf ears. It may be suspected that his honesty regarding the unwillingness of Arab governments to relinquish the refugees as tools of blackmail against the West, and the fact that UNRWA in effect had no plan for resettlement, much less agreement from any Arab state, contributed to the AFSC's decision. The question of AFSC involvement in refugee resettlement then ended.

Part of the futility being sensed during the Fall of 1951 stemmed from the failure of UNRWA's public works projects. As the organization had laconically reported a year before the "time taken to interest refugees and governments in a works program was longer than anticipated."[81] By 1951, UNRWA described the situation in more dire terms, explaining that the refugees' "hostility to all works undertaken by the Agency was based upon their conviction that to accept employment within the host countries would be tantamount to renouncing the right to return home, and perhaps even the right to compensation."[82] Though UNRWA made small loans for refugee business, few of these had the potential for meaningful levels of employment, and consequent removal of refugees from the ration lists. The desires of Arab governments for large-scale projects that would develop national infrastructure were more compelling and would soon be explored through various schemes aimed at reintegration of refugees.[83]

Many of the issues that the AFSC addressed in its relatively brief operations in Gaza were again faced by UNRWA, most notably that of how many refugees actually existed. One of the earliest UNRWA reports to the United Nations, presented during the directorship of Howard Kennedy, noted "it is almost impossible to define closely the word "refugee," as applied to the work of the Agency, without leaving certain groups of deserving people outside those accepted, or conversely, including groups who probably should not be in receipt of relief."[84] In contrast to the "hard-boiled" approach of the AFSC, which in the first instance actually counted the number of persons purporting to be refugees, UNRWA adopted a different approach. Though it purported to have "steadfastly resisted persistent and persuasive efforts to have it become responsible for the care and feeding of citizens of the various countries who are merely needy or destitutes as a result of the war in Palestine," the report asserted that for working purposes, the Agency has decided that a refugee is a needy person, who, as a result of the war in Palestine, has lost his home and his means of livelihood. A large measure of flexibility in the interpretation of the above definition is accorded to chief district officers to meet the many border-line cases which inevitably arise. In some circumstances, a family may have lost part or all of its land from which its living was secured, but it may still have a house to live in. Others may have lived on one side of the boundary but worked in what is now Israel most of the year. Others, such as Bedouins, normally moved from one area of the country to another, and some escaped with part or all of their goods but cannot return to the area where they formerly resided the greater part of the time.[85]

With regard to numbers, the report first accepted the Clapp Mission's figure of 774,000 refugees, and then qualified it by claiming that it "is unlikely that numbers will be reduced below 800,000, and it is possible that that number may be exceeded."[86] It similarly noted:

All earlier attempts at a close census of those entitled to relief have been frustrated, but a comprehensive survey, now under way, is achieving worthwhile results in casting up names of dead people for which rations are still drawn, fraudulent claims regarding numbers of dependents (it is alleged that it is a common practice for refugees to hire children from other families at census time), and in eliminating duplications where families have two or more ration cards.[87]

Finally, with regard to morale, the UNRWA report was far more upbeat than the AFSC's, but cautioned:

Strangely enough the general morale of the refugees is higher than might be expected after spending more than two years in exile under most trying conditions. Real trouble-makers are confined to a very small proportion of the total number of refugees, and food strikes and work stoppages are generally considered to be the result of organized pressure groups. There is considerable evidence indicating that subversive effort is fairly widely diffused amongst the refugees. The Arab is, however, a confirmed individualist and does not offer the most fruitful type of field in which to extol the benefits of any form of government which might propose to alter his traditional mode of life. Otherwise, it is almost inevitable that the misery and suffering of the refugees would already have made them almost completely the tools of pressure groups wishing to exploit their misery for political or other reasons.[88]

This last statement is notable, since it played to the growing Western fears of Communist influence, including those that had shaped UNRWA behind the scenes, and that would help shape American responses to the Middle East throughout the 1950s. Learning to craft the public perception of the refugees and their issues would become an important UNRWA skill. Here too the organization repeated some of the steps that had been taken by AFSC, but in a different political and strategic environment.

# 8. International Security and the Question of Reintegration ✧

After much contention and debate United Nations General Assembly adopted Resolution 393 (V) on December 2, 1950. The Resolution stated:

> without prejudice to the provisions of paragraph of General Assembly resolution 194 (III) of 11 December 1948, the reintegration of the refugees into the economic life of the Near East, either by repatriation or resettlement, is essential in preparation for the time when international assistance is no longer available, and for the realization of conditions of peace and stability in the area.[1]

The Resolution went on to direct UNRWA "to establish a reintegration fund which shall be utilized for projects requested by any government in the Near East and approved by the Agency for the permanent re-establishment of refugees and their removal from relief." The AFSC had discussed reintegration for close to a year, but with its adoption by the United Nations it became an international goal. Defining reintegration, however, was subject to changing geopolitical contingencies.

Throughout 1949 and 1950 a series of developments fundamentally reshaped the global scene and changed the Western, and especially American, perspectives on the Middle East generally, and the Palestine Arab refugee question specifically. Western defense interests had been given new shape and urgency by the Communist takeover of northern China in January 1949, the creation of NATO in April, and the detonation of the Soviet Union's first atomic weapon in August. Cold War issues began to dominate foreign policy planning as never before, and reached new levels with the issuing in April 1950 of NSC-68, a classified national security report, which situated the conflict with the Soviet Union as central and existential for the West, and that moved the United States closer toward a policy of containment.[2] The beginning of the Korean War in June 1950 also shifted American priorities still further, particularly in the areas of military alliances and the conduct of the war through the United Nations.

For the United States and Great Britain, Middle East affairs, including arms control efforts such as the Tripartite Declaration and refugee policy, were being viewed increasingly through the lenses of superpower competition and anti-communism.[3] Foreign aid would also be restructured in view of the larger Cold War situation, such as through the US Mutual Security Act of 1951, and regional defense projects such as "Middle East Command" and the "Middle East Defense Organization" would be launched.[4] The October 1951 proposal for a "Middle East Defense Command" relied heavily on Western basing rights in the Canal Zone but came a week after Egypt repudiated the Anglo-Egyptian Treaty of 1936, and the Anglo-Egyptian Agreement of 1899. Egypt quickly rejected the new proposal.[5] Stable relations with both Israel, which was moving away from its brief early position of official neutrality toward the West, and with the Arab states, which were feared could fall under Communist sway, then became central concerns for both the State Department and the National Security Council.[6]

In November 1951 the American Chiefs of Middle East Missions again met in Istanbul but with a completely different strategic outlook. In a document generally concerned with power politics, the threat of Communism, and the need to strengthen Greece, Turkey, Israel, and the Arab regimes, the Palestine Arab refugee issue found a central place. It was stated, with some apparent relief, by the participants that while during the course of 1950 "the Arabs have not abandoned the principle of repatriation, and may be expected to reaffirm it, they show signs of becoming more realistic as to the obstacles to any satisfactory implementation of this principle, and are giving serious thought to the alternative of compensation and to the concept of reintegration."[7]

The conference also expressed some satisfaction that Israel had voiced interest in resolving the issue of the refugees' blocked bank accounts that was regarded as evidence of Israeli "good will." But the official American orientation toward the refugee issue was stated clearly, "The hard core of approximately 800,000 refugees, on relief and in temporary shelter, constitutes a serious threat to stability, and an important impediment to peace between the Arab states and Israel." With stability in mind, the report endorsed the goal of "reintegration" but it also made clear that the term was being used in a specific sense with respect to UNRWA's task of "direct reintegration, especially in rural areas, financed by international funds." It recommended that "reintegration should be approached as an economic undertaking and service to the refugees, and political issues should be kept to a minimum. There is great need to prepare the minds of 600,000 refugees to move from present locations near Palestine to new countries, new climates, and new economies, and to encourage their acceptance by the publics of the countries to which they must move."[8]

The US National Security Council concurred with the State Department. In a memorandum updating NSC-47/2 on US policy toward Israel and the Arab states, State's James E. Webb report to the Executive Secretary of the National Security Council, James S. Lay notes that UNRWA had not received full funding and was "perforce confined chiefly to relief measures and to very limited works projects." But he added with regard to the Arab states' "by their public acceptance of this resolution [creating UNRWA] and by private statements, Arab representatives have indicated that they regard resettlement of most of the refugees in Arab territory as inevitable."[9] It should be noted that the AFSC's last efforts at becoming involved in resettlement schemes came precisely in the period of October and November 1951. Paul Johnson was not the only participant who thought that resettlement was the future.

The same policies regarding resettlement were echoed a year later in a Top Secret memorandum to the State Department's Near Eastern Affairs bureau from Donald C. Bergus, second secretary at the American Embassy in Beirut and political advisor to the American representative to UNRWA. The primary issues addressed in Bergus's memorandum were refugee compensation, resettlement, and regional defense. After speculations regarding the political connections of American Jews to Israel, more revealing of his own attitudes and those of the State Department, Bergus noted that the Arab and Israeli concepts of compensation differed vastly. Israel was willing to consider paying for real property that had been lost, while the Arab states factored in damages. Bergus estimated that the Israeli concept would entail about $500,000,000, while the Arab version would cost many billions of dollars. Either way, "Ultimate reintegration of refugees now on relief will require an additional expenditure of at last half a billion dollars and the U.S. will probably have to pay most of this bill as well." But he added that "The political barriers to the UNRWA program have almost been completely dissolved. The time has now come for us to press forward with positive action on the refugee program to a point where receiving states are fully convinced that refugee resettlement means a significant economic development"[10]

Reintegration, though vague, had become firmly understood as resettlement, at least in some official US circles, just as it had earlier for most senior

AFSC leaders. Reflected the British understanding, Sir Henry Knight, the British representative to the Advisory Committee commented in July 1951 that "Reintegration is interpreted as assistance to refugees in finding homes and jobs," an analysis that was tantamount to resettlement.[11] This understanding harmonized with clues emanating from elsewhere throughout 1951 and 1952. Specifically, the same sorts of tantalizing rumors regarding Arab states suddenly becoming willing to accept refugees were reaching the Advisory Committee as had been floated at the Lausanne Conference some two years earlier, only to be dashed just days later.[12]

The appointment of John Blandford, Jr. as Director of UNRWA to replace Howard Kennedy was telling of the mindset regarding reintegration at the United Nations and its patrons. Rather than a military quartermaster like Kennedy, who specialized in operational logistics, Blandford had been a manager at the Tennessee Valley Authority, administrator of the wartime National Housing Authority, deputy chief the United States Bureau of the Budget and then the US Economic Cooperation Administration in Greece, and a consultant to President Truman on the Marshall Plan.

In short, Blandford was a professional development administrator with experience in managing large-scale construction projects, budgets, and in negotiating the surrounding politics. His efforts building housing for defense workers during World War II had, among other things, entailed cutting through bureaucratic obstacles and in some cases, tens of thousands of residences were constructed in a matter of months.[13] The American postwar housing crisis, where hundreds of thousands of new residences needed to be built in short order for demobilized troops, was far larger still. Blandford himself went on record envisioning the construction of 12 million new homes in the decade after the war, mostly by private industry.[14] Blandford also had overseas experience in Latin America and Greece. If anyone could put UNRWA back on track, and bring it into sync with regional development plans, it was Blandford. As for Kennedy, a note to the Foreign Office from Knight's deputy captured his frustration, saying "General Kennedy is getting more and more excited about his approaching departure. He said yesterday that nothing would stop him leaving on June 19th."[15]

But by mid-1951 the Advisory Committee, which presumably directed UNRWA's overall strategy, was also becoming frustrated with the unfounded rumors regarding Arab willingness to accept refugee resettlement. Commenting on UNRWA Director John Blandford's conversations with Iraqi officials, Sir Henry Knight commented "One of the Iraqi officials told Blandford that all the Arab States agree that the refugees must be resettled but not on who should 'bell the cat' by accepting refugees!"[16] Despite the frustrations, large-scale resettlement of Palestine Arab refugees remained the preferred American policy through the Suez Crisis.[17]

The UNRWA Advisory Committee also addressed yet again the same political and financial issues, particularly with respect to Gaza, that it had with UNRPR. In a January 1951 note to the Foreign Office, for example, Sir Henry Knight commented:

> The situation of the original inhabitants of Gaza, who have been deprived of any means of livelihood, but who are not strictly speaking refugees, is giving cause for great anxiety, lest starvation and epidemics should shortly start. Kennedy has telegraphed to the United Nations for authority to provide emergency food for these people. The voluntary agencies, whom we had hoped would look after them, have proved entirely broken reeds. Something will probably also have to be done for similar destitute non-refugees in Jerusalem, Hebron, etc. It will be difficult to see them starve while we feed refugees alongside. It seems unlikely that Egypt and Jordan will be prepared to provision them.[18]

The AFSC's concerns regarding the United Nations' and especially UNRWA bureaucracy were also repeated by Knight. In a February 1951 note to the Foreign Office he commented:

> There seems a tendency to constitute a permanent centralized bureaucracy in Beirut, when what is required (in the opinion of the Advisory Committee) is flexibility and the utmost decentralization to officers at Damascus, Amman, and probably Cairo. Whether this is Byzantine bindweed springing up again in this ancient country, or a transatlantic importation from the garden of Lake Success, I cannot say—possibly a hybrid.
>
> I only hope that UNRWA's new director has an effective hand with a hoe.[19]

Even the AFSC's issue of "moral degeneration" was revisited by the UNRWA Advisory Committee and UNRWA personnel. For example, in his informal outgoing report to the UNRWA Advisory Committee, Kennedy recounted the injustices that Israel and the United Nations had created for the refugees. With unwitting condescension he noted that with "subversive elements constantly reminding them of their complaints, it is a tribute to their patience, rather than otherwise, that the situation has remained as peaceful as has been the condition to date. Unfortunately there are now some indications in a few camps of a slackening of moral ethics, a sad commentary to have to make concerning these once-proud people whose traditions and religion have in the past generally maintained a high standard of sexual behavior."[20]

Later, in May 1951, Knight forwarded a brief study on the "mind of the Palestinian refugees in the Lebanon" by an UNRWA official. It repeated all the usual aspects of the refugee narrative, including their own blamelessness, lack of faith in the United Nations, and the great powers, and the conviction that only a war would rectify their situation, and added that "Contrary to all expectation, there exists among the refugees a substantial fall in moral values," including prostitution and dishonesty.[21] But unlike AFSC, the UNRWA report concluded that "Nevertheless we insist on the fact that in spite of all the appearances of intransigence, the refugees will accept any humanitarian solution which will remove once for all this distressing uncertainty in which they live and will guarantee some sort of security."

Reintegration would be the paradigm of UNRWA and the international community for the next several years. On January 26, 1952 the United Nations General Assembly adopted Resolution 513 (VI) "which envisages the expenditure of US$ 50 million for relief and $200 million for reintegration over and above such contributions as may be made by local government, to be carried out over a period of approximately three years starting as of 1 July 1951."[22]

As part of the reintegration paradigm UNRWA, in tandem with the US government, explored a variety of regional development projects. A primary focus for UNRWA, the United States, Israel, and Jordan were comprehensive studies for developing regional water resources. State development was the explicit goal of these studies while refugee resettlement was implicit. The inspiration for the scale and complexity of these efforts is clearly shown in the title of a book on one of the plans, which became the basis for the Israeli water program, James B. Hays' *T.V.A. on the Jordan, Proposals for Irrigation and Hydro-Electric Development in Palestine*. For Israel these efforts culminated in the construction of the National Water Carrier system, beginning in 1953.[23]

In 1952 and 1953, UNRWA undertook a project with Syria and Jordan to develop water resources on the Yarmuk River but disagreement with the United States regarding the specifications and conflicts with Israel regarding potential diversions from the Jordan River delayed implementation. Disagreements and military clashes also led to plans being repeatedly revised as well as another round of American technical diplomacy in 1953 by Eric Johnston. More ambitious still were UNRWA funded studies to channel water from the Nile River to the north Sinai to irrigate the region for agriculture and settlement, and ultimately requests for UNRWA to contribute $83 million in financing for Egypt's Aswan High Dam Project.[24] France, however, developed its own plan based on the concept of an international agency to pay compensation to refugees for lost property. This, too, however, was never adopted for fear that such an agency would be dominated by the United States and would reduce French influence in the region.[25]

The three-year plan pushed the interests of Palestine Arab refugees, as opposed to those of the West and Arab states, further into the background. The impact on UNRWA was at least made clear to British observers. In May 1952 a remarkable report—part of which remains classified—was received by the Foreign Office from British diplomat Sir Edwin Chapman-Andrews that, according to the covering note, originated with "the Friends friends."

The report noted "Everything has been sacrificed to his [Blandford's] lone effort to "sell" the three-year plan to the Arab states—and SYRIA in particular—while measures which might influence the success of the negotiations are left undone."[26] It lamented UNRWA's lack of a press campaign, educational and vocational training programs, or any successful agricultural resettlement programs in Jordan. The report also showed how deep dissent within UNRWA had become over Blandford's efforts. "It may be argued that the generous minded and optimistic manner of his approach constituted the best chance of success. In the eyes of James KEEN and his senior staff however, his disinclination to face facts and adopt a firm line were simply attributed to wishful thinking or intellectual dishonesty."[27]

The report concluded savagely by saying that "much stress has been laid by the Director on how the three year plan should be described. It has been called successively "Reintegration," "Resettlement," "Self-Support," and the present formula (since beginning of June) is in his words "Improving the refugees' living conditions by means of training, loans and employment with the use of government facilities supplies by the Agency." The play with words hoodwinks nobody and the Arabic has remained throughout "توطين ('settlement')."[28]

Who "the Friends friends" were is unknown, but the tone is "hard-boiled" in a way that reminds the reader of AFSC personnel like Alwin Holtz. Sir Henry Knight, however, was unimpressed and in a hand-written note commented, "This is a poor report."

Still, the "envisaged" $200 million had not materialized. Without the funding, dreams of reintegration, whether construed as resettlement or public works, was effectively dead, and UNRWA would concentrate thereafter on relief and in the 1960s, education. The changing geostrategic situation in the Middle East, particularly rising Egyptian nationalism, also soon culminated in the 1956 Suez War that ended large-scale regional development schemes by the West.[29]

In 1959 the connection between reintegration, regional development, and the Palestine Arab refugee problem was raised briefly by United Nations Secretary General Dag Hammarskjold. In a report he suggested "The unemployed population represented by the Palestinian refugees should be regarded not as a liability but, more justly, as an asset for the future; it is a reservoir of manpower which in the desirable general economic development will assist in the creation of standards for the whole population of the area."[30] Even this mild and encouraging formula, which viewed reintegration as a "fairly long process," was rejected by the Arab states. Hammarskjold was forced to insist publicly and privately that his proposal had been misunderstood and that it did not intend for resettlement to be the primary means of reintegration. He defended the proposal throughout 1959 but a letter from the Arab League rejecting reintegration effectively ended the concept at the United Nations.[31]

## AFSC RETROSPECTIVES ON THE UNRPR AND UNRWA

Pickett's 1953 retrospective regarding AFSC's efforts to shape UNRWA was terse, and reflected the organization's and his own personal frustrations with the outcome. It also reflected the position that resettlement was the best solution. Pickett suggested ruefully that there "was a clear feeling among the Arabs that the United States had taken the side of Israel in the conflict" and that this had damaged the "long-standing good will" of the Arab countries. He went on to stress the importance of voluntary groups who would continue to approach the refugee problem from a neutral standpoint, and he noted that the AFSC had been asked by the State Department to develop a plan for Gaza. But this brought the political reality into higher relief:

> This was clear admission of the fact that the refugees' basic problem would remain unsolved for a long time to come. And it has proved to be so. We

responded to this request to the best of our ability before turning the work over to the UN. After several postponements, the transfer finally occurred as of the end of April 1950 and the new UN organization —United Nations Relief and Works Agency—assumed complete responsibility for the Arab refugees, including the problem of their resettlement.[32]

Pickett's memoirs also provide a slightly more candid take on the experience as a whole, which was uncharacteristically prideful regarding AFSC's accomplishments in the face of adversity. He described the work in Gaza in straightforward terms and praised the "great imaginativeness and vigor" of other aid organizations and above all, the AFSC's personnel:

> It was one of the most difficult jobs our Committee ever undertook. Facilities which our workers usually take for granted in setting up relief projects were almost totally lacking: practically no tools or materials available in the desert locale, even wood being virtually nonexistent; with the exception of a few abandoned mosques, no public buildings available as distribution centers; no public-welfare or social service organizations to build on; no local government outside the town of Gaza; communications possible only through UN truce observers' radio; no telephones, no regular mail delivery. It is greatly to the credit of our staff of about fifty volunteers from nine countries that the program was actually carried out in a relatively effective and orderly manner.[33]

Pickett also took pains to praise the "dignity, stability, and responsiveness" of the refugees themselves, despite the "near riots" that occurred, and expressed gratitude for the assistance received from the Egyptian army. But he was uncharacteristically critical of the treatment AFSC received in the Egyptian media:

> One thing which troubled our Unit during the entire operation was that it received such a consistently bad press in Egypt — a country in which the press was government-controlled. This is not the usual experience of Quaker overseas workers. Thirty-five years of service in some twenty-five countries have accustomed us to a considerable amount of co-operation from the press, which made this Egyptian experience stand out more vividly. However, I am sure it was to be interpreted as part of the general feeling against the West, and not as directed against our Unit personally.[34]

This charitable interpretation regarding the Egyptian press's anti-Western bias is probably correct, but his sense of distress is evident.

The attitudes of AFSC staff members also were changed by the experience. Speaking decades later for an AFSC oral history project, Howard McKinney spoke of his altered attitudes toward Arabs:

> A number of us tended to say we did not find the Arab people particularly likable:
> Two things: One, we started out to be philosophical, but for an Arab a person who looks after his family is the good man. If you don't look after your family…this is not a question, in our standards, of stealing or cheating if your family needs it. The other thing was this sort of perpetual whine for baksheesh or special treatments or that kind of thing. There are traits that we found hard to take. Various individuals we would get acquainted with, but to say that you like Arabs en mass was fairly difficult. I remember I had at some point said something about not finding the Arab traits all that endearing … I was not enamored of the Arab as a people.[35]

In a characteristically blunt contribution to the AFSC's oral history of the Gaza experience Alwin Holtz, however, was much more to the point regarding the UN operation and its contrasts with the AFSC: "The U.N. was digging in for, as Howard Wriggins said, fifty years, and there was no way we were going to…I mean, if Quakers can't settle a problem overnight—forget it. I mean, none of this long-term nonsense. We go in and do our good thing and get out and everybody lives happily ever after."[36] Holtz was even more blunt regarding the way the United Nations ran its operation and the personnel it employed:

> Anyway, I was interested in the transition, one, because I wanted to help maintain what I thought we would do, and I wanted to learn. I thought these big professional experts were going to teach me something. I found out very quickly that was ridiculous. But little by little then, after the transition four or five of us stayed on, and they started replacing us with the flotsam and jetsam of Europe. Some of them were all right, but, I mean, most of them were political appointments of one kind or another, which was real obvious, and had instructions to shake this ingrown nonsense that the Quakers were going on, which was dumb to even do it.[37]

Holtz went on to characterize the new management style of UNRWA: "The day I left, on the plane I left on, a guy came down the day before who was taking my place—at that time I was acting director or something and he was replacing me—and I said to him, "Look, tomorrow I'll take you out, I'll introduce you to all the people." He said, "Hold it,

Al. None of that. I came down here with a case of scotch and was told to get along with the Egyptians." He was a nice guy but this is what he was told, and he was a political appointee and that's what he was going to do. He went the next morning right over to see the Egyptians and pat them on the back and hand them a bottle of scotch and get along with them. That must have shocked them, too, because they weren't used to that from us."[38]

## AFSC AND THE MIDDLE EAST AFTER 1953

After 1953, AFSC was no longer involved in field operations in Gaza or Israel. The interests of the AFSC leadership had already shifted away from the Middle East to other global trouble spots. In 1951 Pickett had become involved in the American Food Committee for India, a charitable organization comprised primarily of American Protestant groups.[39] That year he also received an award from the Jewish Theological Seminary in New York, along with David Sarnoff, the chairman of the board of the Radio Corporation of American, for "advancing the cause of international fraternity."[40]

By 1952 Elmore Jackson of the AFSC had become involved in negotiations between India and Pakistan and efforts by Frank Graham, the United Nations Representative for India and Pakistan, to resolve the Kashmir situation.[41] Pickett remained consistent to his growing position of political engagement when he co-authored a letter published in the *New York Times* gently castigating the United States for considering a military alliance with Pakistan at the expense of relations with India.[42] But he was the subject of controversy at the end of 1952 when he was publicly accused of having associated with a "Communist front group" by US Senator Pat McCarran, author of the McCarran-Walter Immigration and Nationality Law. Pickett was reported to "have chuckled after being told of the accusations" that were quickly forgotten.[43]

A few small-scale AFSC projects were undertaken in the region between the end of the Gaza mission and the Suez War of 1956. The Acre operation in Israel was closed in 1953 but an additional small education and social welfare project was initiated that year in northern Jordan. The November 1953 report by AFSC's representatives Moses and Mabel Bailey cheerfully described the primitive conditions that the organization's personnel found and commented that "we anticipate that four or five years of steady (and discouraging) work here will greatly increase the total welfare of the five thousand persons who will be directly reached. Furthermore, from a comparatively limited undertaking of this sort there is sure to radiate a more widely significant influence."[44]

The Baileys sounded positively relieved by the prospect of hard work and frustration, and implied that this effort was a return to traditional AFSC pursuits. They also quote, however, another AFSC staff member then working in Jordan, Roy Lucas, who had been a member of the "Quaker Teamsters of Gaza in 1949", saying, "His criticism of the points of failure toward the Refugees and toward the several governments involved is needed." Three years after the Gaza mission ended, the sting of the experience was still present for field personnel. The Quaker schools in Ramallah continued in operation but without any direct relationship to the AFSC.

In 1955 Jackson and the AFSC were drawn into a series of back channel negotiations between Egypt and Israel that included high level contacts with Nasser and Moshe Sharett.[45] These limited contacts were terminated before the 1956 Suez War.[46] The assessment of American ambassador to Egypt Henry Byroade was the Jackson initiative "made considerable contribution, and as such is an exception to my general thinking that individuals privately operating in such capacity usually do more harm than good."[47]

The American Protestant environment also began to change during the 1950s, particularly with the rise of evangelical denominations whose theologies were dramatically opposed to those of the Quakers. With the formation of the National Council of Churches in 1950, in which the Friends United Meeting was a member, there was a new forum for ecumenical cooperation on social issues, and the Friends were no longer at the forefront. After the mid-1950s, particularly with the publication of *Speak Truth to Power,* the AFSC instead began to reemphasize pacifism as a formal ideology, as a response to the larger context of the Cold War, and with education and community organizing as its preferred means of operation. *Speak Truth to Power* critiqued the Cold War, nuclear weapons, and what would in the next decade be called "mass society," foreshadowing the "personalist" politics of the New Left during the 1960s,[48] and called for world government. The pamphlet sold over 100,000 copies during the course of the 1950s and was extensively discussed in newspapers and other media.

But AFSC's Middle Eastern field operations were strictly limited. In 1957, in the wake of the Suez Crisis the organization sent a small amount of financial aid to refugees in Egypt, and it did so again a year later during the Lebanon crisis.[49] In 1959 the AFSC sent substantial quantities of material aid to Algeria.[50] Pickett's final word on the Palestine refugee problem also came in 1959, when he authored a letter on the issue to President Dwight D. Eisenhower that was signed by twenty-five prominent Americans. In it Pickett "proposed limited resettlement of Arab refugees in Israel and resettlement elsewhere for the rest, all financed by a United Nations-administered loan."[51]

The AFSC did become involved in religious diplomacy in other settings, such as the India-Pakistan War of 1965 and the Nigerian Civil War of 1970, but the organization placed far more emphasis on the nuclear disarmament, superpower relations, and its pacifist agenda.[52] The period when Quakers could successfully represent an unusual form of both radical and establishment heritage had reached its pinnacle during the late 1940s and early 1950s; "they were, by and large, not quite elite, not quite cold warriors, and not communists either."[53] Thereafter the organization became too charged to reconcile these heritages, and the Cold War too unforgiving. In the domestic American arena, containing, rolling back, and unmasking Communism became the overriding issue of the day both at home and abroad.

Within the strands of the pacifist movement, the perception that the Cold War was the greatest threat humanity had ever seen also continued to grow. From 1947 onward the AFSC by choice adopted radical pacifist and internationalist positions that put it decisively on the side of the Left and the growing protests movements of the 1960s, and at odds with American policy. The organization's efforts to lead a mainstream peace movement, and Clarence Pickett's personal impulse to assail American nuclear weapons[54] and to defend Alger Hiss, came to dominate AFSC. The frustrations of the organization's leadership during the Gaza operations was not simply operational but reflected this growing radical pacifist—or better, anti-imperialist—rather than Quaker, ideology.

In general, during the later 1950s and after the AFSC appears to have found that peace-making and conflict resolution at an abstract level was more compelling. Its work during 1960s and 1970s during the Vietnam War, however, was anything but abstract and also proved immensely controversial, putting it decidedly on the side of the American Left. It also paradoxically aligned the organization not with pacifism but violent anti-imperialism.[55] Following up on its 1949 pamphlet that called for normalization of American relations with the Soviet Union, in 1965 the AFSC issued a controversial pamphlet calling for the United States to recognize the People's Republic of China, and for Taiwan to be expelled from the United Nations and its seat to be given to the People's Republic.[56] During the 1960s the regional youth work camps that had formed such an important part of the AFSC and the national network of Friends committees were also closed, a move that caused considerable disappointment.

Even more controversial were AFSC's furious denunciations of American policy in Vietnam, from the escalation of military operations to all forms of aid to South Vietnamese governments, and of the conduct of the war itself. The AFSC also directly violated American embargoes and sent medical aid directly to North Vietnam. As late as 1972 AFSC leadership, in particular, Executive Secretary Bronson Clark, participated in international rallies castigating the United States and South Vietnam. Clark was quoted as stating he believed that official American criticism of the rallies were "another attempt to cast aspersions, [at] red-baiting and McCarthyism."[57] Still, as if scarred by its very brief experience in the Gaza Strip, the AFSC did not become involved in the Arab-Israeli arena again until the 1970s.

Its first foray back into the Arab-Israeli conflict was a pamphlet entitled *Search for Peace in the Middle East* that was notably hostile toward Israel. The pamphlet took special note of the Arab refugee situation and concluded "That the Arab governments cannot resettlement Palestinian refugees in more or less permanent situations against their will should be obvious. Moreover, both the refugees and the host governments have been constantly haunted by the fear that successful resettlement would help the Israelis and the world to forget the injustice done to the Palestinians and to accept a large-scale *fait accompli*.[58]

After harshly criticizing Israel and expressing understanding toward "Palestinian commandos" the document concluded by suggesting the possibility of a regional confederation, the end of Western arms sales to the region, and "Large-scale, long-term technological and economic development of all units within the federation but with each group protected in the maintenances of its cultural and political autonomy."[59] But in an ironic twist, the report also stated that a "temporary United Nations Trusteeship or some type of international administration should replace the Israeli military occupation for Gaza and the West Bank."[60] AFSC had effectively rejected this notion when they left Gaza in 1950 and then abandoned the contractual relationship with UNRWA. Why, and under whose influence, the organization changed its direction so decisively toward anti-imperialism in the guise of pacifism remains to be examined.

But with the publication of *Search for Peace in the Middle East* many other threads came together. The AFSC's 1947 abandonment of political neutrality in the context of the early Cold War, the passionate advocacy of the Gaza Unit's letter to Clarence Pickett from the Fall of 1949 that gave voice to the refugees, were woven with the grandiose regional development schemes of Clarence Pickett, Gordon Clapp, the State Department and the Foreign Office, and the idea of an open-ended international trusteeship, and became AFSC policy in the 1970s.

# 9. Assessing the AFSC as an Early NGO ᴓ

I n historical terms AFSC provides a small but important precedent for some of the types of attitudes and approaches displayed by later NGOs, and a strong contrast to others. At its outset, during World War I, the AFSC was careful to position itself as a patriotic American organization, but its ideals and missions were fundamentally international in scope. AFSC also functioned within a domestic American and international Quaker network of organizations and volunteers, and by the end of World War I had generated sufficient social capital that its services were in demand globally. The AFSC's Quaker religious agenda of pacifism declined to endorse nations and nationalism, even as it was necessary to deal continually on a practical level with states and their institutions, both to execute relief missions and undertake religious diplomacy. This image of impartiality was another important source of social capital and operational flexibility. The organization's convergent values with the New Deal and particularly its close association with the figure of Eleanor Roosevelt also immeasurably enhanced its standing in American political and social life.

But as has been shown above, a conscious decision was made in 1947 under the leadership of Clarence Pickett and Henry Cadbury to change the AFSC's longstanding policy of political and religious neutrality and to work aggressively for world peace and disarmament in the context of the Cold War, in the manner of a secular left-liberal pressure group. This new policy was directed in the first instance at the United States and became most evident in the criticisms the AFSC lodged against American policies during the course of the later 1950s and especially the 1960s. Pickett and Cadbury's new direction created a tension within the organization that was played out as a subtext of the Gaza relief mission and which, by the mid-1950s, overtook the AFSC as a whole.

The failed "Truce of God," Municipal Governorship for Jerusalem, and Vail-Castle missions all showed how ill-suited the AFSC's religious diplomacy was to the bitterness and complexities of the Middle East crisis. Apparently stung by this, the AFSC welcomed the opportunity to participate in traditional relief efforts that carried with them liberal religious diplomatic messages, and that would serve to rehabilitate the organization's reputation, at least in its own eyes. But the AFSC's subsequent public stance on the mission and on the substantive political issues was low-key. In the case of the Gaza relief mission for UNRPR, AFSC personnel appear to have largely avoided commenting publicly on what might be called national political issues, but at the same time the organization's retreat from neutrality is apparent in many instances.

Internally, individuals such as Donald Stevenson, made their dislike of Israel and Israelis clear, and even senior Quakers like Clarence Pickett and Delbert Replogle voiced frustration over Israeli policies and politics. The AFSC's public stance was neither overtly critical of Israel, nor of Egypt, whose representatives were occasionally also found to be obstructive, particularly to the AFSC's field personnel. At the same time, the AFSC's calls for development solutions would necessarily have been viewed by Arab leaders, and possibly the Palestine Arab refugees themselves, as explicitly political statements, although of what sort is unclear. More research is needed in Arab media and other sources such as Egyptian diplomatic sources to determine how AFSC was perceived by their "clients." What is clear is that once development schemes were hatched, Arab states sought to raise the ante as high as possible.

But the Gaza Unit's October 1949 letter to Clarence Pickett regarding the decaying condition of their refugee charges constituted a severe erosion of the organization's internal and external stances of neutrality. Caught in the "humanitarian trap" on the ground, the Gaza Unit chose a passive-aggressive means to go public, doing so with what is by now the tried and true means of "giving voice" to the allegedly voiceless. As has been seen, this letter was immediately put to use publicly by Pickett, United Nations Secretary General Tryvgie Lie, and by the Egyptian ambassador to the United Nations. How the refugees perceived this use of their "voice" is unknown.

But despite this clear-cut shift on the ground, the organization's move toward the refugee narrative at the leadership was not complete. Neither the Gaza Unit nor the AFSC leadership could reconcile to long-term involvement as long as no resolution was in sight. Nor could the contradiction noted earlier, that practical solutions to the refugee problem were also political solutions, be overcome, even as the organization's positive moved decidedly to that of reintegration that was understood as resettlement. But publicly endorsing any solution would lead to its rejection by one or the other party. One result of this contradiction was the redefinition of the UNRPR mission into the UNRWA mission, from the stark choices of repatriation or resettlement to the vagueness of rehabilitation and reintegration. For the AFSC the situation in Gaza was bad enough; stasis had led to "moral degeneration" and playing a role in prolonging the situation was unacceptable.

Writer David Rieff has famously suggested that humanitarian actions have become "a sop to western conscience" and a "substitute for Western political engagement."[1] The desire to do something for someone, propelled by the "CNN Effect"[2] of media driven crises, by organizational requirements to market interventions, regardless of effectiveness, and often in partnership with private corporations, are among the features of what Rieff and others have called the "humanitarian trap."[3] Decades before the term was invented, AFSC had become mired briefly in the "humanitarian trap" and decided not to participate further. The same would not be said of UNRWA.

The way AFSC used its considerable "soft power" was also distinctive. Considerable capital had been expended on the "Truce of God" scheme and involvement in the plan for a Municipal Commissioner in an internationalized Jerusalem. Both had failed badly, and while AFSC was neither blamed nor tarred, it may have both propelled them back to the types of low-key relief missions with which they were most experienced, and toward a liberal and practical approach regarding the Gaza operation itself. Refugee relief was also an opportunity for the AFSC to reestablish its credibility and even leadership within the American Protestant environment, particularly those with overseas missions in the Middle East.

At best, Quaker ideals of modesty and an unknown measure of embarrassment and fear constrained AFSC from doing more than a minimal job of publicizing its operations and proposals. As noted above, the AFSC had pursued a quiet strategy of publicizing its American activities through film during the 1930s, and had begun using radio broadcasts after World War II to oppose racial segregation in the American South.[4] But the Gaza operation never warranted a full public relations effort by the organization. Clarence Pickett, never shy regarding self-promotion, may have written opinion pieces for newspapers about the Gaza relief effort, but as has been seen, after his two personal failures over Jerusalem, volunteers undertaking their jobs in a more or less Quakerly way appear to have been regarded as a more appropriate and sufficient form of publicity.[5]

Mobilization of public opinion on Gaza and Palestine refugees, or Middle East peace, was never an AFSC priority, even as it adopted an ever-larger public profile on Cold War and pacifist issues during the 1950s. Neither Elmore Jackson's request to Clarence Pickett "for thee to take the lead in setting up a committee in the United States" nor Paul Johnson's more impassioned call for "broadest-gauge and most influential international Quaker delegation you can contrive" could move the organization to use its considerable "soft power." A full AFSC public stance on the Middle East did not come until the late 1960s, long after the organization already had recrafted its image to that of an international peace organization, rather than an American Protestant relief group, and had gained immense experience in publicizing its controversial stances on world affairs. Why this was not done during the brief Gaza mission or shortly thereafter is unclear, but for whatever reasons the organization did not expend or risk its considerable political capital on the issue. Insecurity regarding failure, felt acutely after the failures of early 1948 and expressed at the outset of the Gaza mission by Colin Bell in the Nineteen Points, may have set limits on the AFSC's willingness to generate or court publicity.

But despite the lack of publicity, after the conclusion of the Gaza mission the AFSC, in the person of Elmore Jackson, again undertook religious diplomacy with Egyptian and Israeli officials, leveraging its reputation for fairness and honesty to gain entry and as a source of influence. And both before and after the Gaza mission AFSC's leadership also moved interacted freely with American, British and United Nations officials, advising and politicking with them, even as the United States. and Great Britain in particular pursued their own political agendas. AFSC's influence on governmental and United Nations' decision-making seems minimal, although arguably Clarence Pickett's support of the regional development solutions helped root the idea in State Department planners. The AFSC's interactions with other voluntary organizations, facilitated by Arthur Ringland at the State Department, and with apparent government and oil industry front groups like that of Kermit Roosevelt, Jr., were even less satisfactory. In short, AFSC's use of "soft power" with respect to the Gaza mission and the Middle East generally appears minimal, in strong contrast to their controversial approaches to Cold War affairs, and subsequent Middle East policies.

It is worth noting, however, in this discussion of "soft power" that a large number of AFSC staff members went on to academic careers. Channing

Richardson, Howard Wriggins, Don Peretz, and James Read became university professors where they were well-positioned to exercise a familiar form of "soft power" over students, colleagues, and through the media. This may have been a more Quakerly avenue to modestly shape the future. Wriggins, along with Elmore Jackson, also served in the State Department. Wriggins worked in ambassadorial and policy positions and Jackson was Special Assistant for Policy Planning to the Assistant Secretary of State for International Organization Affairs.[6] The "soft power" they exercised in these varied positions complemented that of other American Protestant missionaries and particularly their offspring, who formed an important part of the American foreign policy apparatus during the second half of the twentieth century.[7]

In a piece on the AFSC, Feldman argued that the organization's Quaker values, including pacifism and the emphasis on personal interaction, constituted what she calls "ethical labor."[8] In her view these values were immediately challenged by the operational requirements of the Gaza mission, including, for example, the need to work closely with Egyptian military officials in a zone where Egyptian state sovereignty was dubious but its selective control was unmistakable. Her reading of the AFSC oral history accounts emphasizes the outrage of individual field workers at Egyptian military stupidity, even as some admitted that the military presence was critical for maintaining law and order and the effective distribution of relief.

In Feldman's view the fundamental contradiction was that the AFSC's relief mission was also part of a specific pacifist mission to find a political solution to the refugee crisis that necessitated debilitating moral compromises. Feldman also emphasizes the moral quandary of the AFSC having to establish personal relationships with refugees on a practical level, and as a matter of Quaker doctrine, but then also to take steps such as cutting refugee rolls in order to minimize fraud and maintain costs and order. She concludes that neutrality on the part of relief organizations in humanitarian situations is unsustainable and unrealistic. Interestingly, though Feldman notes that humanitarian organizations have advocated military interventions, she does not fully address the issue of the "humanitarian trap" as articulated by Rieff and others.

Her reading weighs the pacifist dimension of AFSC too heavily against that of the relief mission as well as the complexities of Quaker theology and Protestant politics. AFSC had received the Nobel Prize and had been asked to participate in the UNRPR program on the basis of its European relief experience that was represented as non-political rather than pacifist.

It later became fashionable, however, for the organization and its supporters to represent the Nobel Prize as having been rewarded for "tireless efforts to promote peace and reconciliation."[9] Only one small element of the Nineteen Points, which eschewed armed protection for AFSC convoys, even implied a pacifist dimension to the operation. The AFSC entered into the Gaza operation with a hard-boiled relief agenda rather than explicit pacifist goals.

Feldman is correct that the AFSC's field personnel in particular were drawn from pacifist backgrounds, as was senior leadership. But it has been shown that the senior leadership had far more political experience and sophistication than field personnel, and a corresponding willingness to live with contradictions in order to execute the relief mission. They had, after all, worked with far worse regimes such as the Soviets and the Nazis in the past. It is also necessary to recall that only a third of AFSC personnel were Quakers It is true that Clarence Pickett and Henry Cadbury were leading the organization toward a public pacifist stance after 1947, a dramatic change that Feldman does not mention. But the AFSC personnel in charge of the Gaza mission in Philadelphia and Geneva were sufficiently "hard-boiled" and expressed far fewer qualms than the field personnel. For example, she cites the moral qualms field personnel expressed in an October 1949 camp meeting over the question of cutting refugee ration lists:

> One camp leader pointed out that we are not supposed to cut real refugees from our lists, and that to do so is a real injustice. Another suggested that the Quaker technique demands trust; and that in this situation we cannot trust—therefore we must be prepared to use some kind of force. At another point in the meeting a further concern was expressed that non-Quaker means for achieving the desired end should not be used. One suggested that we are here, as any Quaker group is in any field, to spread good will, and that we cannot do that if we are too "tough." On the other hand, one pointed out that carrying false names without taking action against the fraud is also out of harmony with Quaker methods of procedure...It was felt that further sharing of opinions in an effort to achieve common understanding must be the basis of all action taken in the matter.[10]

But Feldman neglects to cite this as the background to the impassioned October 12, 1949 from the Gaza Unit to Clarence Pickett, in which such concerns were very much played down, or were, perhaps, projected onto the depiction of refugee misery. The contrast between field personnel and more senior staff members elsewhere is, in fact, demonstrated by another letter that she cites, from Donald Stevenson to Bronson Clark, in which Stevenson states "While I have every respect for the right of every individual conscience on the problem of "using food as a weapon," I could not help but think that those who consider this problem a strong moral issue are the same ones who are unable to tackle the job of list reduction in what I would call a brave and honest way."[11]

The lesson of these examples may be that the political realities of relief work and the "humanitarian trap," rather than pacifism as such, force senior leaders and field personnel of NGOs into contradictions that result in irresolvable situations, "hard-boiled" mentalities, and flirtations with cynicism.

In another piece on the AFSC's Gaza experience, Feldman addresses the issue of "who is a refugee" in order to understand evolving international humanitarian norms. She argues, for example, that there were no real social, cultural, or other distinctions between the refugees and the Gaza residents.[12] This is despite documentary accounts, such as those of AFSC and UNRWA personnel, and even personal testimonies provided to her by Gaza residents attesting to such distinctions. Her goal instead is to argue that "Gaza's population categories have been derived from legal definitions that do not quite apply in this territory (international refugee conventions), shaped by institutions that do not have jurisdiction over it (UNHCR), and influenced by long absent political forms (the sovereign state)."[13] In this way Gazans—and it is unclear whether she means indigenous populations, refugees, Bedouin or all—"came to see themselves in the terms used by humanitarian practitioners." But as has been shown, the contrasts between these groups were mentioned repeated by the AFSC and the United Nations, and treating them as a whole was accepted only with reluctance.

Feldman's vision of a unified Palestinian population divided, at best, by class distinctions is also not fully supported by historical evidence. Though the Gaza population shared familial and economic relations with inland groups, it is clear from historical and ethnographic evidence that during the late nineteenth and early twentieth centuries their primary cultural and economic connections were with Egypt and southern caravan routes. In addition, by the early twentieth century Gaza's harbor had been eclipsed by Haifa and Jaffa, and the town was routinely subjected to raiding by Negev Bedouin.[14] Prior to the 1936–1939 Arab revolt Gaza also appears to have to be marginal to evolving Palestinian nationalism and politics.

Above all Feldman is concerned with what she deems as arbitrary and imposed categories that cut against the grain of an essential "Palestinian" identity. She therefore ignores data showing the diversity of the populations. In this way, she privileges the concept of shared "citizenship" for indigenous Gazans, refugees and presumably, Bedouins as well, to suggest that their shared experience, and brief relegation by the AFSC and other relief organizations such as UNRPR and UNRWA into the category of "citizens" during the period 1948–1950, helped activate modern Palestinian identity.[15] This may have been the case, but the road to creating "Palestinians" and unity was far longer for Gaza than what she describes. Only UNRWA itself has continually enlarged the definition of "who is a refugee" and thus de facto expanded the scope of a unified Palestinian population.[16]

Feldman does make interesting observations regarding the development of attitudes among refugees regarding relief as a "right" that "came to serve as 'evidence' both of dispossession and of international responsibility for it."[17] She fails, however, to fully articulate the background and role of this dual self-conception in Palestinian identity. Instead, she sees this evasive dualism as a window into larger global problems of "refugeedom and citizenship." In doing so she effectively endorses "Palestinian exceptionalism" and proposes to extend it globally.

Arguably, however, the self-image of Palestine Arabs as victims had begun forming much earlier, at least the 1930s, and had been given specific content by many factors. These included the participation of Arab states and organizations such as the Muslim Brotherhood in the cause, the religious vision of the Grand Mufti Haj Amin al-Husseini, and in the local manifestation of Eastern Mediterranean honor-shame culture.[18] Ultimately Feldman usefully raises the issue of the AFSC's role in facilitating aspects of Palestinian identity development. This is a question that must also be asked regarding UNRWA.

Part of the facilitation of Palestinian identity stemmed from the AFSC's approach to its own religion. Adhering to its liberal humanitarian and non-conversionist tradition, and conscious of the potential dangers to Quaker and other Christian institutions should allegations of proselytizing be lodged, the AFSC frowned on the promotion of specifically Quaker or even broadly Christian values in the field. As AFSC volunteer Vern Pings put it, "The Quaker thing was tolerance. You came there with attitudes about what you're going to do, how you're going to do it, and what the limits were. They had to be worked out, and how Quakerly they were, I have no way of judging. I don't know if anybody who was a birthright Quaker could say that this was a real Quaker enterprise. We started off with this is the way Quakers talk with one another and this is how we act. That was all there."[19]

This low-key and seemingly secular approach had been the reason why the organization had been invited to participate in Gaza operations in the first place by the United Nations. AFSC personnel at all levels appear to have been willing to discuss religious issues with refugees and in diplomatic settings, such as in Pickett and Replogle's meeting with the Grand Mufti, but there is no hint that they proselytized in any way. Like modern NGOs whose ideology is effectively the secular religion of humanitarianism, and arguably paternalistic, the AFSC did not challenge the identities of refugees or Gazans in any meaningful way, but merely treated them in the functional categories, as Feldman describes, of refugee, local Gazan, and "citizen." The deeper cultural sources of the dual rights-entitlement identity she describes must be sought elsewhere.

With regard to their own religious mission, the AFSC appears to have had few qualms regarding interactions with governments. Personnel participated in numerous discussions with American and United Nations officials regarding its Gaza operations and larger issues of religious diplomacy, such as the status of Jerusalem. There is no indication that AFSC personnel felt uncomfortable or compromised by these interactions, which necessarily enmeshed them still further in the geopolitical agendas of states, the details of which they could not have known. AFSC leadership, in their letters and memoirs, appear to have had no trouble trying to use their access to political power to further goals that were always defined in terms of the refugees. But as AFSC's "soft power" was reaching its peak after the Nobel Peace Prize in 1947 and in the following decade, the specifically Quaker content was drained away in favor of a pacifist agenda that was directed at the largest issues, rather than a local crisis. It is again worth noting that this power was not used on behalf of the Palestine Arab refugees, but was reserved for Cold War issues, particularly in opposition to the United States.

Finally, it is necessary to emphasize that AFSC's decision-making, operations, and religious and political orientation and operations were not transparent or accountable to anyone outside the organization. During the late 1940s and early 1950 the organization's broader and operational direction were largely set by Clarence Pickett and Henry Cadbury, who would jointly make decisions and then together guide the monthly meetings of the AFSC board toward their desired conclusions.[20] AFSC's Foreign Service Executive Committee appears to have had some say regarding strategic goals and operational considerations, such as personnel and funding, and a variety of senior leaders and managers then had wide latitude to carry out operations.

But neither external mechanisms for demanding or enforcing NGO transparency existed during that era, nor were there any apparent AFSC internal metrics for success except overt operational success or failure. From the outset and the Nineteen Points, the AFSC's leadership made plain their sensitivity to the bad publicity that would result from the failure of their Gaza mission, but that fear does not appear to have been the primary driver of their decision-making. Even the decision to withdrawn from Gaza was not made on the basis of fear of impending failure, although, to be sure, in its final report to the United Nations, as well as in private exchanges, the leadership put the best face possible on the matter. The contracting agencies, UNRPR and UNRWA, also appear to have demanded little accountability from AFSC, despite a late few hints at dissatisfaction, particularly under UNRWA, regarding AFSC's methods and personnel. The praise lavished on AFSC, LRCS, and ICRC by the United Nations for their participation in the UNRPR program might have been genuine and well-earned, but it was also instrumental and intended to promote the next phase of Palestine relief, UNRWA.

AFSC's political economics were unlike those of modern NGOs, and this is demonstrated by the decision they took to withdraw from Gaza, and indeed, the logic of their decision. The AFSC's experience with UNRPR had been unsatisfactory. While the organization had been largely left to its own devices in the field, the constant worries about funding were a severe constraint. UNRWA was even worse in AFSC's view. It was ill-conceived and inefficient, staffed with ineffective, incompetent, and self-aggrandizing individuals, and worst of all, offered no hope to the refugees.

For political and moral reasons AFSC was anxious to remove itself from an insoluble situation, and at no time did either the leadership or field personnel argue that more funding should be sought in order to prolong its operations, either directly or under contract to the United Nations. At no time did the AFSC become a rent-seeking organization seeking to expand or prolong its mission in the interest of economic gain. However conflicted individuals may have become, and however mired the organization itself may have been in contradictory humanitarian and political logics, the AFSC's religious values were an important if difficult to quantify source of accountability and the guiding light of its decision-making throughout its involvement in Gaza. These religious values, above all modesty and practical self-reliance, though stretched toward the standpoint of the Palestine Arab refugees, in the end fundamentally sensitized the AFSC to the "humanitarian trap" and the problem of moral hazard.

## AFSC, NGOS, UNRWA, AND MORAL HAZARD

Moral hazard is the situation where a party that is insulated from risk behaves differently than if it lacked that protection. Parties with protection undertake riskier behavior, while those without protection pay the price or otherwise suffer the consequences of failure. Parties that have some form of security or protected status need not worry about failure, as do those who are willing to blame others for failure, or in situations where it is difficult to determine precisely who is accountable. In terms of economics, moral hazard describes when one party enters into a transaction in bad faith, has or operates under misleading information, or takes unusual risks to earn a profit. The concept of moral hazard is frequently applied, for example, to the areas of welfare, insurance, as well as in financing.

Less well understood is the role of moral hazard in international civil society and the world of NGOs. Some studies have shown that NGOs in developing economies are increasingly involved as participants in political and economic processes that redistribute risk and uncertainty between specific populations and state or international institutions.[21] As participants or mediators, they stand to gain but are exposed to little or no risk themselves should policies or programs fail. The transnational and networked basis of modern NGOs is another source of insulation from risk and from failure. Things may go badly in one place but the organization, and more broadly speaking, the "cause," can survive or reconstitute itself elsewhere on the globe.

During its brief Gaza mission AFSC's exposure to moral hazard was relatively minor, despite the fact that AFSC, LRCS, and ICRC were the only official contractors providing services to the UNRPR program. In the case of AFSC, there was some minimal fear of overt failure since that would have had a negative impact on both the refugees and the organization's reputation that was then at a high point. But there is no indication that the AFSC or any of the relief organizations proceeded with a sense that they were protected from failure by a special status or relationship with the United Nations. The reverse may in fact have been true. In the case of ICRC, it has been noted above that its moral and practical failures during World War II, and threats to its existence in the postwar era, gave it particular incentives for participation in the Palestine relief mission and for performance to the best of its abilities.

In contrast with the relief organizations participating in UNRPR, it was the United Nations itself that assumed the moral hazard with respect to the Palestine refugee problem.[22] The UNRPR program was protected from any consequences by the United Nations General Assembly, and by external political dynamics. These included the Western powers that brought the program into being and funded it, the Arab states who stridently demanded that the program continue, and the refugees themselves, who in the absence of having their own maximalist demands for repatriation met, demanded the United Nations maintain them. There were no consequences for UNRPR inefficiency, waste, abuse or failure. These dynamics have been carried over and been multiplied many fold with respect to UNRWA.

Gottheil makes the point that UNRWA could have proposed to the United Nations that its mandate be allowed to expire in 1952 and that its functions be assumed by the United Nations High Commissioner for Refugees.[23] Indeed, in 1950 the organization, facing a funding crisis, proposed to Israel that it take over responsibilities for refugees within Israel, but then withdrew the proposal. But negotiations on the same issue were resumed in 1952 and the organization ended its operations there on September 1.[24] In the Arab countries, however, the opposite path was chosen. The fundamental politicization of UNRWA, and the UNHCR mandate that explicitly excluded Palestine Arab refugees, along with the concurrent interests of UNRWA as an organization, Israel, the host countries, and indeed, the refugees themselves, all led to the renewal of UNRWA. No party bore the moral hazard for failure, or conversely, perceived significant benefits for solving the refugee problem in difficult circumstances. Any solution would have been far from optimal for several of the participants; the loss of institutional existence for UNRWA, foreign exchange and employment opportunities for host countries, and resettlement for the refugees. Only Jordan offered a partial solution by offering citizenship to Palestine Arabs, while at the same time annexing the West Bank.

The implicit and explicit threat of increasing radicalization of the Middle East and destabilizing various states as a result of reducing aid to the Palestinians was explicitly recognized in the early 1950s but cast in terms of the perceived potential for Communist influence. But with the failure of development schemes in the mid-1950s, and with the generalized anger in the wake of Suez, Western states recognized that "the political repercussions in the Middle East would have been disastrous"[25] if they curtailed, much less ended, aid to the Palestine Arab refugees, or made Arab states responsible for supporting refugees on their territories. With the fixing of Palestinian national identity and the gradual radicalization of Palestinian culture around the figure of the *fedayeen* and the idea of "resistance" the possibility of withdrawing aid was even more fraught with peril. To do so would, presumably, radicalize Palestinians still further, destabilize friendly or allied states, and reduce Western influence in the region still further.[26]

It has been noted earlier that AFSC criticized both organizations, as did the UNRWA Advisory Committee of political appointees. But despite criticism and periodic reforms the mission itself was regarded as too politically important to fail, and hence little changed except the scale of inefficiency, waste, and abuse. The continued and rapidly escalating support for UNRWA and the various regional development schemes proposed by the United States and to a lesser extent by Great Britain were motivated as much by political as humanitarian needs. Perversely, these served to intensify the moral risk assumed by UNRWA. The regional development programs promoted by the United States also served to create dependencies on foreign financing and expertise that undermined local processes and transfer moral hazard to the sponsoring nations and organizations.[27] Doubly perverse is that the "moral degeneration" decried by AFSC and UNRWA was at least partially a consequence of the deliberate transfer of moral hazard onto UNRPR and UNRWA by all parties, not least of all the refugees themselves. Breaking this pattern is more difficult than ever. As in 1949, real or received cuts to UNRWA activities today produce riots in Gaza while UNRWA officials proclaim impending disaster and seek additional emergency funding.[28]

## AFSC, UNRWA, AND THE QUESTION OF ANTI-SEMITISM

Defense of Christian interests in the Holy Land was not an explicit part of the AFSC's mission but it was a consideration within larger Quaker circles, and certainly within the larger British and American Protestant environments. British Friends in particular had long exhibited explicit hostility toward Zionism, as did American Quakers working in the Holy Land. These issues were of paramount important within the American Protestant community in 1947 and 1948 and arguably influenced the AFSC's decision to become involved in the Middle East.

During the late 1940s the AFSC was undergoing an unprecedented transformation under the direction of Clarence Pickett and Henry Cadbury, from an American Quaker relief organization with a global reach to a global pacifist organization. It was, however, still an organization whose mission and personnel were shaped by traditional Quaker theology, including attitudes toward Jews. As has been shown, Quakers who had worked in Palestine like Mildred E. White had unconsciously absorbed the anti-Zionism and Arab nationalism of their local charges. This was even more the case for a Palestinian Christian like Khalil Totah. Like other Protestants, they saw themselves as defenders of the Christian community and a status quo that was being overturned by partition and the creation of the State of Israel.

The AFSC's leadership was put in a difficult situation. The organization's by then traditional relationship with and sympathy for Jews was challenged by the situation in Palestine. Quakers never expressed the same theological sympathy for Jews and Zionism that characterized a few liberal Protestants like Reinhold Niebuhr, but while Anglicans and Congregationalists in Palestine and the United States publicly attacked Zionism, and implicitly Jews, in harsh terms, Quakers did not. Individual Quakers, from Clarence Pickett on down, periodically expressed frustration with Jews for their unyielding and unchristian ways, but they did so privately. Even Donald Stevenson, whose dislike for Jews in general, the Jewish state, and Don Peretz in particular, was palpable, never appears to have made his criticisms public.

Other personnel, both in the leadership and the field, later expressed the view that the Jews, previously the victims, had become the victimizers of the Palestine Arabs. This is a more complex attitude to explain. The example of Howard Wriggins has been mentioned above. In her "Oral History," Josina Vreed Burger, a Dutch-born nurse and non-Quaker, also stated, "There was a time that I regret having been there because I feel I can't do enough to change this miserable situation, the way they are treated, the way America doesn't do anything because they want to have Israel, even if Israel is a robbing country of everything of those people. They don't know anything about it. If another country does it they make a lot of noise and send armies in. It's just terrible, and I still think so. I have friends that when I meet them 27 years ago they say, "Maybe you were right. I never thought about it."[29]

Volunteer David Walker added another comment regarding Quaker perceptions of the AFSC. In explaining why he was no longer involved with the AFSC but rather with other Quaker groups he noted, "we were rather disillusioned and felt that, in particular, the Middle East part of the AFSC was dominated by pro-Israeli sentiment at one time. This was about 10, 12 years ago, and we weren't very supportive of that. We were in an institute in Washington, and it may not have been the fault of the person who was the Middle East rep from AFSC employed by the AFSC, it may have just been the audience was loaded with pro-Israelis, but it didn't leave a good taste in my mind at all."[30] The suggestion that the AFSC was dominated by pro-Israel sentiment during the 1970s and 1980s is unusual given the hostility expressed by the organization in its publications.

Overall, it may be suggested that individual Quakers had become accustomed on a practical level to dealing with Jews as victims through their World War II relief efforts. Other American Protestant denominations were simultaneously horrified by the Holocaust but opposed both Jewish immigration to the United States and a Jewish state on practical and theological grounds.[31] The AFSC, however, had endorsed partition and the creation of Israel and, despite warnings from Quaker missionaries, did not have the same theological or practical opposition to Israel as other denominations. Once confronted with the Palestine Arab refugee situation from a human basis, however, individual fieldworkers began to sympathize both with their charges and their cause. This heightened the contrast between the "proper" or at least well-understood role of Jews as victims, and put them into the new role of victimizers.

For senior personnel, both on the scene like Stevenson and the leadership in Philadelphia, not being exposed to the situation on a daily basis enabled them to retain a more abstract Quaker perspective. The lack of Quakerly values among Israelis with whom they interacted on a political basis, or the AFSC's own employee like Don Peretz, who was "too Zionist" (in addition to being Jewish), reflects an almost theological confrontation between abstract beliefs and expectations and complex realities. The examples of Josina Vreed Burger and David Walker both suggest that the immense sympathy and identification the AFSC's field personnel felt for the Palestine Arab refugees could be generalized into disapproval of Israel that contained elements of modern anti-Semitic views, namely that Israel is fundamentally illegitimate and that the United States is dominated by Israel.

The AFSC's public stance was neutral toward Israel and the Arab-Israeli conflict, even though internally the sympathies of staff, certainly field personnel, shifted strongly toward the Palestine Arab refugees. But unlike members of other American Protestant denominations, such as Bayard Dodge or Harry Emerson Fosdick, no AFSC staff member ever publicly questioned the legitimacy of Israel or accused it of destroying Christian civilization in the Holy Land. In this sense, despite Quaker supersessionist theology, and the attitudes of individuals like Donald Stevenson, as an organization it cannot be accused of anti-Semitism. In this sense perhaps Henry Cadbury's early search for the "historical Jesus" that found him as a Galilean Jew may have carried the day, at least with most Quakers at AFSC offices in Philadelphia.

The same, however, cannot be said of the AFSC after 1970. Long after the Gaza mission, its complete radicalization as an American leftist organization, and the passing of the leadership of Rufus Jones and Clarence Pickett, the organization took stances that clearly put the entire onus for the Arab-Israeli conflict solely on Israel. Beginning with the pamphlet *Search for Peace in the Middle East,* later statements such as *A Compassionate Peace-A Future for the Middle East,*[32] and continuing through today, the organization has actively supported the Palestinian cause through fieldwork, lobbying, and activism, including boycotts of Israel.[33] The AFSC itself has also helped organize Palestinian groups involved in civil disobedience in the West Bank.[34] In the process, the AFSC and the Quakers have moved ever-closer to embracing Palestinian liberation theology that casts the Palestinians as a sacralized people and a moral force acting against an oppressor whose covenant is obsolete and whose religious ideology is outdated if not barbaric.[35]

Ties between Quakers, Jews, and Jewish organizations have long become frayed and shrill.[36] This has occurred even as American Quakerism itself has become so diluted and diffuse that it now includes the ahistorical, indeed oxymoronic, concept of "Jewish Quakers."[37] In a broad sense, the AFSC itself and some unknown proportion of Quaker practice appears in the 1960s to have adopted anti-imperialism in the name of pacifism as its primary political doctrine. In a narrower way, contemporary Quaker doctrine drawing on these sources has on the question of the Middle East converged with both secular left wing critiques of Israel, especially those from "peace studies" perspectives,[38] and, most ironically, the anti-Zionist American Protestant theology of the 1940s and the modern era.[39] In an era when American religion continues to shape public opinion, political affairs, and foreign policy, these questions remain at the forefront of contentious debates in the American public square.[40]

For UNRWA's part, its consistent support of a Palestinian "right of return" and espousal of a Zionist "original sin" with regard to the refugees and the creation of the State of Israel places it in a difficult and morally complex situation.[41] The "right of return" necessarily entails the dissolution of Israel as such and the establishment of a new state, either binational or Palestinian. In either scenario Jewish sovereignty, as envisioned by the Zionist movement and the 1947 partition plan, would be ended, and Jewish political and cultural rights necessarily curtailed. Whether this constitutes anti-Semitism is an unresolved issue.

# 10. Conclusions ⟶

Across some sixty years of the Palestine refugee problem, statements such as this are common:

> The next few months will hold the answer to the questions: are the Arab states willing to face reality, that is, the presence of Israel in their midst, to accept the financial and economic aids offered to them by the Relief and Works Agency and thus to begin to solve the refugee problem? If they do so, they can utilize the refugees to start the slow process of economic and social betterment for which the entire Middle East cries out. If they thus eliminate the use of the refugee problem as a political weapon against Israel and as a bargaining weapon against the West, they will serve their own long-range interests. If, however, they allow unsolved political issues, internal or external, to continue to dominate the refugee problem, they add one more large piece of fuel to the fires of unrest and instability which threaten each government in the Middle East.[1]

The sense of urgency that the Channing B. Richardson perceived in 1950, that time is running out, that hard choices must be made immediately, and that compromise on both sides is necessary, can be still found in the pages of any contemporary Middle East policy journal or newspaper discussion of the Palestinian situation. Successful resolution of the Palestine Arab refugee crisis then and now is posited as the key to the larger question of peace or war in the Middle East, even as it is admitted that the refugee issue is also used as a weapon against Israel and the West. The question of the refugees as individuals is in a sense secondary, as is the role that refugee relief plays in perpetuating larger political problems. The frequent statements from Palestinian leaders, Western scholar-advocates, NGOs and UNRWA itself regarding the "inviolable" "right of return" cast us back to the very same dilemma recognized by the AFSC in 1949. There are only two solutions, repatriation and resettlement, either or both of which would require immense political will and nearly inconceivable cultural willingness on the part of deeply alienated populations to be even considered. The centrality of the "right of return" to Palestinian identity, along with the concept of "resistance" as a means to restore both "justice" and "honor" have reliably thwarted any consideration of resettlement. Israeli concerns over security and national identity have obviated anything but nominal or symbolic repatriation of refugees or their descendents.

This study has demonstrated that the AFSC and the Palestine Arab refugee relief were from the very beginning enmeshed in politics and preconceptions as large as superpower competition and as subtle as nuances of Protestant theology. If anything, the scale and complexity of issues surrounding the Palestine Arab refugee problem have grown exponentially since the AFSC left Gaza. The solution they initially participated in, refugee relief and rehabilitation, with the goal of resettlement, on the familiar European and Indian-Pakistani models, was direct, but soon became mired in proposals for ever-larger solutions. Regional development, which the AFSC also supported, was to be the tide to lift all boats, change all attitudes, and bring a new, enlightened age of social and economic progress across the Middle East. In the process nearly all parties attempted to manipulate and blackmail one another for political or economic gain. But the fundamental refusal of the Arab states or the refugees themselves to accept any type of resettlement thwarted this, and indeed any, resolution of the problem.

In the interim, with UNRWA's help, Palestinian nationalism developed fully, based on the twinned ideas that "the world owes them a living" and that resistance to Israel and steadfastness were the only ways to restore lost honor. But the AFSC was opposed to dependence, "moral degeneration," and unbridled nationalism. The decision of the AFSC to withdraw from refugee relief, done in the name of religious and humanitarian values, and pure pragmatism, was the fateful path not taken by the international community at any point during the subsequent six decades. A similar decision is difficult to imagine today.

# Notes ✌

## INTRODUCTION

1. United Nations General Assembly Resolution 302 (IV) of 8 December 1949.
2. United Nations General Assembly. Resolution 212 (III), para. 12, of 19 November 1948.

## 1 STUDYING THE PALESTINE ARAB REFUGEE PROBLEM

1. For example, J. C. Hurewitz's fundamental, *The Struggle for Palestine* (New York: Schocken Books, 1976), treats the questions of UNRPR and UNRWA in less than three paragraphs (see pages 321 and 326). A recent book on Palestinian refugees in Egypt only mentions UNRPR or AFSC in passing. See Oroub El-Abed, *Unprotected: Palestinians in Egypt since 1948* (Washington, DC: Institute for Palestine Studies, 2009).
2. Marta Rieker, "Uses of Refugee Archives for Research and Policy Analysis. Reinterpreting the Historical Record," in *The Use of Palestinian Refugee Archives for Social Science Research and Policy Analysis*, ed. S. Tamari, and E. Zureik (Jerusalem: Institute of Jerusalem Studies, 2001), 11–23.
3. Michael R. Fischbach, *Records of Dispossession: Palestinian Refugee Property and the Arab-Israeli Conflict*, (New York: Columbia University Press, 2003).
4. Stéphanie L. Abdallah, "Regards, visibilité historique et politique des images sur les réfugiés palestiniens depuis 1948," *Le Mouvement social* no. 219–220 (2007): 65–91.
5. Channing B. Richardson, "The United Nations and Arab Refugee Relief, 1948–1950; a Case Study in International Organization and Administration" (doctoral dissertation, Columbia University, 1951).
6. Robert Simon, "Channing Richardson, Professor of International Relations (1952–1983)," Hamilton College, last accessed June 12, 2013.: www.hamilton. edu/history/memorial-minutes/Channing-Richardson.
7. Channing B. Richardson, "The United Nations Relief for Palestine Refugees," *International Organization* 4, no. 1 (1950): 44–54.
8. Richardson, "United Nations Relief," 50.

9.  Channing B. Richardson, "The Refugee Problem," *Proceedings of the Academy of Political Science* 24, no. 4 (1952): 43–50.

10. Richardson, "The Refugee Problem," 48.

11. Don Peretz, "Israel and the Arab Refugees" (doctoral dissertation, Columbia University, 1955).

12. Don Peretz, "Vignettes – Bits and Pieces," in *Paths to the Middle East: Ten Scholars Look Back*, ed. T. Naff (Albany: SUNY Press, 1993), 231–261.

13. Don Peretz, *The Rights of the Palestinians* (Washington, DC: Middle East Institute, 1974); Don Peretz, *The West Bank: History, Politics, Society, and Economy* (Boulder: Westview, 1986); Don Peretz, *Palestinians, Refugees, and the Middle East Peace Process* (Washington, DC: United States Institute of Peace Press, 1993).

14. Don Peretz, *Israel and the Palestine Arabs* (Washington, DC: Middle East Institute, 1958).

15. Peretz, *Israel and the Palestine Arabs*, 7.

16. Roni E. Gabbay, *A Political Study of the Arab-Jewish Conflict. The Arab Refugee Problem (A Case Study)* (Paris: Libraire Minard, 1959).

17. Gabbay, *Political Study*, 54–112.

18. David P. Forsythe, "UNRWA, the Palestine Refugees, and World Politics: 1949–1969," *International Organization* 25 (1971): 26–45.

19. Forsythe, "UNRWA," 27.

20. Forsythe, "UNRWA," 30–31.

21. Forsythe, "UNRWA," 45.

22. Amos Perlmutter, "Patrons in the Babylonian Captivity of Clients: UNRWA and World Politics," *International Organization* 25, no. 2 (1971): 306–308.

23. Perlmutter, "Patrons," 306.

24. Perlmutter, "Patrons," 307.

25. David P. Forsythe, "Further on the United Nations Relief and Works Agency: Refugees from Objectivity: Comment," *International Organization* 25 (1971): 950–952.

26. David P. Forsythe, *United Nations Peacemaking: the Conciliation Commission for Palestine* (Baltimore: Johns Hopkins University Press, 1972). See also J. C. Hurewitz, "The United Nations Conciliation Commission for Palestine: Establishment and Definition of Functions," *International Organization* 7, no. 4 (1953): 482–497.

27. Edward H. Buehrig, *The UN and the Palestinian Refugees: a Study in Nonterritorial Administration* (Bloomington: Indiana University Press, 1971).

28. Buehrig, *The UN and the Palestinian Refugees*, 43.

29. Buehrig, *The UN and the Palestinian Refugees*, 43–53, 167–179.

30. Marx and Nachmias also note that the UNRWA Commissioner General does not require any approval or confirmation from the General Assembly and that the individual reports directly to the Fifth Committee (administrative and

budgetary) before being forwarded to the General Assembly. See Emmanuel Marx and Nitza Nachmias, "Dilemmas of Prolonged Humanitarian Aid Operations: The Case of UNRWA (UN Relief and Works Agency for Palestinian Refugees)," *Journal of Humanitarian Assistance* (2004), available at http://sites.tufts.edu/jha/archives/834.

31. Buehrig, *The UN and the Palestinian Refugees*, 90–92.

32. Benjamin N. Schiff, *Refugees unto the Third Generation: UN Aid to Palestinians* (Syracuse, NY: Syracuse University Press, 1995).

33. Schiff, *Refugees*, 5–20.

34. Benny Morris, *The Birth of the Palestinian Refugee Problem, 1947–1949* (Cambridge: Cambridge University Press, 1988).

35. Efraim Karsh, "Benny Morris and the Reign of Error," *Middle East Quarterly* 4 (1999): 15–28; Efraim Karsh, *Fabricating Israeli History: the "New Historians"* (London: Frank Cass, 2000). See also Shabtai Teveth, "The Palestine Arab Refugee Problem and its Origins," *Middle East Studies* 26, no. 2 (1990): 214–249.

36. See Benny Morris, *The Birth of the Palestinian Refugee Problem Revisited* (Cambridge: Cambridge University Press, 2004), 1–9, and Benny Morris, *One State, Two States: Resolving the Israel/Palestine Conflict* (New Haven: Yale University Press, 2009).

37. Benny Morris, "The Historiography of Deir Yassin," *Journal of Israeli History* 24, no. 1 (2005): 79–107.

38. See generally Yoav Gelber, "The History of Zionist Historiography, From Apologetics to Denial," in *Making Israel*, ed. Benny Morris (Ann Arbor: University of Michigan Press, 2007), 47–80; Joseph Heller, "Alternative Narratives and Collective Memories: Israel's New Historians and the Use of Historical Context," *Middle Eastern Studies* 42, no. 4 (2006): 571–586; Anita Shapira, "Historiography and Politics: The Debate of the New Historians," *History and Memory* 7, no. 1 (1995): 9–40; Amos Perlmutter, "The Post-Zionist war against Israel," *Totalitarian Movements and Political Religions* 1, no. 2 (2000): 93–112. Compare Assaf Likhovski, "Post-Post-Zionist Historiography," *Israel Studies* 15, no. 2 (2010): 1–23.

39. For example, Ilan Pappé, *The Making of the Arab-Israeli Conflict, 1947–1951* (London: I.B. Taurus, 1992); Avi Shlaim, *The Politics of Partition: King Abdullah, the Zionists, and Palestine, 1921–1951* (New York: Columbia University Press, 1990).

40. Walid Khalidi, *From Haven to Conquest; Readings in Zionism and the Palestine Problem until 1948* (Beirut: Institute for Palestine Studies, 1971); Walid Khalidi, *All That Remains: The Palestinian Villages Occupied and Depopulated by Israel in 1948* (Washington, DC: Institute for Palestine Studies, 1992); Ibrahim Abu-Lughod, ed. *The Transformation of Palestine: Essays on the Origin and Development of the Arab-Israeli Conflict* (Evanston, Northwestern University Press, 1971).

50. For example, UNRWA's Senior Ethics Officer Lex Takkenberg's "UNRWA and the Palestinian Refugees After Sixty Years: Some Reflections," *Refugee Survey Quarterly* 28, nos. 2–3 (2009): 253–259. See also former UNRWA Commissioner-General Karen Abu Zayd's "UNRWA and the Palestinian Refugees After Sixty Years: Assessing Developments and Marking Challenges," *Refugee Survey Quarterly* 28, no. 2–3 (2009): 227–228.

51. Lance Bartholomeusz, "The Mandate of UNRWA at Sixty," *Refugee Survey Quarterly* 28, no. 2–3 (2009): 452–474.

52. For example, Rex Brynen and Roula El-Rifai, eds., *Palestinian Refugees: Challenges of Repatriation and Development* (London: I.B. Taurus, 2007). In contrast, Howard Adelman, noted that the original recommendations by United Nations Mediator Folke Bernadotte on the return of refugees included an important qualification: "The vast majority of the refugees may no longer have homes to return to and their resettlement in the State of Israel presents an economic and social problem of great complexity. Whether the refugees are resettled in the State of Israel or in one or another of the Arab States, a major question to be faced is that of placing them in an environment in which they can find employment and a means of livelihood. But in any case their unconditional right to make a free choice should be fully respected." He argued that the Bernadotte's murder "lent great support to his report" and noted the conditional language in the final text of U.N. Resolution 194 III makes the humanitarian assertion that refugees *ought* to be *permitted* to be repatriated. It does not demand this. See Howard Adelman, "Home and Homeland: The Bequest of Count Folk Bernadotte," in *Palestinian and Israeli Environmental Narratives*, ed. Stuart Schoenfeld (Toronto: Ontario, Centre for International and Security Studies, York University, 2005), 213–219.

53. For example, Randa Farah, "UNRWA: Through the Eyes of its Refugee Employees in Jordan," *Refugee Survey Quarterly* 28, no.14 (2009): 392; Dominique Vidal and Joseph Algazy, *Le péché originel d'Israël: l'expulsion des Palestiniens revisitée par les "nouveaux historiens" israéliens* (Paris: Edition de l'Atelier, 1998); Ricardo Bocco, "UNRWA and the Palestinian Refugees: A History within History," *Refugee Survey Quarterly* 28, nos. 2–3 (2009): 229–252.

54. For example, Arlene Kushner, "UNRWA, The United Nations Relief and Works Agency for Palestine Refugees in the Near East, A Report," Jerusalem: Israel Resource News Agency, 2003; Arlene Kushner, "The UN's Palestinian Refugee Problem," *Azure* 22 (2005): 57–77; Arlene Kushner "UNRWA, Overview and Policies," Jerusalem: Center for Near East Policy Research, 2008.

55. For example, James G. Lindsay, *Fixing UNRWA: Repairing the UN's Troubled System of Aid to Palestinian Refugees* (Washington, DC: Washington Institute for Near East Policy, 2009).

56. Salim Tamari, and Elia Zureik, eds., *The Use of Palestinian Refugee Archives for Social Science Research and Policy Analysis* (Jerusalem: Institute of Jerusalem Studies, 2001).

57. Julie M. Peteet, "AFSC Refugee Archives on Palestine, 1948–50,' in *The Use of Palestinian Refugee Archives for Social Science Research and Policy Analysis*, eds. Salim Tamari and Elia Zureik (Jerusalem: Institute of Jerusalem Studies, 2001), 109–128.

58. Julie M. Peteet, *Landscape of Hope and Despair: Palestinian Refugee Camps* (Philadelphia: University of Pennsylvania Press, 2005): 57–61.

59. Nancy Gallagher, *Quakers in the Israeli-Palestinian Conflict: the Dilemmas of NGO Humanitarian Activism* (Cairo: American University in Cairo Press, 2007).

60. Ilana Feldman, "Difficult Distinctions: Refugee Law, Humanitarian Practice, and Political Identification in Gaza," *Cultural Anthropology* 22, no. 1 (2007): 129–169.

61. Ilana Feldman, "The Quaker Way: Ethical Labor and Humanitarian Relief," *American Ethnologist* 34, no. 4 (2007): 689–705.

62. Clarence Pickett, *For More than Bread, an Autobiographical Account of Twenty-two Years' Work with the American Friends Service Committee* (Boston: Little, 1953); Walter Kahoe, *Clarence Pickett, a Memoir* (Privately printed, 1966); Elmore Jackson, *Middle East Mission, The Story of a Major Bid for Peace in the Time of Nasser and Ben Gurion* (New York: W.W. Norton & Company, 1983); William H. Wriggins, *Picking up the Pieces from Portugal to Palestine: Quaker Refugee Relief in World War II, A Memoir* (Lanham, MD: University Press of America, 2004).

## 2   THE QUAKERS AND THE AMERICAN FRIENDS SERVICE COMMITTEE: ORIGINS OF THE QUAKERS AND QUAKER IDEOLOGY

1. Thomas Alexander Lacey, *The Acts of Uniformity: Their Scope and Effect* (London: Rivingtons, 1900).

2. George Fox, *Journal of George Fox* (Glasgow: W.G. Mackie & Co. 1852), 54.

3. Thomas Evans, *A Concise Account of the Religious Society of Friends* (Philadelphia: Religious Society of Friends, 1856).

4. David Yount, *How the Quakers Invented America* (Lanham, MD: Rowman & Littlefield, 2007).

5. Thomas D. Hamm, *The Quakers in America* (New York: Columbia University Press, 2003), 37–63, 120–155; Pink Dandelion, *The Quakers: A Very Short Introduction* (Oxford: Oxford University Press, 2008), 19–36.

6. Rufus M. Jones, *A Service of Love in War Time, American Friends Relief Work in Europe, 1917–1919* (New York: Macmillan, 1920), 4.

7. Jones was scion of a well-established Quaker family. In addition to his work with the AFSC he taught psychology and philosophy at Haverford College and wrote widely on Christian and humanitarian themes. His orientation

was liberal, modernist, and mystical, and his work comprises an important element of what passes for twentieth-century American Quaker theology.

8. Jones, *A Service of Love in War Time*, 8–9.
9. Jones, *A Service of Love in War Time*, 85–108.
10. Jones, *A Service of Love in War Time*, 191.
11. Jones, *A Service of Love in War Time*, 202–203.
12. Jones, *A Service of Love in War Time*, 260.
13. Sonja Wentling, "The Engineer and the Shtadlanim: Herbert Hoover and American Jewish Non-Zionists, 1917–28," *American Jewish History* 88 (2000): 377–406.
14. Allan W. Austin, "'Let's do away with walls!': The American Friends Service Committee's Interracial Section and the 1920s United States," *Quaker History* 98, no. 1 (2009): 1–34; Mary Hoxie Jones, *Swords into Ploughshares; An Account of the American Friends Service Committee, 1917–1937* (New York: Macmillan, 1937).
15. Hamm, *Quakers in America*, 174–175.
16. Howard Haines Brinton, *A Religious Solution to the Social Problem* (Wallingford, PA: Pendle Hill, 1934).
17. Frank Fox, "Quaker, Shaker, Rabbi: Warder Cresson, the Story of a Philadelphia Mystic," *The Pennsylvania Magazine of History and Biography* 95 (1971): 146–193.
18. Ela Greenberg, *Preparing the Mothers of Tomorrow: Education and Islam in Mandate Palestine* (Austin: University of Texas Press, 2009): 22–24. See also Christina Jones, *Friends in Palestine* (Richmond, IN: American Friends Board of Missions, 1944); Catherine C. B. Baylin, *Quaker Activity in Ramallah: 1869–1914* (Masters Thesis, American University of Cairo, 2010).
19. Theophilus Waldmeier, *The Autobiography of Theophilus Waldmeier, Missionary: Being Ten Years' Life in Abyssinia; and Sixteen Years in Syria* (London: S.W. Partridge & Co., 1886), 253, 277, 280.
20. Greenberg, *Preparing the Mothers*, 85–86.
21. See generally Abdul Latif Tibawi, *American Interests in Syria, 1800–1901: A Study of Educational, Literary and Religious Work* (Oxford: Oxford University Press, 1966); Bayard Dodge, "American Educational and Missionary Efforts in the Nineteenth and Early Twentieth Centuries," *Annals of the American Academy of Political and Social Science* 401 (1972): 15–22; Ghada Yusuf Khoury, *The Founding Fathers of the American University of Beirut* (Beirut: American University of Beirut, 1992); Fruma Zachs, "From the Mission to the Missionary: The Bliss Family and the Syrian Protestant College, 1866–1920," *Die Welt des Islams* 45, no. 2 (2005): 255–291; Fruma Zachs, "Toward a Proto-Nationalist Concept of Syria Revisiting the American Presbyterian Missionaries in the Levant," *Die Welt des Islams* 41, no. 2 (2001): 1–29; Betty S. Anderson, *The American University of Beirut: Arab Nationalism and Liberal Education* (Austin: University of Texas Press, 2011).

22. See generally Gershon Greenberg, *The Holy Land in American Religious Thought, 1620–1948: The Symbiosis of American Religious Approaches to Scripture's Sacred Territory* (Lanham, MD and Jerusalem: University Press of America and the Avraham Harman Institute of Contemporary Jewry, The Hebrew University of Jerusalem, 1994); Lester Vogel, *To See A Promised Land, Americans and the Holy Land in the Nineteenth Century* (State College, PA: Penn State Press, 1995); Hilton Obenzinger, *American Palestine, Melville, Twain, and the Holy Land Mania* (Princeton: Princeton University Press, 1999).

23. Joseph L. Grabill, *Protestant Diplomacy and the Near East; Missionary Influence on American Policy, 1810–1927* (Minneapolis, MN: University of Minnesota Press, 1971).

24. Suzanne E. Moranian, "The Armenian Genocide and American Missionary Relief Efforts," in *America and the Armenian Genocide of 1915*, ed., J. M. Winter (Cambridge: Cambridge University Press, 2003), 185–213; Merrill D. Peterson, *"Starving Armenians": American and the Armenian Genocide, 1915–1930 and After* (Charlottesville, VA: University of Virginia Press, 2004).

25. William Ernest Hocking, ed. *Re-Thing Missions, a Layman's Inquiry after One Hundred Years* (New York: Harper & Brothers Publishers, 1932).

26. Thomas M. Ricks, "Khalil Totah, The Unknown Years," *Jerusalem Quarterly* 34 (2008): 51–77.

27. Khalil Totah, "Education in Palestine," in *Palestine: A Decade of Development*, eds. Harry Viteles and Khalil Totah (Philadelphia: American Academy of Political and Social Science, 1932), 155–166.

28. Ricks, "Khalil Totah, The Unknown Years," 64.

29. Great Britain, Palestine Royal Commission. *Palestine Royal Commission Report, Presented by the Secretary of State for the Colonies to Parliament by Command of His Majesty, July 1937* (London: His Majesty's Stationary Office, 1937), 351.

30. Haverford College, Quaker & Special Collections, Khalili A. Totah and Eva Marshall Totah Papers. Khalil Totah to Palestine Watching Committee, Friends House London, May 11, 1936.

31. "Proposals of the British Quakers Palestine Watching Committee, September 4, 1938, Friends Services Council, London," *The Friend* 97 (1939): 49–50.

32. Edgar B. Castle, *Palestine Pamphlets: A Constitution for Palestine; Reconciliation in Palestine* (London: Friends' Book Centre, 1945).

33. Farah Mendlesohn, "Denominational Difference in Quaker Relief Work During the Spanish Civil War: The Operation of Corporate Concern and Liberal Theologies," *Journal of Religious History* 24, no. 2 (2000): 180–96.

34. Allen Smith, "The Renewal Movement: The Peace Testimony and Modern Quakerism," *Quaker History* 85, no. 2 (1996): 1–23. See also Allen Smith, "The Peace Movement at the Local Level: The Syracuse Peace Council, 1936–1973," *Peace & Change* 23, no. 1 (1998): 1–26.

35. Robert H. Abzug, *America Views the Holocaust, 1933–1945: A Brief Documentary History* (New York: Bedford/St. Martin's, 1999), 28–33.
36. Rufus M. Jones, "Our Day in the German Gestapo," *The American Friend*, July 10, 1947. Reprinted as a pamphlet for distribution. Last accessed June 12, 2013. www.afsc.org/sites/afsc.civicactions.net/files/documents/Our_Day_in_the_German_Gestapo_by_Rufus_Jones.pdf
37. For another account of the meeting see Elizabeth Gray Vining, *Friend of Life: The Biography of Rufus M. Jones* (New York: J. B. Lippincott, 1958): 280–293.
38. See generally Hans A. Schmitt, *Quakers and Nazis: Inner Light in Outer Darkness* (Columbia: University of Missouri Press, 1997); Gallagher, *Quakers in the Israeli-Palestinian Conflict*, 13–17.
39. Melanie J. Wright, "The Nature and Significance of Relations Between the Historic Peace Churches and Jews During and After the Shoah," in *Christian-Jewish Relations Through the Centuries*, eds., Stanley E. Porter and Brook W. R. Pearson (Sheffield: Sheffield Academic Press, 2000), 400–425.
40. For the activities of British Friends in post-war relief with the UNRRA see Fiona Reid and Sharif Gemie, "The Friends Relief Service and Displaced People in Europe after the Second World War, 1945–48," *Quaker Studies* 7, no. 2 (2013): 223–43.
41. *New York Times*, "World Needs After UNRRA," February 12, 1947, p. 24.
42. Pickett, *For More than Bread*, 191, 198.
43. The purchasing power of $8,000,000 in 1947 dollars is roughly equivalent to $82,200,000 in 2012 dollars. Calculated at www.measuringworth.com/ppowerus/. Last accessed June 12, 2013.
44. *New York Times*, "A Message to Our Fellow Americans Concerning World Hunger," February 19, 1947, p. C19.
45. Smith notes that over 90 percent of eligible Quakers did military service during World War II. The reach of Quaker beliefs and AFSC ideology was evidently limited. See Smith, "The Renewal Movement," 400.
46. Cadbury was a prominent New Testament scholar at Harvard Divinity School and brother-in-law of Rufus Jones. See Mary Hoxie Jones, "Henry Joel Cadbury: A Biographical Sketch," in *Then and Now, Quaker Essays: Historical and Contemporary*, ed., Anna Cox Brinton (Philadelphia: University of Pennsylvania Press, 1960), 11–70. Cadbury's book *The Peril of Modernizing Jesus* (New York: Macmillan, 1937) was an extended argument to "demodernize" Jesus and see him as a Galilean Jew rather than a twentieth-century liberal or an American icon. As such it is an important indication of American Quaker attitudes toward Jews and presages arguments that reemerged decades later in Biblical studies, even as Quakers have moved toward supersessionism.
47. H. Larry Ingle, "The American Friends Service Committee, 1947–49: The Cold War's Effect," *Peace & Change* 23, no. 1 (1998): 27–48. Compare Allen Smith, "Comments on Ingle," *Peace & Change* 29, no. 3 (1998): 399–401.

48. Ingle, "The Cold War's Effect," 30.
49. Ingle, "The Cold War's Effect," 35, 36.
50. Ingle, "The Cold War's Effect," 29.
51. Ingle, "The Cold War's Effect," 28. Compare Irwin Abrams, "The Quaker Peace Testimony and the Nobel Peace Prize, Presented at the International Conference: 'The Pacifist Impulse in Historical Perspective,'" (University of Toronto, May 1991). Last accessed June 12, 2013. www2.gol.com/users/quakers/quaker_peace_testimony.htm
52. American Friends Service Committee, *The United States and the Soviet Union: Some Quaker Proposals for Peace* (New Haven: Yale University Press, 1949).
53. American Friends Service Committee, *Steps to Peace: A Quaker View of U.S. Foreign Policy*, (Philadelphia, 1951). American Friends Service Committee, *Toward Security through Disarmament* (Philadelphia, 1952).
54. American Friends, Service Committee, *Speak Truth to Power: A Quaker Search for an Alternative to Violence* (Philadelphia, 1955). See also Elizabeth Walker Mechling and Jay Mechling, "Hot Pacifism and Cold War: The American Friends Service Committee's Witness for Peace in 1950s America," *Quarterly Journal of Speech* 78, no. 2 (1992): 173–196; H. Larry Ingle, "'Speak Truth to Power': A Thirty Years' Retrospective," *Christian Century* 102 (1985): 383–385.
55. *New York Times*, "Truman is Urged to Bar Atom Bomb," August 20, 1945, p. 21; *New York Times*, "Theologians Assail New Bomb Decisions," February 2, 1950, p. 6.
56. *New York Times*, "Protection Asked in Loyalty Tests," January 12, 1948, p. 10.
57. Ingle, "The Cold War's Effect," 40.
58. *Washington Post*, "Witnesses Praise Hiss' Reputation," December 14, 1949, p. 2. See generally Larry Miller, "Clarence Pickett and the Alger Hiss Case," *Friends Journal*, November 1994, December 1994: 9–13, 12–15.
59. *Chicago Daily Tribune*, "How Reds Lure Intellectuals to Their Side," June 6, 1948, p. 11.
60. Smith, "Renewal Movement."
61. Gunnar Jahr, Award Ceremony Speech, www.nobelprize.org/nobel_prizes/peace/laureates/1947/press.htm. Last consulted June 12, 2013.

## 3   THE AFSC IN THE MIDDLE EAST: THE OFFICIAL ORIGINS OF AFSC INVOLVEMENT IN THE MIDDLE EAST

1. Pickett, *For More than Bread*, 260–261.
2. Pickett, *For More than Bread*, 262.

3. Kahoe, *Clarence Pickett*, 23. See also Gallagher, *Quakers in the Israeli-Palestinian Conflict*, 36; David Hinshaw, *Rufus Jones, Master Quaker* (New York: G. P. Putnam's Sons, 1951): 237–239.

4. American Friends Service Committee Achive, Philadelphia, PA (henceforth AFSC) 1950. Marshall Sutton to Corrine Hardesty, January 30, 1950.

5. See generally H. Eugene Bovis, *The Jerusalem Question, 1917–1968* (Palo Alto: The Hoover Institution, 1971): 41–43.

6. See the summary in Marshal J. Breger and Thomas A. Idinopulos, *Jerusalem's Holy Places and the Peace Process* (Washington, DC: Washington Institute for Near East Policy, 1998).

7. United Nations General Assembly, Resolution 181 (III), of 29 November 1947.

8. Bovis, *Jerusalem Question*, 47–55.

9. Ricks, "Khalil Totah, The Unknown Years," 70, no. 55. See also Khalil Totah, *Dynamite in the Middle East* (New York: Philosophical Library, 1955), 182, 206.

10. Former US President Herbert Hoover had, in a private capacity, endorsed Zionism since the 1920s. In 1945 he published a plan for resettling Palestine Arabs in Iraq to make way for a Jewish state. This had evidently been developed in part with the help of Revisionist Zionist operative Eliahu Ben-Horin. Hoover approached the issue from a purely technocratic, and as he saw it, pragmatic, point of view. Transferring Jewish and Arab populations would encourage the development of both Iraq and Palestine. The proposal, like other population transfer proposals, met with bitter rejection from Arab representatives. But at no time were these efforts identified in any way as a Quaker initiative. See Rafael Medoff, "Herbert Hoover's Plan for Palestine: A Forgotten Episode in American Middle East Diplomacy," *American Jewish History* 79 (1990): 449–476; Chaim Simons, *International Proposals to Transfer Arabs from Palestine* (Hoboken, NJ: Ktav Publishing, 1988), 133, 146–166; W. D. Blanks, "Herbert Hoover and the Holy Land: A Preliminary Study Based upon Documentary Sources in the Hoover Presidential Library," in *With Eyes Toward Zion, Scholars Colloquium on America-Holy Land Studies*, ed. M. Davis (New York: Arno Press, 1977), 163–176.

11. Bernard Wasserstein, *Divided Jerusalem, The Struggle for the Holy City* (New Haven: Yale University Press, 2002), 148. For additional Quaker versions see Larry Miller, *Witness for Humanity: The Biography of Clarence E. Pickett* (Wallingford, PA: Pendle Hill Publications, 1999), 154; Daisy Newman, *A Procession of Friends: Quakers in America* (New York: Doubleday, 1972), 223. Compare Pablo de Azcárate, *Mission in Palestine, 1948–1952* (Washington, DC: Middle East Institute, 1966), 49–50. Compare also U.S. Department of State, *Foreign Relations of the United States, 1948*. Vol. V, The Near East, South Asia, and Africa, (in two parts) (Washington, DC: Government Printing Office, 1975–1976), 917, that only indicates that Harold Evans of

AFSC was the agreed upon "Special Commissioner for Palestine." [Hereafter *FRUS*]. Compare Vining, *Friend of Life*, 311.

12. Vining, *Friend of Life*, 308–311. Sayre was a prominent international lawyer. He married Woodrow Wilson's daughter Jessie in 1913 and prior to World War II served as the US Ambassador to Siam, Assistant Secretary of State, and High Commissioner to the Philippines. After his retirement in 1952 he served as president of the House of Deputies of the Episcopal Church of America in Japan. See Williams College, Archives & Special Collections, Francis B. Sayre (1885–1972) Papers, 1914–1917. Last accessed June 12, 2013. http://archives. williams.edu/manuscriptguides/sayre/bio.php

13. Hinshaw, *Rufus Jones*, 237–238.

14. AFSC 1948. Report of Friends Mission to Palestine: April 15–20, 1948, James Vail, Edgar B. Castle. Compare Vining, *Friend of Life*, 310–311.

15. Edgar B. Castle, "Jerusalem Now," *The Spectator*, May 14, 1948, 578.

16. Gelber, *Palestine 1948*, 120–129.

17. David Barnett and Efraim Karsh, "Azzam's Genocidal Threat," *Middle East Quarterly* 18 (2011): 85–88.

18. Eyal Naveh, "Unconventional "Christian Zionist": the Theologian Reinhold Niebuhr and His Attitude toward the Jewish National Movement," *Studies in Zionism* 11 (1990): 183–196, 12 (1991): 85–88.

19. See generally Hertzel Fishman, *American Protestantism and a Jewish State* (Detroit: Wayne State University Press, 1973), 64–126; William L. Burton, "Protestant America and the Rebirth of Israel," *Jewish Social Studies* 26, no. 4 (1964): 203–14; Caitlen Carenen, "The American Christian Palestine Committee, the Holocaust, and Mainstream Protestant Zionism, 1938–1948," *Holocaust and Genocide Studies* 24, no. 2 (2010): 273–296.

20. Thomas Lippman, "The View From 1947: The CIA and the Partition of Palestine," *Middle East Journal* 61, no. 1 (2007): 17–28.

21. Gardiner H. Shattuck, Jr., ""True Israelites": Charles Thorley Bridgerman and Anglican Missions in Palestine, 1922–1948," *Anglican and Episcopal History* 77, no. 2 (2008): 115–149; Gardiner H. Shattuck, Jr., "Weeping over Jerusalem: Anglicans and Refugee Relief in the Middle East, 1895–1950," *Anglican and Episcopal History* 80, no. 2 (2011): 117–141. Compare Laura Robson, "Church, State, and the Holy Land: British Protestant Approaches to Imperial Policy in Palestine, 1917–1948," *The Journal of Imperial and Commonwealth History* 39, no. 3 (2011): 457–477.

22. AFSC 1948, Paul Sturge to Colin Bell, July 28, 1948.

23. AFSC 1948. Colin Bell to A. Willard Jones, September 1, 1948.

24. *New York Times*, "U.N. Relief Expert Asks Aid to Arabs," August 8, 1948, p. 28.

25. AFSC 1948. Colin Bell to Paul Sturge, August 24, 1948.

26. AFSC 1948. Bernard G. Lawson to Colin Bell, August 25, 1948.

27. Cilento was an Australian physician and specialist in public health and tropical diseases who had worked with the United Nations Relief and Rehabilitation Administration and the Social Activities Division of the United Nations. Well-known as a conservative social Darwinist and racialist, his statement regarding the equivalence of the European Jewish refugee crisis and the Palestine Arab crisis evoked anger from Jewish and Israeli sources, who accused him of having pro-Arab sympathies that verged onto anti-Semitism. After the end of the Disaster Relief Programma Cilento briefly headed the United Nations Social Welfare Seminar for Arab States in the Middle East. He was later active in right-wing Australian politics. See Fedora Gould Fisher, *Raphael Cilento: A Biography* (Brisbane: University of Queensland Press, 1994).

28. AFSC 1948. Outline of a Proposed Plan for a Quaker Team in Palestine, September 28, 1948. The document is unsigned.

29. *Nebraska Yearly Meeting of Friends, Thirteenth Annual Assembly*, Held at Central City, Nebraska, 1920, 32.

30. AFSC 1948. Mildred E. White to Colin Bell, December 2, 1948.

31. *FRUS 1948*, Vol. V, The Special Representative of the United States in Israel (McDonald) to President Truman, October 17, 1948, 1486.

32. *FRUS 1948*, Vol. V, The Special Representative of the United States in Israel (McDonald) to the Acting Secretary of State, November 10, 1948, 1567–1568.

33. *New York Times*, "Twenty U.S. Groups Map Palestine Relief," October 6, 1948, p. 5.

34. *New York Times*, "Child Fund Plans New Palestine Aid," *New York Times*, 19 October, 1948, p. 3.

35. *New York Times*, "Text of Encyclical," *New York Times*, 24 October, 1948, p. 7.

36. AFSC 1948. Statement, American Appeal for Holy Land Refugees, October 21, 1948; *New York Times*, "Joint Appeal to Aid Holy Land Refugees," October 22, 1948, p. 6.

37. W. C. Klein, "Pause in Palestine," *The Living Church*, October 3, 1948, p. 8. See also Shattuck, "Weeping over Jerusalem," 139–139.

38. Wassserstein, *Divided Jerusalem*, 160–165; Shlomo Slonim, "Israeli Policy on Jerusalem at the United Nations, 1948," *Middle Eastern Studies* 30, no. 3 (1994): 590–593.

39. AFSC 1948. Minutes of the Foreign Service Executive Committee meeting, November 17, 1948, submitted by Julia E. Branson.

40. AFSC 1948. Minutes of the Foreign Service Executive Committee meeting, November 17, 1948, submitted by Julia E. Branson.

41. Elmore Jackson Papers, RG 5/202, Friends Historical Library of Swarthmore College. Elmore Jackson to Clarence Pickett and Charles Read, December 5, 1948. Box 5.

42. *Manchester Guardian*, "Aid to Palestine Refugees: U.N. Begins its Task," December 18, 1948, p. 6; *New York Times*, "U.N. Relief Groups Sign Arab Aid Pacts," December 18, 1948, p. 7.
43. Wriggins, *Picking up the Pieces*, 178.
44. Elmore Jackson Papers, RG 5/202, Friends Historical Library of Swarthmore College. Elmore Jackson to Clarence Pickett and Charles Read, December 5, 1948.
45. W. H. Wriggins, *Picking up the Pieces*, 185.
46. American Friends Service Committee AFSC Oral History Interviews Series #600, 1992. See also Gallagher, "Quakers in the Israeli-Palestinian Conflict," 69–73.
47. AFSC Oral History Interview #609, Narrator: David Walker, Interviewer: Joan Lowe, September 20, 1992, 209.
48. AFSC 1948. Colin Bell to Paul Sturge, November 26, 1948.
49. Jalal al-Husseini, "Red Cross Palestinian Refugee Archives 1948–1950," in *The Use of Palestinian Refugee Archives for Social Science Research and Policy Analysis*, eds. Salim Tamari, and Elia Zureik (Jerusalem: Institute of Jerusalem Studies, 2001), 145–171; David P. Forsythe, *The Humanitarians: the International Committee of the Red Cross* (Cambridge: Cambridge University Press, 2005), 55–57.
50. Sydney D. Bailey, "Review of D. P. Forsythe, The Humanitarians: the International Committee of the Red Cross, Cambridge: Cambridge University Press," *International Affairs* 55, no. 2 (1979): 270.
51. Jean-Claude Favez, *The Red Cross and the Holocaust* (New York: Cambridge University Press, 1999).
52. Dominique-D. Junod, *The Imperiled Red Cross and the Palestine-Eretz-Yisrael Conflict, 1945–1952: the Influence of Institutional Concerns on a Humanitarian Operation* (London: Keegan Paul International, 1996). Compare Forsythe, *The Humanitarians*, 55–57.
53. Jacques de Reynier, *1948 à Jérusalem* (Paris: Éditions de la Baconnière, 1969). See also the largely descriptive piece by René Bovey, "L'aide du Comité international aux Réfugiés de Palestine," *International Review of the Red Cross* 31, no. 364 (1949): 265–270. Compare Catherine Rey-Schyrr, "Le CICR et l'assistance aux réfugiés arabes palestiniens (1948–1950)," *International Review of the Red Cross* 83, no. 843 (2001): 739–761.
54. Laszlo Ledermann, "The International Organization of the Red Cross and the League of Red Cross Societies," *American Journal of International Law* 42, no. 3 (1948): 635–644; Lili Petschnigg, "The League of Red Cross Societies," *American Journal of Nursing* 50, no. 9 (1950): 516–517.
55. Clyde E. Buckingham, *Red Cross Disaster Relief, its Origin and Development* (Washington, DC: Public Affairs Press, 1956); Clyde E. Buckingham, *For Humanity's Sake: The Story of the Early Development of the League of Red Cross Societies* (Washington, DC: Public Affairs Press, 1964).

56. W. de St. Aubin, "Peace and Refugees in the Middle East," *Middle East Journal* 3 (1949): 249–259.
57. United Nations General Assembly, Resolution 194 (III), of 11 December 1948. See generally Forsythe, *United Nations Peacemaking* 1972.
58. United Nations General Assembly, Resolution 194 (III), of 11 December 1948, Para. 11.
59. Gabbay, *Arab-Jewish Conflict*, 125.
60. United Nations General Assembly, Resolution 212 (III), of 19 November 1949, Para. 2.
61. *New York Times*, "He Will Ask Congress to Appropriate 50% of Sum Sought from U.N.—Griffis Shapes Relief Distribution for 507,000," December 8, 1948, p. 18.
62. *New York Times,* "Extra $5,000,000 on Hand," December 8, 1948, p. 18.
63. Gabbay, *The Arab-Jewish Conflict*, 126.
64. Efraim Karsh, "How Many Palestinian Arab Refugees Were There?" *Israel Affairs* 17, no. 2 (2011): 224–246. See also Teveth, "The Palestine Arab Refugee Problem and Its Origins," 219–220 for a critique of Morris's four stage reconstruction and the general problem of periodization, and cause and effect, in reconstructing the refugee problem.
65. See for example Itamar Radai, "The Collapse of the Palestinian-Arab Middle Class in 1948: The Case of Qatamon," *Middle Eastern Studies* 43, no. 6 (2007): 961–982; Efraim Karsh, "Nakbat Haifa: The Collapse and Dispersion of a Major Palestinian Community," *Middle Eastern Studies* 37, no. 4 (2001): 25–70.
66. *New York Times*, "Refugees Create Big Arab Burden," December 12, 1948, E 5.
67. Gabbay, *Arab-Jewish Conflict*, 167; Karsh, "How Many Palestinian Arab Refugees," 225.
68. Chaim Herzog, and Shlomo Gazit, *The Arab-Israeli Wars: War and Peace in the Middle East from the 1948 War of Independence to the Present* (London: Greenhill Books, 2004), 97–103.
69. William Roger Louis, *The British Empire in the Middle East, 1945–1951: Arab Nationalism, the United States, and Postwar Imperialism* (Oxford: Clarendon Press, 1984), 564–565.

## 4   AFSC IN THE FIELD: DECEMBER 1948–DECEMBER 1949

1. Ilana Feldman, "Mercy Trains and Ration Rolls Between Government and Humanitarianism in Gaza (1948–67)," in *Interpreting Welfare and Relief in the Middle East,* eds. N. Naguib and I. M. Okkenhaug (Leiden: Brill, 2008), 175–194.

2. AFSC 1948. John Devine to Stanton Griffis, December 13, 1948.

3. AFSC 1948. John Devine to Stanton Griffis, December 13, 1948.

4. In fact, in October 1949 Egypt moved between 5,000 and 6,000 refugees from their territory back to Gaza, gave responsibility to UNRPR, and "made overtures requesting UNRPR to assume responsibility for the remaining Palestinian refugees in Egypt." *FRUS 1949*, Vol. VI, The Minister in Lebanon (Pinkerton) to the Secretary of State, October 1, 1949, 1415, note 1.

5. AFSC 1948. John Devine to Stanton Griffis, December 13, 1948.

6. *FRUS 1949*, Vol. VI, The Acting Secretary of State to the United States Representative at the United Nations (Austin), January 11, 1949, 642.

7. *FRUS 1949*, Vol. VI, The Acting Secretary to the President, January 14, 1949, 663–665.

8. AFSC 1948. United Nations Relief for Palestine—A New Pattern in International Welfare Administration, December 1948. Published as Elmore Jackson, "Meeting Human Needs in the Near East," *New York Herald Tribune*, February 24, 1949.

9. *Manchester Guardian*, "Aid to Palestine Refugees: U.N. Begins its Task," December 18, 1948, p. 6.

10. United Nations General Assembly, Progress Report of the United Nations Mediator on Palestine Submitted to the Secretary-General for Transmission to the Members of the United Nations, A/648, 16 September 1948.

11. E. Jackson, *Middle East Mission*, 23–24.

12. Wriggins, *Picking up the Pieces*, 188.

13. AFSC 1950. Alwin Holtz to James Keen, January 20, 1950.

14. AFSC Oral History Interview #604, Narrator Alwin Holtz, Interviewer: Joan Lowe, 19 September 1992, 59.

15. Wriggins, *Picking up the Pieces*, 191; Gallagher, *Quakers in the Israeli-Palestinian Conflict*, 73–88.

16. AFSC 1949. M. Zaki, 'Schools of the Gaza Area,' April 14, 1949, attached to a memorandum from Corrinne Hardesty to John Kavanaugh and George Mathues, April 27, 1949.

17. Emmet W. Gulley, *Tall Tales by a Tall Quaker* (privately published, 1973), 6.

18. *New York Times*, "Arab Refugee Aid Well Under Way," January 5, 1949, p. 16.

19. Wriggins, *Picking up the Pieces*, 184.

20. AFSC Oral History Interview #604, Narrator Alwin Holtz, Interviewer: Joan Lowe, 19 September 1992, 65.

21. *New York Times*, "Medical Aid Set for Arabs," January 20, 1949, p. 22; *New York Times* "Epidemic of Measles Hits Arab Refugees," January 23, 1949, p. 27.

22. AFSC 1949. Notes on Delbert Replogle and Douglas Cornog, Faluja, February, 11. See also the longer account of the meeting with Shertok in AFSC 1949. Delbert Replogle to Clarence Pickett, February 24, 1949 (received March 21, 1949).

23. See generally Martin Kolinsky, "The Efforts of the Truman Administration to Resolve the Arab-Israeli Conflict," *Middle Eastern Studies* 20 (1984): 81–94.
24. Forsythe, *United Nations Peacemaking*, 42–43; Peretz, *Israel and the Palestine Arabs*, 58–71.
25. *New York Times*, "Arab Refugees Get Food," January 22, 1948, p. 5.
26. AFSC 1949. Elmore Jackson to Clarence Pickett, et al. February 23, 1949.
27. *New York Times*, "Senate Unit Urges Palestine Aid Gift," February 3, 1949, p. 10.
28. AFSC 1949. Clarence Pickett to Trygve Lie, March 2, 1949.
29. AFSC 1949. Delbert Replogle to Mohamad Abbasay, March 6, 1949.
30. AFSC 1949. Delbert Replogle to Mohamad Abbasay, March 6, 1949.
31. AFSC 1949. Delbert Replogle to Mohamad Abbasay, March 6, 1949.
32. See generally Zvi Elpeleg, *The Grand Mufti, Haj Amin al-Hussaini, Founder of the Palestinian National Movement* (London: Frank Cass, 1993); Philip Mattar, "The Mufti of Jerusalem: Muhammad Amin al-Husayni, a Founder of Palestinian Nationalism" (doctoral dissertation, Columbia University, 1981); Joseph B. Schechtman, *The Mufti and the Fuehrer; the Rise and Fall of Haj Amin el-Husseini* (New York: T. Yoseloff, 1965). The Mufti's meeting with Pickett and Replogle is not mentioned in any of these biographies.
33. AFSC 1949. Memo of Visit of Clarence Pickett and Delbert Replogle with the Grand Mufti of Jerusalem and Zamalih, Cairo, February 1949.
34. AFSC 1949. Memo of Visit of Clarence Pickett and Delbert Replogle with the Grand Mufti of Jerusalem and Zamalih, Cairo, February 1949.
35. Compare this with Gallagher's misleading statement that the Mufti had told Pickett and Replogle that the refugees should return to Israel. Gallagher, *Quakers in the Israeli-Palestinian Conflict*, 101.
36. AFSC 1949. Memo of Visit of Clarence Pickett and Delbert Replogle with the Grand Mufti of Jerusalem and Zamalih, Cairo, February 1949.
37. AFSC 1949. Press release, March 20, 1949. The point regarding the unanticipated need for schools was also reflected in media coverage of the AFSC press release. See *New York Times*, "Arab Refugees Aided By Quaker Schools," March 20, 1949, p. 5.
38. See generally Gallagher, *Quakers in the Israeli-Palestinian Conflict*, 119–123, 130–142. In his autobiographical sketch (*Vignettes*) Peretz discusses his AFSC work only briefly and does not mention the matter of Stevenson's criticism of him or of the Acre unit.
39. AFSC 1949. Press release, March 20, 1949.
40. AFSC 1949. Press release, March 20, 1949.
41. AFSC 1949. Howard Wriggins to George Mathues et al., March 11, 1949.
42. AFSC 1949. Howard Wriggins to George Mathues et al., March 11, 1949.
43. AFSC 1949. Howard Wriggins to George Mathues et al., March 11, 1949.
44. AFSC 1949. Howard Wriggins to George Mathues et al., March 11, 1949.

45. The William E. Harmon Foundation of New York City (1922–1967) patronized African American art and artists. It had a small film-making unit. See http://www.npg.si.edu/exh/harmon/. Last accessed June 12, 2013
46. Clarence E. Pickett, "Friends Feed Exiled Arabs," *Philadelphia Inquirer*, March 20, 1949.

## 5   AFSC AND THE POLITICS OF REGIONAL DEVELOPMENT

1. AFSC 1949. George Mathues to James Read, March 28, 1949. See also AFSC 1949. Tony Meager to James Read, March 18, 1949, on the same meeting.
2. AFSC 1949. George Mathues to James Read, March 18, 1949.
3. See Michael J. Cohen, "William A. Eddy, the Oil Lobby and the Palestine Problem," *Middle Eastern Studies* 30 (1994): 166–180. For American Zionist efforts to influence the politics of Middle East oil companies prior to partition see Zohar Segev, "Struggle for Cooperation and Integration: American Zionists and Arab Oil, 1940s," *Middle Eastern Studies* 42, no. 5 (2006): 819–830.
4. *FRUS 1949*, Vol. VI, Memorandum by the Coordinator on Palestine Refugee Matters (McGhee) to the Secretary of State, March 15, 1949, 827.
5. *FRUS 1949*, Vol. VI, Policy Paper Prepared in the Department of State, March 15, 1949, 828, 831.
6. *FRUS 1949*, Vol. VI, Policy Paper Prepared in the Department of State, March 15, 1949, 833.
7. U.S. National Archives, Record Group 59, Textual Records from the Department of State. Bureau of Near Eastern, South Asian and African Affairs. Office of Near Eastern Affairs. Container 74, Arc Identifier 2507075–77, U.S. Department of State, Palestine Refugee Problem Secret Folder 1–3.
8. Wiggins, *Picking up the Pieces*, 201.
9. John A. DeNovo, "The Culbertson Economic Mission and Anglo-American Tensions in the Middle East, 1944–1945," *The Journal of American History* 63 (1977): 913–936; Robert Vitalis, "The 'New Deal' in Egypt: The Rise of Anglo-American Commercial Competition in World War II and the Fall of Neocolonialism," *Diplomatic History* 20, no. 2 (1996): 211–240.
10. Peter L. Hahn, *The United States, Great Britain, and Egypt, 1945–1956: Strategy and Diplomacy in the Early Cold War* (Chapel Hill: University of North Carolina Press, 1991), 82–88; Steven L. Spiegel, *The Other Arab-Israeli Conflict: Making America's Middle East Policy, from Truman to Reagan* (Chicago: University of Chicago Press, 1985), 45–46.

11. See the classic statements in Seymour Martin Lipset, "Some Social Requisites of Democracy," *American Political Science Review* 53, no. 1 (1959): 69–105 and Walt W. Rostow, *The Stages of Economic Growth* (Cambridge: Cambridge University Press, 1960).

12. Daniel Lerner, *The Passing of Traditional Society: Modernizing the Middle East* (Glencoe, IL: The Free Press), 79. For the view of a Point IV administrator that illustrates American faith in the program see Jonathan B. Bingham, *Shirt Sleeve Diplomacy-Point 4 in Action* (New York: John Day, 1954).

13. Nicholas Owen, "Britain and Decolonization: The Labour Governments and the Middle East, 1945–1951," in *Demise of the British Empire in the Middle East: Britain's Responses to Nationalist Movements, 1943–55,* eds. Michael J. Cohen and Martin Kolinsky (London: Frank Cass, 1998), 3–22.

14. Wesley K. Wark, "Development Diplomacy: Sir John Troutbeck and the British Middle East Office, 1947–1950," in *British Officials and British Foreign Policy, 1945–1950,* ed. John Zametica (Leicester: Leicester University Press, 1990), 231. See generally Ritchie Ovendale, *The Foreign Policy of the British Labour Governments, 1945–1951* (Leicester: Leicestershire, Leicester University Press, 1984).

15. Martin W. Wilmington, *The Middle East Supply Centre* (Albany: State University of New York Press, 1971).

16. Paul W. T. Kingston, *Britain and the Politics of Modernization in the Middle East, 1945–1958* (Cambridge: Cambridge University Press, 1996).

17. Gregory A. Barton, "Environmentalism, Development and British Policy in the Middle East 1945–65," *The Journal of Imperial and Commonwealth History,* 38, no. 4 (2010): 619–639.

18. Wark, "Sir John Troutbeck," 235–236.

19. CAB 129/32, C.P. (49) 10, Memorandum by the Secretary of State for Foreign Affairs, Palestine, 15 January 1949. See generally Louis, *The British Empire in the Middle East,* 578–588.

20. Mary C. Wilson, *King Abdullah, Britain, and the Making of Jordan* (Cambridge: Cambridge University Press, 1987), 184.

21. CAB 131/7, D.O. (49) 23, Memorandum by the Secretary of State for War, Long Term Policy in Egypt, 22 March 1949.

22. CAB 131/7, D.O. (4) 26 21, March 1949, Memorandum by the Secretary of State for Foreign Affairs, Egyptian Defense Talks.

23. CAB 131/7. Defense Committee, Arms and Equipment for the Egyptians, Report by the Chiefs of Staff, D.O. (49) 58, 25 July 1949. See also David Tal, "Weapons Without Influence: British Arms Supply Policy and the Egyptian-Czech Arms Deal, 1945–55," *The Journal of Imperial and Commonwealth History* 34, no. 3 (2006): 369–388.

24. See generally Elie Kedourie, "Britain, France, and the Last Phase of the Eastern Question," in *Soviet-American Rivalry in the Middle East,* ed. J. C.

Hurewitz, (New York: Praeger, 1969), 189–197; Philippe Rondot, "France and Palestine: From Charles de Gaulle to Francois Mitterand," *Journal of Palestine Studies* 16, no. 3 (1987): 87–100.

25. Alberto Tonini, "International Donors, The Refugees and UNRWA: France, Britain and Italy as Case Studies, 1950–1993," in *The Palestinian Refugees and UNRWA in Jordan, the West Bank and Gaza, 1949–1999* (Beirut: Centre d'Etudes et de Recherche sur le Moyen-Orient Contemporain, 1999), 8.

26. AFSC 1949. Suggested Draft for Submission to UN, March 1949.

27. AFSC 1949. Clarence Pickett to Howard Wriggins, March 29, 1949.

28. United Nations Conciliation Commission for Palestine, A/AC/25/W9 of 9 April 1949. Functions and Composition of the Technical Mission on Refugees.

29. Peretz, *Israel and the Palestine Arabs*, 38–41. See also Neil Caplan, "A Tale of Two Cities: The Rhodes and Lausanne Conferences, 1949," *Journal of Palestine Studies* 21, no. 3 (1992): 5–34; Neil Caplan, *Futile Diplomacy III: The United Nations, the Great Powers and Middle East Peacemaking, 1948–1954* (London: Frank Cass, 1997), 59–100.

30. Joshua Landis, "Early U.S. Policy toward Palestinian Refugees: the Syria Option,' in *The Palestinian Refugees: Old Problems – New Solutions,*" eds. Joseph Ginat and Edward J. Perkins (Norman, OK: University of Oklahoma Press, 2001), 77–87. Compare Jalil al-Husseini, "Arab States and the Refugee Issue: A Retrospective View," in *Israel and the Palestinian Refugees,* ed. Eyal Benvenisti (Berlin: Springer, 2007), 438–439. Al-Husseini neglects to mention the Syria political situation.

31. AFSC 1949. Delbert Replogle to Clarence Pickett, April 7, 1949. Gallagher's suggestion ("Quakers in the Israeli-Palestinian Conflict," 105–106) that the State Department's rationale for the study group was simply resettlement and that the naming of the Economic Survey Mission was to "disguise its purpose" is belied by Replogle's memo. He clearly states the intended purpose of the mission would be "rehabilitation and resettlement."

32. AFSC 1949. Delbert Replogle to Clarence Pickett, April 7, 1949.

33. AFSC 1949. Delbert Replogle to Clarence Pickett, April 7, 1949.

34. AFSC 1949. Delbert Replogle to Clarence Pickett, April 7, 1949.

35. AFSC 1949. Visit of the Quaker team to Faluja, February 26 to March 6, reported by Ray Hartsough, ed. Corrinne Hardesty. See especially Gallagher, *Quakers in the Israeli-Palestinian Conflict*, 123–130.

36. Gallagher claims that this is evidence of more generalized tension between AFSC and the Israeli government. Gallagher, *Quakers in the Israeli-Palestinian Conflict*, 130. Aside from the issue of Donald Stevenson's views that she does not discuss, there is little evidence to suggest tension as such rather than AFSC's frustration.

37. AFSC 1949. Minutes of the meeting of the Coordinating Committee and others Interested in the American Appeal for Holy Land Refugees held in the Offices of the Near East Foundation on Friday, April 22, 1949.

38. FO 371/68679, Raphael Cilento, Beirut to Foreign Office, October 1, 3, 1948, "The Number of Arab Refugees (Revised Version)"; de St. Aubin, "Peace and Refugees," 249; Karsh, "How Many Palestinian Arab Refugees," 226.

39. United Nations Conciliation Commission for Palestine. SR/LM/17. Summary Record of a Meeting between the Conciliation Commission and Representatives of Relief Organizations in Geneva, 7 June 1949.

40. FO 371/75342/E7816, Sir J. Troutbeck, "Summary of general impressions gathered during week-end visit to the Gaza District,'" 16 June 1949.

41. AFSC Oral History Interview #604, Narrator Alwin Holtz, Interviewer: Joan Lowe, 19 September 1992, 74.

42. AFSC Oral History Interview #604, Narrator Alwin Holtz, Interviewer: Joan Lowe, 19 September 1992, 70.

43. Lorton Heusel, *Friends on the Front Line The Story of Delbert and Ruth Replogle* (Greensboro, NC: Friends Historical Society, 1985), 110–111.

44. AFSC Oral History Interview #601, Narrator: Paul Johnson, Interviewer: Joan Lowe, September 19, 1992, 18.

45. AFSC Oral History Interview #601, Narrator: Paul Johnson, Interviewer: Joan Lowe, September 19, 1992, 13.

46. AFSC Oral History Interview #604, Narrator Alwin Holtz, Interviewer: Joan Lowe, 19 September 1992, 70.

47. AFSC Oral History Interview #604, Narrator Alwin Holtz, Interviewer: Joan Lowe, 19 September 1992, 74.

48. AFSC Oral History Interview # 601, Narrator: Paul Johnson, Interviewer: Joan Lowe, September 19, 1992, 20.

49. AFSC Oral History Interview #604, Narrator Alwin Holtz, Interviewer: Joan Lowe, 19 September 1992, 73.

50. Gulley, *Tall Tales by a Tall Quaker*, 17.

51. Compare Feldman, "Difficult Distinctions," 699, and below.

52. Rey-Schyrr, "Le CICR et l'assistance," 28–29.

53. Gabbay, *Arab-Jewish Conflict*, 137; cf. Richardson, "United Nations," 116.

54. United Nations Conciliation Commission for Palestine, A/AC/25/Org11 of May 8, 1949. Restricted. Letter dated May 4, 1949 addressed to the Chairman of the Conciliation Commission by Mr. Howard Wriggins, Geneva Representative, American Friends Service Committee, Enclosing an Analysis of Palestine Population Statistics.

55. AFSC 1949. Emmett Gulley to Colin Bell, May 5, 1949.

56. *New York Times*, "$1,000,000 Waste is Bared in U.N. Middle East Relief," June 16, 1949, p. 1.

57. *New York Times*, "U.N. Relief Waste Denied by Griffis," June 17, 1949, p. 18.

58. *New York Times*, "U.N. Refugee Body Shifts Buying Plan," June 18, 1949, p. 5.

59. AFSC 1949. Colin Bell to Clarence Pickett, June 6, 1949.

## 6 AFSC, THE ECONOMIC SURVEY MISSION, AND REGIONAL DEVELOPMENT

1. United Nations Conciliation Commission for Palestine. A/AC/25/Org8 of 2 May 1949. Restricted. Text of a letter dated 14 April 1949 from M. de Rougé, Secretary-General, League of Red Cross Societies, to the Secretary-General of the United Nations, transmitted for the information of the Conciliation Commission.
2. AFSC 1949. Elmore Jackson to Clarence Pickett. A Committee to stimulate interest in the overall settlement of the Palestine Refugee Problem. May 18, 1949.
3. AFSC 1949. Report on Meeting at New State Department Building, Washington, June 15, 1949, on the Future of the Palestine Refugee Problem.
4. AFSC 1949. Report on Meeting at New State Department Building, Washington, June 15, 1949, on the Future of the Palestine Refugee Problem.
5. AFSC 1949. Report on Meeting at New State Department Building, Washington, June 15, 1949, on the Future of the Palestine Refugee Problem.
6. AFSC 1949. Report on Meeting at New State Department Building, Washington, June 15, 1949, on the Future of the Palestine Refugee Problem.
7. Peretz, *Israel and the Palestine Arabs*, 4. See generally Alexander Bligh, "Israel and the Refugee Problem: from Exodus to Resettlement, 1948–52," *Middle Eastern Studies* 34, no. 1 (1998): 123–147.
8. AFSC 1949. Conference with Aubrey Eban, Israeli Representative to the United Nations on May 20th. See also Caplan, *Futile Diplomacy*, 90–100; Mordechai Gazit, "Ben-Gurion's 1949 Proposal to Incorporate the Gaza Strip with Israel," *Studies in Zionism* 8, no. 2 (1987): 223–243.
9. *FRUS 1949*, VI, The Ambassador in Israel (McDonald) to the Coordinator on Palestine Refugee Matters (McGhee), June 15, 1949, 1140.
10. *FRUS 1949*, Vol. VI, The Ambassador in Israel (McDonald) to the Coordinator on Palestine Refugee Matters (McGhee), June 15, 1949, 1140, note 1, quoting McGhee to McDonald, July 1.
11. AFSC 1949. Prospects for the Palestine Refugee Relief Program, June 24, 1949.
12. See Peter L. Hahn, *Caught in the Middle East: U.S. Policy toward the Arab-Israeli Conflict, 1945–1961* (Chapel Hill: University of North Carolina Press, 2004), 102–106.
13. AFSC 1949. Letter of Byron Price, 314/3/01/PhE, July 8, 1949.
14. Hahn, *Caught in the Middle*, 106; Peter L. Hahn, "The View from Jerusalem: Revelations about U.S. Diplomacy from the Archives of Israel," *Diplomatic History* 22, no. 4 (1998): 514–515.
15. Louis, *The British Empire in the Middle East*, 578–579, 604–609; Wark, "Sir John Troutbeck," 241–242.

16. CAB 129/36, C.P. (49) 188, 25 August 1949, Middle East Policy. Note by the Secretary of State for Foreign Affairs.
17. AFSC 1949. Donald Stevenson to Bronson Clark, Interview with Ambassador Eliahu Elath of Israel at the Israeli Embassy, Washington, on August 9, 1949.
18. AFSC 1949. Don Stevenson to Bronson Clark. Discussions with Mr. Cordier of U.N. on August 10, 1949 at Lake Success on R.P.R.
19. AFSC 1949. Palestine AFSC/UN Agreement, April 4, 1949.
20. AFSC 1949. Colin W. Bell to Clarence E. Pickctt, May 25, 1949.
21. United Nations, Public Information Bureau, Press Release PAL/521 24 August 1949.
22. Compare Maya Rosenfeld, "From Emergency Relief Assistance to Human Development and Back: UNRWA and the Palestinian Refugees, 1950–2009," *Refugee Survey Quarterly* 28, no. 2–3 (2009): 294, n. 24, who appears to believe that the ESM's development paradigm was solely function of Clapp having been a TVA official rather than a policy of the US State Department.
23. See generally Arthur Ernest Morgan, *The Making of the TVA* (Buffalo, NY, Prometheus Books, 1974). Hydraulic engineer Arthur E. Morgan was the president of Antioch College and the first chairman of the Tennessee Valley of Authority. Compare Morgan's account with Richard A. Colignon, *Power Plays: Critical Events in the Institutionalization of the Tennessee Valley Authority* (Albany: State University of New York Press, 1997). Born a Unitarian, Morgan became a Quaker and was also father of AFSC Gaza volunteer Ernest Morgan.
24. David Ekbladh, "Mr. TVA: Grass-Roots Development, David Lilienthal, and the Rise and Fall of the Tennessee Valley Authority as a Symbol for U.S. Overseas Development, 1933–1973," *Diplomatic History* 26, no. 3 (2002): 335–374.
25. Harry S. Truman Library and Museum. Oral History Interview with George C. McGhee Washington, DC 11 June 1975 by Richard D. McKinzie, www.trumanlibrary.org/oralhist/mcgheeg.htm#transcript, 39. Last accessed June 12, 2013.
26. *FRUS 1949*, Vol. VI, The Secretary of State to the Legation in Lebanon, September 3, 1949, 1359, 1360.
27. *FRUS 1949*, Vol. VI, The Secretary of State to the Embassy in the United Kingdom, September 10, 1949, 1374.
28. *FRUS 1949*, Vol. VI, The Near East, South Asia, and Africa, The Chargé in the United Kingdom (Holmes) to the Secretary of State, September 12, 1949, 1375.
29. Louis, *The British Empire in the Middle East*, 612–613.
30. *FRUS 1949*, Vol. VI, Memorandum of Conversation, by the Secretary of State, September 13, 1949, 1376.

31. *FRUS 1949*, Vol. VI, The Secretary of State to the Embassy in the United Kingdom, September 13, 1949, 1382. See also note 1.
32. *FRUS 1949*, Vol. VI, Mr. Stuart W. Rockwell to the Secretary of State, September 14, 1949, 1387.
33. *FRUS 1949*, Vol. VI, The Minister in Lebanon (Pinkerton) to the Secretary of State [from Clapp]. September 1949, 1393.
34. *New York Times*, "Arab Chieftain is Against Resettlement of Palestinians on Newly-Developed Land," September 6, 1949, p. 11.
35. Unsurprisingly, the Ruwalla remained resolutely nomadic throughout the 1950s and 1960s, adopting motor transport and only leaving Syria temporarily in 1959 as a result of drought. See Norman N. Lewis, *Nomads and Settlers in Syria and Jordan, 1800–1980* (Cambridge: Cambridge University Press, 1987), 137.
36. FO 371/75439, E 11297/1821/131, Morton to Foreign Office, 23 September 1949. See also G. Bennett, *Churchill's Man of Mystery: Desmond Morton and the World of Intelligence* (London: Routledge, 2007), 291.
37. AFSC 1949. James Keen to Colin Bell, September 13, 1949.
38. In fact, Griffis had been largely absent from UNRPR since mid-July when he underwent eye surgery in New York. *New York Times*, "Griffis to Undergo Eye Surgery," July 15, 1949, p. 20.
39. *FRUS 1949*, Vol. VI, Memorandum by the Secretary of State to the President, August 4, 1949, 1283, note 2.
40. AFSC 1949. Donald Stevenson to Bronson Clark, October 7, 1949.
41. AFSC 1949. Gaza Unit to Clarence Pickett, October 12, 1949.
42. AFSC 1949. Gaza Unit to Clarence Pickett, October 12, 1949.
43. AFSC 1949. Colin Bell. American Friends Service Committee Program in Israel. 1. Impressions of Israel. October 17, 1949.
44. AFSC 1949. Colin Bell. American Friends Service Committee Program in Israel. 2. Possible Future AFSC Activity in Israel. October 17, 1949.
45. AFSC 1949. Colin Bell. American Friends Service Committee Program in Israel. Appendix A. Outline of Community Centre Program in Acre. October 17, 1949.
46. AFSC 1949. Colin Bell. American Friends Service Committee Program in Israel. Appendix B. Outline of Proposed Agricultural Project as Set Out by Mr. Palmon, Advisor to the Prime Minister on Arab Affairs.
47. AFSC 1949. Charles Read to AFSC headquarters, October 15, 1949.
48. AFSC 1949. Don Peretz to Donald Stevenson, November 7, 1949.
49. AFSC 1949. Donald Stevenson to Bronson Clark, Re: Don Peretz's Letter of November 7th, November 25, 1949.
50. AFSC 1949. Donald Stevenson to Bronson Clark, Re: Don Peretz's Letter of November 7th, November 25, 1949.
51. AFSC 1949. Donald Stevenson to Colin Bell, October 15, 1949.

52. AFSC 1949. Donald Stevenson to Bronson Clark, Re: Don Peretz's Letter of November 7th, November 25, 1949.
53. AFSC 1949. Donald Stevenson to Bronson Clark, Re: Don Peretz's Letter of November 7th, November 25, 1949.
54. *FRUS 1949*, Vol. VI, Memorandum by the Assistant Chief of the Division of International Organization Affairs (Halderman), September 9, 1949, 1372.
55. United Nations, Draft Text, Verbatim Proceedings of the Ad Hoc Advisory Committee on Refugees on Relief to Palestine Refugees, Second Session, Held at Lake Success, New York on Tuesday, 4 October 1949, at 10:45 a.m.
56. United Nations, Draft Text, Verbatim Proceedings of the Ad Hoc Advisory Committee on Refugees on Relief to Palestine Refugees, Second Session, Held at Lake Success, New York on Tuesday, 4 October 1949, at 10:45 a.m.
57. Dillon S. Myer, *An Autobiography of Dillon S. Myer* (University of California, Berkeley, Bancroft Library, Regional Oral History Office, 1970), 246.
58. AFSC 1949. Donald Stevenson to Bronson Clark, October 27, 1949.
59. AFSC 1949. Donald Stevenson to Bronson Clark, October 27, 1949.
60. Myer, *Autobiography,* 248, 250.
61. Harry S. Truman Library and Museum. Oral History Interview with George C. McGhee, Washington, DC 11 June 1975 by Richard D. McKinzie, www.trumanlibrary.org/oralhist/mcgheeg.htm#transcript, 40. Last accessed June 12, 2013.
62. Gordon R. Clapp, "Adventures in Faith and Works," *Ethics* 58 (1947): 60.
63. Included in the Final Report of the United Nations Economic Survey Mission for the Middle East, Part I, A/AC/25/6, of 28 December 1949, 14.
64. AFSC 1949. Cordelia Trimble to Bronson Clark, November 29, 1949.
65. United Nations. Final Report of the United Nations Economic Survey Mission for the Middle East, Part I, A/AC/25/6, of 28 December 1949, 17.
66. United Nations Conciliation Commission for Palestine. A/AC/25/W/28 of 27 October 1949. Restricted. Notes on the Secretary-General's Draft Report on the Work of UNRPR.
67. *FRUS 1949*, Vol. VI, The Secretary of State to the Legation in Lebanon, October 31, 1949, 1459–1460.
68. *FRUS 1949*, Vol. VI, Statement by the United States and the United Kingdom Groups, November 14, 1949, 67.
69. *FRUS 1949*, Vol. VI, Statement by the United States and the United Kingdom Groups, November 14, 1949, 67, 68.
70. *FRUS 1949*, Vol. VI, Memorandum by the Department of State to the President, undated, but presumably November 1949, 1505.
71. Shattuck, "Weeping over Jerusalem," 139–140.
72. A.C. Ringland, *The Organization of Voluntary Foreign Aid: 1939–1953* (Washington, DC, Department of State Bulletin, 1954), 386.
73. *FRUS 1949*, Vol. VI, Statement by the Department of State, 167, note 1.

74. *FRUS 1949*, Vol. VI, Agreed Conclusions of the Conference of Near Eastern Chiefs of Missions, Istanbul, 26–29 November, 1949,. 173. See also James G. McDonald, *My Mission to Israel 1948–1951* (New York: Simon and Schuster, 1951), 179–185.

75. *FRUS 1949*, Vol. VI, Agreed Conclusions of the Conference of Near Eastern Chiefs of Missions, Istanbul, 26–29 November, 1949, 173.

76. *FRUS 1949*, Vol. VI, Recapitulation of Conclusions for Confidential Guidance of Chiefs of Mission in Oral Presentation to Governments, 176.

77. Shlomo Slonim, "Origins of the 1950 Tripartite Declaration on the Middle East," *Middle Eastern Studies* 23 (1987): 135–149. See also Michael B. Oren, "The Tripartite System and Arms Control in the Middle East: 1950–1956," in *Arms Control in the Middle East*, ed. Dore Gold (Boulder, CO: Westview, 1990), 77–87.

78. *FRUS 1949*, Vol. VI, The Near East, South Asia, and Africa: multilateral relations, Statement by the United States and the United Kingdom Groups, November 14 and 15, 1949, 68.

79. AFSC 1949. Bronson Clark to Donald Stevenson and Charles Read, December 1, 1949.

80. AFSC 1949. Clarence Pickett to Trygve Lie, November 1, 1949.

81. AFSC 1949. Bronson Clark to Donald Stevenson and Charles Read, December 1, 1949.

82. *New York Times*, "Quakers Ask Help for Arab Refugees," November 14, 1949, p. 7.

83. AFSC 1949. Statement of the American Friends Service Committee for the Ad Hoc Political Committee of the United Nations on 2 December 1949.

84. United Nations General Assembly, A/648, Progress Report of the United Nations Mediator on Palestine Submitted to the Secretary-General for Transmission to the Members of the United Nations, 16 September 1948. See also Rosenfeld, "From Emergency Relief Assistance to Human Development and Back."

## 7  THE AFSC AND UNRWA: THE END OF UNRPR

1. United Nations General Assembly, A/RES/302 (IV) of 8 December 1949, Assistance to Palestine Refugees.

2. United Nations General Assembly, A/RES/302 (IV) of 8 December 1949, Assistance to Palestine Refugees.

3. *FRUS 1950*, Vol. V, Messers. John W. Halderman and James W. Barco of the Office of United Nations Political and Security Affairs, January 3, 1950, 662.

4. *FRUS 1950*, Vol. V, Memorandum by Messers. John W. Halderman and James W. Barco of the Office of United Nations Political and Security Affairs, January 3, 1950, 664.

5. *FRUS 1950*, Vol. V, The Secretary of State to the Embassy in the United Kingdom, January 5, 1950, 669; The Secretary of State to the Embassy in France, January 10, 1950, 679.
6. *FRUS 1950*, Vol. V, Memorandum of Conversation, by the Assistant Secretary of State for Near Eastern, South Asia, and Africa Affairs (McGhee), January 11, 1950, 681–682. Compare United Nations Conciliation Commission for Palestine, A/AC.25/W.81/Rev.2 of 2 October 1961, Historical Survey of Efforts of the United Nations Conciliation Commission for Palestine to Secure the Implementation of Paragraph 11 of General Assembly Resolution 194 (III), 23–24. See also Michael R. Fischbach, *The Peace Process and Palestinian Refugee Claims: Addressing Claims for Property Compensation and Restitution* (Washington, DC: United States Institute of Peace Press, 2006); M.R. Fischbach, "Palestinian Refugee Compensation and Israeli Counterclaims for Jewish Property in Arab Countries," *Journal of Palestine Studies*, 38 (2008): 6–24.
7. *FRUS 1950*, Vol. V, The Near East, South Asia, and Africa, Memorandum of Conversation, by Mr. Stuart D. Nelson of the Office of African and Near Eastern Affairs, January 17, 1950, 691.
8. United States House of Representatives, Committee on Foreign Affairs, Hearings on Aid to Palestine Refugees. Eighty-First Congress, Second Session, February 16 and 17, 1950. (Washington, DC, Government Printing Office, 1950), 9.
9. *New York Times*, "Give Point Four Aid Through U.N., Witnesses Urge House Group," January 13, 1950, p. 3.
10. AFSC 1950. Memorandum in regard to Work Possibilities in the Gaza Area. January 26, 1950.
11. AFSC 1950. Marshall Sutton to Corrine Hardesty, January 30, 1950.
12. AFSC 1950. Marshall Sutton to Corrine Hardesty, January 30, 1950.
13. AFSC 1949. Charles W. Bronson. Thoughts on Possible AFSC Activities in the Palestine Area after 1949. December 11, 1949.
14. AFSC 1950. Bronson Clark to the Foreign Service Executive Committee, February 9, 1950.
15. AFSC 1950. Bronson Clark to the Foreign Service Executive Committee, February 9, 1950.
16. United Nations General Assembly Resolution 303 (IV), of 9 December 1949. Palestine: Question of an International Regime for the Jerusalem Area and the Protection of the Holy Places.
17. AFSC 1949. Colin Bell to Clarence Pickett, October 27, 1949.
18. AFSC 1950. Donald Stevenson to Bronson Clark, January 27, 1950. The letter is labeled 'Personal and Unnumbered' and was thus not intended to be entered into the standard AFSC record-keeping system.
19. AFSC 1950. Donald Stevenson to Bronson Clark, January 27, 1950.
20. Slightly over one month later, at the beginning of March 1950, the Iraqi Parliament and Regent authorised a bill that denaturalized any Jews who

chose to leave Iraq. See Moshe Gat, "Between Terror and Emigration: The Case of Iraqi Jewry," *Israel Affairs* 7 (2000): 1–2.

21. AFSC 1950. Donald Stevenson to Bronson Clark, March 4, 1950.

22. AFSC 1950. Donald Stevenson to Bronson Clark, March 4, 1950. See generally Arnon Golan, "Postwar Spatial Reorganization: The Resettlement of Greek Refugees, 1922–1930" in *Population Resettlement in International Conflicts: A Comparative Study*, eds. A. M. Kacowicz and P. Lutomski (Lanham, MD: Lexington Books, 2007), 21–40.

23. AFSC 1950. Donald Stevenson, Report to the American Friends Service Committee on the position of the Arab Community in Israel, March 22, 1950, at 5.

24. AFSC 1950. Donald Stevenson, Report to the American Friends Service Committee on the position of the Arab Community in Israel, March 22, 1950, at 5.

25. AFSC 1950. Charles Read to James Goble, March 15, 1950.

26. AFSC 1950. Memorandum in Regard to Work Possibilities in the Gaza Area. January 26, 1950.

27. AFSC 1950. Arthur Ringland to Clarence Pickett, March 20, 1950.

28. AFSC 1950. Bronson Clark to Donald Stevenson and Paul Johnson. Meeting in New York with Blandford and Knight. March 23, 1950.

29. AFSC 1950. Bronson Clark to Paul Johnson. Proposed AFSC Projects in Gaza after April. April 4, 1950.

30. AFSC 1950. Bronson Clark to Paul Johnson. Proposed AFSC Projects in Gaza after April. April 4, 1950.

31. AFSC 1950. Bronson Clark to Paul Johnson. Proposed AFSC Projects in Gaza after April. April 4, 1950.

32. AFSC 1950. Summary Statement of the American Friends Service Committee Operation for the Period 1 August 1949 to 30 April 1950.

33. The 27 October draft report of the UNRPR noted that Director Stanton Griffis did "not consider it practical to ask all the relief agencies to undertake a census, although he requested them to take all possible steps to ensure that aid was distributed only to *bona fide* refugees." United Nations Conciliation Commission for Palestine. A/AC/25/W/28 of 27 October 1949. Restricted. Notes on the Secretary-General's Draft Report on the Work of UNRPR, 1.

34. AFSC 1950. Summary Statement of the American Friends Service Committee Operation for the Period 1 August 1949 to 30 April 1950.

35. AFSC 1950. Summary Statement of the American Friends Service Committee Operation for the Period 1 August 1949 to 30 April 1950.

36. AFSC 1950. Summary Statement of the American Friends Service Committee Operation for the Period 1 August 1949 to 30 April 1950.

37. AFSC 1950. Summary Statement of the American Friends Service Committee Operation for the Period 1 August 1949 to 30 April 1950.

38. AFSC 1950. James Keen to Clarence Pickett, reproduced in a letter from Charles Read to Bronson Clark, May 20, 1950.

39. AFSC 1950. Cable from James Keen to Clarence Pickett, November 20, 1950.
40. AFSC 1950. Bronson Clark to Ernest Morgan, June 9, 1950.
41. AFSC 1950. Paul Johnson to Clarence Pickett, June 15, 1950.
42. AFSC 1950. Bronson Clark to Hugh Jenkins, November 21, 1950. AFSC 1950. Delbert Replogle to Hugh Jenkins, November 22, 1950.
43. AFSC 1950. Bronson Clark to Lewis Hoskins, Bayard Dodge Luncheon, June 16, 1950.
44. Ricks, "Khalil Totah, The Unknown Years," 51–57.
45. Kermit Roosevelt, Jr., "Partition of Palestine: A Lesson in Pressure Politics," *Middle East Journal* 2 (1948):1–16. For the Institute for Arab American Affairs generally H. J. Bawardi, "Arab American Political Organizations from 1915 to 1951: Assessing Transnational Political Consciousness and the Development of Arab American Identity," (doctoral dissertation, Wayne State University, 2009); Eliezer Tauber, "The Jewish and Arab Lobbies in Canada and the UN Partition of Palestine," *Israel Affairs* 5, no. 4 (1999): 229–244.
46. *New York Times,* "Against Palestine Partition," November 21, 1947, p. 26.
47. Robert Kaplan, *The Arabists, The Romance of an American Elite* (New York: Free Press, 1993), 80.
48. *New York Times,* "American Zionists Warned on Tactics," June 18, 1948, p. 15; *New York Times,* "Expansion by War Held Israel's Aim," August 1, 1948, p. 45. For Roosevelt's cooperation with leading British anti-Zionist Sir Edward Spears see Rory Miller, "Sir Edward Spears' Jewish Problem: A Leading Anti-Zionist and His Relationship with Anglo-Jewry, 1945–1948," *Journal of Israeli History* 19, no. 1 (1998): 57–58.
49. Thomas A. Kolsky, *Jews Against Zionism: The American Council for Judaism, 1942–1948* (Philadelphia: Temple University Press, 1992), 184.
50. Shattuck, "True Israelites," 145.
51. Eddy was born to Presbyterian missionaries in Lebanon. After military service in World War I he taught at the American University of Cairo and was later President of Hobart College. He served in the Office of Strategic Services during World War II and was President Franklin D. Roosevelt's translator during his meeting with Saudi Abdul-Aziz Al Saud. See Thomas Lippman, *Arabian Knight: Colonel Bill Eddy USMC and the Rise of American Power in the Middle East* (Vista, CA: Selwa Press, 2008); Cohen, "William A. Eddy."
52. *New York Times,* "Liaison Body Formed for Near East Relief," September 12, 1949, p. 8. On October 12, 1949 former Office of Strategic Services official, and future Central Intelligence Agency director Allan W. Dulles resigned from HELP, saying that he had not in fact given permission for his name to be used as a member of the executive committee. See *Jewish Telegraph Agency,* "Former State Department Official Resigns from Holyland Emergency Liaison Program," October 13, 1949.
53. *FRUS 1949*, Vol. VI, Policy Paper Prepared in the Department of State, March 15, 1949, 840.

54. Robert M. Miller, *Harry Emerson Fosdick: Preacher, Pastor, Prophet* (New York: Oxford University Press, 1985), 192. See also Fishman, *American Protestantism*, 101–107; Ofira Seliktar, *Divided We Stand: American Jews, Israel, and the Peace Process* (Westport, CT: Praeger, 2002), 13; Hugh Wilford, *The Mighty Wurlitzer: How the CIA Played America*, (Cambridge, MA: Harvard University Press, 2008), 236–237.

55. AFSC 1950. Bronson Clark to Lewis Hoskins, Bayard Dodge Luncheon, June 16, 1950.

56. AFSC 1950. Bronson Clark to Lewis Hoskins, Bayard Dodge Luncheon, June 16, 1950.

57. *New York Times*, "Dorothy Thompson Gets Refugee Award," May 18, 1950, p. 27.

58. AMIDEAST. "About AMIDEAST." www.amideast.org/about/how-amideast-making-difference. Last accessed June 12, 2013.

59. AFSC 1950. Bronson Clark to Cassius Fenton and Corrine Hardesty, September 24, 1950.

60. Compare Clark's assessment of Keen with that of Howard Wriggins, who stated that Keen, a retired British Army officer, was "a first class administrator, but his distant manner and intolerance of muddle won him respect rather than affection." Wriggins, *Picking up the Pieces*, 187.

61. AFSC 1950. Bronson Clark to Cassius Fenton and Corrine Hardesty, September 24, 1950.

62. AFSC 1950. Alwin Holtz to Corrine Hardesty, November 10, 1950. A similar issue had been faced in August 1949 when AFSC personnel had to deal with Egyptian authorities and Palestine Arab teachers using "schools for indoctrination purposes and for creating hatred of Jews." AFSC 1949. Corrine Hardesty to Colin Bell and Tony Meager, August 22, 1949.

63. AFSC 1950. Alwin Holtz to Corrine Hardesty, November 10, 1950. Neither Gallagher nor Feldman mentions this incident. In the AFSC Oral History Pings described the incident as a conflict with an Egyptian officer over building supplies. AFSC Oral History Interview #612, Narrator: Vern Pings, Interviewer: Paula Goldberg, 19 September 1992, 251.

64. Gallagher (*Quakers in the Israeli-Palestinian Conflict*, 118, no. 280) reports interviewing a Palestinian in Gaza "who recalled that one Quaker leader, "Frank" (Hunt) told some refugees through their mukhtar that they should boycott the food distribution for a week to protest the lack of progress in repatriation. He regretted that the refugees did not take Frank's advice and argued that Frank's idea showed that the Quakers were "not imperialistic." This incident occurred when Hunt, a British volunteer from the Friends Service Council, was working under UNRWA rather than AFSC. It is not reflected in any AFSC documentation. Hunt later went on to head the AFSC's agricultural project at Tur 'an in the Galilee.

65. AFSC 1950. Report on Gaza operations dated October 14, 1950 attached to a letter from James Keen to Clarence Pickett, November 15, 1950.
66. AFSC 1950. Report on Gaza operations dated October 14, 1950 attached to a letter from James Keen to Clarence Pickett, November 15, 1950.
67. AFSC 1950. Report on Gaza operations dated October 14, 1950 attached to a letter from James Keen to Clarence Pickett, November 15, 1950.
68. AFSC 1950. Clarence Pickett to James Keen, December 26, 1950.
69. For example, Memorandum enclosing copy of letter from Charles P. Taft, Chairman of the Advisory Committee on Voluntary Foreign Aid, to Willard Thorp, Assistant Secretary for Economic Affairs, Department of State, on the Point IV Program, copied to William Datt, et. al., 27 June 1950. Harry S. Truman Library, http://www.trumanlibrary.org/oralhist/ringland. htm#appendix. Last accessed June 12, 2013.
70. AFSC 1951. James Keen to Clarence Pickett, 2 February 1951.
71. AFSC 1951. Clarence Pickett to James Keen, 26 February 1951.
72. US National Archives, Record Group 59, Textual Records from the Department of State. Bureau of Near Eastern, South Asian and African Affairs. Office of Near Eastern Affairs. (1951–1958). ARC Identifier 2558731/MLR Number A1 1437. UNRPR. Minutes of the meeting of UNRWA representatives held on Saturday 20 October and Monday 22 October 1951. The Role of the AFSC in Refugee Reintegration. Presumably the UNRWA minutes were forwarded to the State Department by the American representative to the Advisory Committee or by Blandford himself. Johnson, a Quaker, had been an employee of the TVA. AFSC Oral History Interview #601, Narrator: Paul Johnson, Interviewer: Joan Lowe, September 19, 1992, 5–6.
73. U.S. National Archives, Record Group 59, Textual Records from the Department of State. Bureau of Near Eastern, South Asian, and African Affairs. Office of Near Eastern Affairs. (1951–1958). ARC Identifier 2558731/MLR Number A1 1437. UNRPR. Minutes of meeting of UNRWA representatives held on Saturday 20 October and Monday 22 October 1951. The Role of the AFSC in Refugee Reintegration.
74. AFSC 1951. Minutes of the Sub-committee on Social and Technical Assistance, November 1, 1951.
75. AFSC 1951. Paul Johnson to Clarence Pickett, November 5, 1951.
76. AFSC 1951. Paul Johnson to Clarence Pickett, November 5, 1951.
77. AFSC 1951. Paul Johnson to Clarence Pickett, November 6, 1951.
78. AFSC 1951. Paul Johnson, November 20, 1951, letter addressed "Dear Friends." Presumably this was addressed to the AFSC's Foreign Service Executive Committee or the Sub-committee on Social and Technical Assistance.
79. AFSC 1951. Paul Johnson, November 20, 1951, letter addressed "Dear Friends." Johnson did not mention these events in his AFSC Oral History.

80. AFSC 1951. Minutes of the Sub-committee on Social and Technical Assistance, December 3, 1951. See also Schiff, *Refugees unto the Third Generation*, 34–35 for a discussion of UNRWA's small-scale exploration of refugee resettlement in Libya that by 1953, when all discussion finally ended, had consisted of 13 artisans, eight of whom had been returned to Lebanon.

81. United Nations General Assembly, A/1451/Rev.1, Interim Report of the Director of the United Nations Relief and Works Agency for Palestine Refugees in the Near East, para. 42 (2), 6 October 1950.

82. United Nations General Assembly, A/1905, Report of the Director of the United Nations Relief and Works Agency for Palestine Refugees in the Near East. para. 44, of 28 September 1951.

83. Schiff, *Refugees to the Third Generation*, 30–33.

84. United Nations General Assembly, A/1451/Rev.1, Interim Report of the Director of the United Nations Relief and Works Agency for Palestine Refugees in the Near East, para. 13, of 6 October 1950.

85. United Nations General Assembly, A/1451/Rev.1, Interim Report of the Director of the United Nations Relief and Works Agency for Palestine Refugees in the Near East, para. 15, of 6 October 1950.

86. United Nations General Assembly, A/1451/Rev.1, Interim Report of the Director of the United Nations Relief and Works Agency for Palestine Refugees in the Near East, para. 16, of 6 October 1950.

87. United Nations General Assembly, A/1451/Rev.1, Interim Report of the Director of the United Nations Relief and Works Agency for Palestine Refugees in the Near East, para. 18, of 6 October 1950. Schiff notes, on the basis of interview with participants in the surveys that UNRWA hired several hundred people to carry out a census from May 1950 to June 1951 but that the "whole operation 'went corrupt.'" The census was then suspended and when the results were reviewed, refugees rioted. Schiff, *Refugees unto the Third Generation*, 22–23.

88. United Nations General Assembly, A/1451/Rev.1, Interim Report of the Director of the United Nations Relief and Works Agency for Palestine Refugees in the Near East, para. 26, of 6 October 1950.

# 8   INTERNATIONAL SECURITY AND THE QUESTION OF "REINTEGRATION"

1. United Nations General Assembly. Resolution 393 (V), of 2 December 1950. For the political background to Resolution 393 (V), see Gabbay, *Arab-Jewish Conflict*, 386–393.

2. See generally Paul Nitze, "The Development of NSC-68," *International Security* 4, no. 4 (1980): 170–176; Ernest R. May, ed. *American Cold War Strategy: Interpreting NSC 68* (New York: Bedford/St. Martin's, 1993).

3. For George McGhee's comments on the perception of Communism in the Middle East during this period see his *On the Frontline in the Cold War: An Ambassador Reports* (Westport, CT: Greenwood, 1997), 48–50.

4. See Michael J. Cohen, *Fighting World War Three from the Middle East: Allied Contingency Plans 1945–1954,* (London: Frank Cass, 1997), 239–270.

5. Majid Khadduri, 'The Anglo-Egyptian Controversy,' *Proceedings of the Academy of Political Science* 24, no. 2 (1952): 82–100. See also P. L. Hahn, "Containment and Egyptian Nationalism: The Unsuccessful Effort to Establish the Middle East Command, 1950–53," *Diplomatic History* 11 (1987): 23–40.

6. Hahn, *Caught in the Middle*, 137–142.

7. *FRUS 1951,* Vol. V, Agreed Conclusions and Recommendations of the Conference of Middle Eastern Chiefs of Missions, Istanbul, February 14–21, 1951, 62.

8. *FRUS 1951,* Vol. V, Agreed Conclusions and Recommendations of the Conference of Middle Eastern Chiefs of Missions, Istanbul, February 14–21, 1951, 63.

9. *FRUS 1951,* Vol. V, Memorandum by the Under Secretary of State (Webb) to the Executive Secretary, National Security Council (Lay), Third Progress Report on NSC-47/2, January 29, 1951, 18–19. Webb would go on to greater acclaim as the second administrator of NASA, under whose leadership US manned space flight was first accomplished.

10. U.S. National Archives, Record Group 59, Textual Records from the Department of State. Bureau of Near Eastern, South Asian and African Affairs. Office of Near Eastern Affairs. Office of the Country Director for Israel and Arab-Israel Affairs. Container 72, Folder 2, ARC Identifier 2507045, Memorandum of Donald G. Bergus, Beirut, "An American Policy for Arab-Israeli Peace," December 2, 1952.

11. FO 371/91417, EE 18211/19, Sir Henry Knight to Francis Evans, letter of 17 July 1951.

12. Compare F0 371/91417/345481, Sir Henry Knight to Francis Evans, 19 April 1951 with Knight's follow up on 24 April 1951. See also the correspondence in FO 371/98520 from 1952. For the negative implications of publicizing US negotiations and potential agreements with Arab governments on refugee and development issues see Harry S. Truman Library and Museum, Oral History Interview with Harry N. Howard, Washington, DC, 5 June 1975 by Richard D. McKinzie, www.trumanlibrary.org/oralhist/howardhn.htm, 92–93. Last accessed June 12, 2013.

13. *Chicago Daily Tribune*, "Chicago Faces Critical Housing Shortage, Builders Warn," June 14, 1942, p. 21; *Dubuque The Telegraph Herald*, "Simplified Order for War Housing," July 12, 1942, p. 4.

14. J. B. Blandford, Jr. "Wanted: 12 Million New Houses," *National Municipal Review* 34 (1945): 376–385.

15. FO 371/91417, EE 18211/9, letter to Francis Evans, 4 April 1951. Schiff states that Blandford had been the "real power" behind Kennedy but offers no documentation. Presumably this would have been because Blandford was chairman of the UNRWA Advisory Committee prior to becoming director. See Schiff, *Refugees unto the Third Generation*, 36.

16. FO 371/91417/345481, Sir Henry Knight to Francis Evans, 16 August 1951.

17. Salim Yaqub, *Containing Arab Nationalism: the Eisenhower Doctrine and the Middle East* (Chapel Hill: University of North Carolina Press, 2004), 29.

18. FO 371/91417, Sir Henry Knight to Francis Evans, letter of 16 January 1951.

19. FO 371/91417, EE 18211/6, Sir Henry Knight to Francis Evans, letter of 20 February 1951.

20. FO 371/91430, "Informal Report of the Retiring Director of the United Nations Relief and Works Agency for Palestine Refugees to the Secretary-General, United Nations." Knight was characteristically unimpressed and in his covering note to the report to Evans, he comments about Kennedy "He has had his grouse at the Adcom! Which I don't think will [*sic*] will worry much over that. His troubles there were mostly of his own fault, although not entirely."

21. FO 371/91426, Sir Henry Knight to Francis Evans, 8 May 1951, forwarding "Analysis of the State of Mind of the Palestinian Refugees in the Lebanon," by UNRWA Chief District Officer R. M. Courvoisier of 26 April 1951, 5.

22. United Nations General Assembly Resolution 513 (VI), para. 2, of 26 January 1952.

23. James B. Hayes, *T.V.A. on the Jordan, Proposals for Irrigation and Hydro-Electric Development in Palestine* (Washington, DC: Public Affairs Press, 1948). For the other primary architect of Israel's water system, leading pro-Zionist American Christian and former US Soil Conservation Service engineer Walter Clay Lowdermilk, see Rory Miller, "Bible and Soil: Walter Clay Lowdermilk, the Jordan Valley Plan and the Battle over Palestine in the Final Mandatory Era," *Middle Eastern Studies* 39, no. 2 (2003): 55–81. See generally Nadav Morag, "Water, Geopolitics and State Building: The Case of Israel," *Middle Eastern Studies* 37, no. 3 (2001): 179–198.

24. Mriaim R. Lowi, *Water and Power: The Politics of a Scarce Resource in the Jordan Valley* (Cambridge: Cambridge University Press, 1993), 79–103. Schiff, *Refugees to the Third Generation*, 36–45; Gabbay, *Arab-Jewish Conflict*, 532–536.

25. Tonini, "International Donors, The Refugees and UNRWA," 8–9.

26. FO 371/98512. "Summary of Paper on UNRWA Activities." 20 May 1952. The file was marked, "Top Secret." It should be noted that a portion of this file remains classified and a Freedom of Information request was denied by the Foreign and Commonwealth Office.

27. FO 371/98512. "Summary of Paper on UNRWA Activities." 20 May 1952.

28. FO 371/98512. "Summary of Paper on UNRWA Activities." 20 May 1952.

29. See generally Jon B. Alterman, *Egypt and American Foreign Assistance, 1952–1956: Hopes Dashed* (New York: Palgrave Macmillan, 2002).
30. United Nations General Assembly, A/4121, Proposals for the Continuation of United Nations Assistance to Palestine Refugees, Submitted by the Secretary General, para. 11, 15 June 1959.
31. Andrew W. Cordier and Wilder Foote, eds., *Public Papers of the Secretaries General of the United Nations* (New York: Columbia University Press, 1974), 414–436, 492–493.
32. Pickett, *For More than Bread*, 286.
33. Pickett, *For More than Bread*, 285.
34. Pickett, *For More than Bread*, 286.
35. AFSC Oral History Interview #605, Narrator: Howard McKinney, Interviewer: Joan Lowe. November 11, 1992, 118.
36. AFSC Oral History Interview #604, Narrator Alwin Holtz, Interviewer: Joan Lowe, September 19, 1992, 87.
37. AFSC Oral History Interview #604, Narrator Alwin Holtz, Interviewer: Joan Lowe, September 19, 1992, 87.
38. AFSC Oral History Interview #604, Narrator Alwin Holtz, Interviewer: Joan Lowe, September 19, 1992, 87.
39. *New York Times*, "American Food Committee for India," April 6, 1951, p. 17.
40. *New York Times*, "Sarnoff Receives Seminary Award, March 19, 1951, p. 36.
41. *FRUS 1952–1954*, Vol. IX, The United States Representative at the United Nations (Austin) to the Department of State, February 26, 1952, 1194.
42. *New York Times*, "Our Relations with India," December 17, 1953, p. 36. Pickett, along with Albert Einstein and Pearl Buck, had telegraphed Nehru in 1948 urging him to take the initiative in world affairs, particularly with regard to the issue of nuclear weapons. Pickett also met Nehru in 1949 when the latter visited the United States. See Lawrence S. Wittner, *The Struggle Against the Bomb* (Palo Alto: Stanford University Press, 1995), 308.
43. *New York Times*, "Text of McCarran Statement on New Act," December 25, 1952, p. 4; *New York Times*, "Two Laugh at Charges," December 26, 1952, p. 15.
44. AFSC 1953. Newsletter #4 from Moses and Mabel Bailey, November 27, 1953.
45. Elmore Jackson, "The Developing Role of the Secretary-General," *International Organization* 11, no. 3 (1957): 431–445; Sydney D. Bailey, "Non-Official Mediation in Disputes: Reflections on Quaker Experience," *International Affairs* 61 (1985): 205–222; Gallagher, *Quakers in the Israeli-Palestinian Conflict*, 145–152.
46. *FRUS 1952–1954*, Vol. IX, Telegram from the Embassy in Israel to the Department of State, September 1, 1955, 441; Telegram from the Embassy in Israel to the Department of State, September 7, 1955, 445.

47. *FRUS 1952–1954*, Vol. IX, Telegram from the Embassy to Egypt to the Department of State, September 12, 1955, 463.

48. Allen Smith, "Mass Society and the Bomb," *Peace & Change* 18, no. 4 (1993): 347–372. See also James J. Farrell, *The Spirit of the Sixties: Making Postwar Radicalism* (New York: Routledge, 1997), 115–116. Compare Robert O. Byrd, *Quaker Ways in Foreign Policy* (Toronto: University of Toronto Press, 1960), 189–191.

49. *New York Times*, "Aid Sent to Suez Refugees," February 11, 1957, p. 3; *New York Times*, "U.S. Group Helps Lebanon," July 3, 1958, p. 6.

50. *New York Times*, "Aid Sent to Algeria Refugees," March 1, 1959, p. 20.

51. *New York Times*, "Appeal on Mideast Sent to Eisenhower," December 8, 1959, p. 25.

52. C. H. Mike Yarrow, *Quaker Experiences in International Conciliation* (New Haven: Yale University Press, 1978). AFSC had called for negotiations between the United States and the Soviet Union as early as 1948. See the appeal published in the *New York Times*, "Not by Might, Nor by Power, But by My Spirit," April 21, 1948, p. 19.

53. Robert S. Ellwood, *The Fifties Spiritual Marketplace: American Religion in a Decade of Conflict* (New Brunswick, NJ: Rutgers University Press, 1997), 66.

54. In 1958 Pickett participated in a lawsuit against the United States government to force it to stop all nuclear testing. *Washington Post and Times Herald*, "Nuclear Weapons Fought in Suit," April 5, 1958, p. 3.

55. Guenter Lewy, *Peace and Revolution: The Moral Crisis of American Pacifism* (Grand Rapids, MI: William B. Eerdmans Publishing Company, 1988).

56. American Friends Service Committee, *A New China Policy: Some Quaker Proposals*, (Philadelphia, 1965).

57. *Washington Post*, "Paris Rally Attacks Nixon," February 12, 1972, A 11.

58. American Friends Service Committee, *Search for Peace in the Middle East*, (Philadelphia, 1970), 20.

59. American Friends Service Committee, *Search for Peace*, 69.

60. American Friends Service Committee, *Search for Peace*, 58. See also *Washington Post*, "Quakers List Mideast Plan," May 9, 1970, p. D 28.

## 9   ASSESSING THE AFSC AS AN EARLY NGO

1. David Rieff, "The Humanitarian Trap," *World Policy Journal* 12, no. 5 (1995), 8.

2. Steven Livingston, "Clarifying the CNN Effect: An Examination of Media Effects According to Type of Military Intervention," Research Paper R-18, (Cambridge, MA: The Joan Shorenstein Center on the Press, Politics and Public Policy, Harvard University, 1997).

3. See also Fiona Terry, *Condemned to Repeat?: the Paradox of Humanitarian Action* (Ithaca: Cornell University Press, 2002); Jonathan Benthall, *Disasters, Relief and the Media*: (New York: I.B. Tauris, 1993); Stephen Hopgood, "Saying No to Wal-Mart? Money and Morality in Professional Humanitarianism," in *Humanitarianism in Question: Politics, Power, Ethics*, eds. Michael Barnett and Thomas G. Weiss (Ithaca: Cornell University Press, 2008), 98–123.

4. Brian Ward, "Broadcasting Truth to Power: The American Friends Service Committee and the Early Southern Civil Rights Movement," *Quaker Studies* 10, no. 1 (2005): 87–108. Ward notes that the AFSC's radio program founded in the late 1950s was a result of the tension between the organization's absolute commitment to featuring only supporters of integration and the practical difficulty of finding Southern radio stations that would broadcast the programs. He notes that wider distribution for progressive programming became possible once the AFSC ended its support and restrictions. The contradiction between idealism and practicality experienced in Gaza was thus played out elsewhere.

5. See also Peteet's survey of AFSC documents, "AFSC Refugee Archives on Palestine, 1948–50," 112–113, that notes minimal publicity files.

6. Elmore Jackson Papers, RG 5/202, Friends Historical Library of Swarthmore College. www.swarthmore.edu/library/friends/ead/5202elja.xml. Last accessed June 12, 2013.

7. See R. Kaplan, *The Arabists*.

8. Feldman, "The Quaker Way," 693.

9. Wriggins, *Picking up the Pieces*, 180.

10. AFSC 1949. Minutes of Camp Leader's Meeting, October 6, 1949. Compare Feldman, "The Quaker Way," 699.

11. AFSC 1949. Donald Stevenson to Bronson Clark, October 24, 1949.

12. Feldman, "Difficult Distinctions," 131.

13. Feldman, "Difficult Distinctions," 134.

14. See Beshara Doumani, *Rediscovering Palestine: Merchants and Peasants in Jabal Nablus, 1700–1900* (Berkeley: University of California Press, 1995), 24; Clinton Bailey, "The Ottomans and the Bedouin Tribes of the Negev," *Ottoman Palestine 1800–1914, Studies in Economic and Social History*, ed. Gad C. Gilbar (Haifa: Gustav Heinemann Institute of Middle Eastern Studies, University of Haifa, 1990), 321–332.

15. Feldman expanded her thesis of Gaza as a unique space that nevertheless produced typical Palestinians in "Government Without Expertise?: Competence, Capacity, and Civil Service Practice in Gaza (1917–67)," *International Journal of Middle East Studies* 37, no. 4 (2005): 485–507, and "Everyday Government in Extraordinary Times: Persistence and Authority in Gaza's Civil Service, 1917–1967," *Comparative Studies in Society and History* 47, no. 4 (2005): 863–891.

16.  Alexander H. Joffe, "UNRWA Resists Resettlement," *Middle East Quarterly* 19 (2012): 11–25.

17.  Feldman, "Difficult Distinctions," 144.

18.  For the pre-partition role of the Arab states in the Palestine issue see generally Barry Rubin, *Arab States and the Palestine Conflict,* (Syracuse, NY: Syracuse University Press, 1981), 23–164; Elie Kedourie, "The Bludan Congress on Palestine," *Middle Eastern Studies* 17, no. 1 (1981): 107–125; and Basheer M. Nafi, *Arabism, Islamism and the Palestine Question, 1908–1941: a Political History* (London: Ithaca Press, 1998). For the role of the Grand Mufti see Elpeleg, *The Grand Mufti*. For the role of honour, shame, and clientalism in the construction of modern Palestinian identity, see N. T. Anders Strindberg, "'From the River to the Sea?' Honour, Identity and Political in Historical and Contemporary Palestinian Rejectionism" (doctoral dissertation, University of St. Andrews, 2001), 44–76.

19.  AFSC Oral History Interview #612, Narrator: Vern Pings, Interviewer: Paula Goldberg. September 19, 1992, 262.

20.  Ingle, "The Cold War's Effect," 30–31.

21.  John Cameron, "Development Economics, the New Institutional Economics and NGOs," *Third World Quarterly* 21 (2000): 627–635.

22.  Fred M. Gottheil, "UNRWA and Moral Hazard," *Middle Eastern Studies* 42, no. 3 (2006): 409–421.

23.  Gottheil, "UNRWA and Moral Hazard," 411–414.

24.  Bligh, "From UNRWA to Israel," 9.

25.  FO 371/127871/ VE1827/11, Minutes by Rose, April 11, 1957.

26.  Forsythe, "UNRWA," 44.

27.  Kingston, *Britain and the Politics of Modernization*, 7.

28.  On the April 2013 riots in Gaza see http://unispal.un.org/UNISPAL.NSF/0 /5840640903D5342E85257B430065EE0B. For UNRWA's Commissioner-General, Filippo Grandi statement regarding the need for a "quantum and sustained leap" in his organization's funding see www.un.org/News/Press/ docs/2012/gaspd518.doc.htm. Last accessed June 12, 2013.

29.  AFSC Oral History Interview # 602, Narrator: Josina Vreed Burger, Interviewer: Paula Goldberg, September 19, 1992.

30.  AFSC Oral History Interview # 609, Narrator: David Walker, Interviewer: Joan Lowe, September 20, 1992, 227.

31.  Fishman, *American Protestantism*, 53–63.

32.  American Friends Service Committee, *A Compassionate Peace-A Future for the Middle East* (New York: Hill and Wang, 1982). Khoury noted that Arab-American groups had criticized *Search for Peace in the Middle East* for not recognizing the PLO, and he criticizes *A Compassionate Peace* for not condemning "Zionist ideology and militarism." P. S. Khoury, "Review of *A Compassionate Peace-A Future for the Middle East,*" *Journal of Palestine Studies* 12 (1983): 72–76. Compare Arnold M. Soloway and Edwin Weiss, *Truth and*

*Peace in the Middle East: A Critical Analysis of the Quaker Report* (New York: Friendly House, 1971).

33. See the summaries of pro-Palestinian Quaker activities at http://afsc.org/search/node/palestine, http://www.quakerpi.org/default.shtml, http://afsc.org/story/jean-zaru. Last accessed June 12, 2013. See also the older comments in John P. Richardson, "Tug-of-War: American Voluntary Organizations in the West Bank," *Journal of Palestine Studies* 14, no. 2 (1985): 137–148.

34. Ofira Seliktar, *Doomed to Failure? The Politics and Intelligence of the Oslo Peace Process* (Santa Barbara, CA: Praeger, 2009): 16.

35. Hamm, *Quakers in America*, 156, 165; Duncan L. Clarke and Eric Flohr, "Christian Churches and the Palestine Question," *Journal of Palestine Studies,* 21 (1992): 67–79; Naim Ateek, Cedar Duaybis, and Maurine Tobin, *Challenging Christian Zionism: Theology, Politics and the Israel-Palestine Conflict* (London: Melisende, 2005); Laura C. Robson, "Palestinian Liberation Theology, Muslim-Christian Relations and the Arab-Israeli Conflict," *Islam and Christian-Muslim Relations* 21, no. 1 (2010): 39–50.

36. For example, H. David Kirk, *The Friendly Perversion. Quakers as Reconcilers: Good People and Dirty Work* (New York: Americans for a Safe Israel, 1979); Marvin Maurer, "Quakers in Politics: Israel, PLO, and Social Revolution," *Midstream* 23 (1977): 36–44; Rael Jean Isaac, "From Friendly Persuasion to PLO Support," *Midstream* 25 (1979): 23–29.

37. For example, Claire Gorfinkel, *I Have Always Wanted to be Jewish: And Now, Thanks to the Religious Society of Friends, I Am* (Wallingford, PA, Pendle Hill Publications, 2000). Predictably, "Jewish Quakers" are deeply involved in Arab-Israeli peacemaking and supporting the Palestinians. See for example http://archive.peacemagazine.org/v09n2p06.htm. Last accessed June 12, 2013. See also H. Larry Ingle, "Can We Be Friends," *Christian Century* 112 (1995): 412–413, on the controversial issue of adding non-Quakers to the AFSC's board of directors.

38. Gerald M. Steinberg, "Postcolonial Theory and the Ideology of Peace Studies," *Israel Affairs* 13, no. 4 (2007): 786–796. The quasi-religious nature of "peace studies" and "conflict resolution" and the influence of Quaker ideology, especially pacifism, have yet to be fully acknowledged. Note for example that the first chair of Peace Studies at the University of Bradford was created in 1972 with a grant from the Quaker Peace Studies Trust. See http://www.brad.ac.uk/peace/qpst/. Last accessed June 12, 2013. "Peace Studies" are especially prominent at church-related colleges and universities. See Ian M. Harris, Larry J. Fisk, and Carol Rank, "A Portrait of University Peace Studies in North America and Western Europe at the End of the Millennium," *International Journal of Peace Studies* 3 (1998), available at http://www.gmu.edu/programs/icar/ijps/vol3_1/Harris.htm. Last accessed June 12, 2013. Gerald M. Steinberg, "The Thin Line between Peace Education and Political Advocacy: Towards a Code of Conduct," in *Educating Toward a Culture of*

*Peace*, eds. Yaacov Iram, Hillel Wahrman, and Zehavit Gross (Charlotte, NC: Information Age Publishing, 2006), 13–22.

39. For example, http://www.kairospalestine.ps/sites/default/Documents/English.pdf. Last accessed June 12, 2013. See generally Dexter Van Zile, "Mainline American Christian 'Peacemakers' against Israel," (Jerusalem: Jerusalem Center for Public Affairs, 2009), http://jcpa.org/article/mainline-american-christian-peacemakers-against-israel/. Last accessed June 12, 2013; Dexter Van Zile, "Broadcasting a Lethal Narrative: The World Council of Churches and Israel" (Jerusalem: Jerusalem Center for Public Affairs), http://jcpa.org/article/broadcasting-a-lethal-narrative-the-world-council-of-churches-and-israel-6/. Last accessed June 12, 2013.

40. Jody C. Baumgartner, Peter L. Francia, and Jonathan S. Morris, "A Clash of Civilizations? The Influence of Religion on Public Opinion of U.S. Foreign Policy in the Middle East," *Political Research Quarterly* 61, no. 2 (2008): 171–179.

41. For a detailed articulation of UNRWA's view on the "right of return" see the statement by spokesman Chris Gunness, "Exploding the myths: UNRWA, UNHCR and the Palestine refugees," www.unrwa.org/etemplate.php?id=1029. Last accessed June 12, 2013. Compare Ruth Lapidoth, "The Right of Return in International Law, with Special Reference to the Palestinian Refugees," *Israel Yearbook on Human Rights* 16 (1986): 107–108.

## 10   CONCLUSIONS

1. Richardson, "The Refugee Problem," 49.

# Bibliography ❧

## BOOKS AND JOURNAL ARTICLES

Abdallah, Stéphanie Latte. "Regards, Visibilité Historique Et Politique Des Images Sur Les Réfugiés Palestiniens Depuis 1948." *Le Mouvement social* 219/220 (2007): 65–91.

Abu-Lughod, Ibrahim, ed. *The Transformation of Palestine: Essays on the Origin and Development of the Arab-Israeli Conflict.* Evanston: Northwestern University Press, 1971.

Abu Zayd, Karen. "UNRWA and the Palestinian Refugees after Sixty Years: Assessing Developments and Marking Challenges." *Refugee Survey Quarterly* 28 (2009): 227–228.

Abzug, Robert H. *America Views the Holocaust, 1933–1945: A Brief Documentary History.* New York: Bedford/St. Martin's, 1999.

Adelman, Howard. "Home and Homeland: The Bequest of Count Folk Bernadotte." In *Palestinian and Israeli Environmental Narratives*, ed. Stuart Schoenfeld, 213–19. Toronto, Ontario: Centre for International and Security Studies, York University, 2005.

Alterman, Jon B. *Egypt and American Foreign Assistance, 1952–1956: Hopes Dashed.* New York: Palgrave Macmillan, 2002.

American Friends Service Committee. *The United States and the Soviet Union: Some Quaker Proposals for Peace.* New Haven: Yale University Press, 1949.

———. *Steps to Peace: A Quaker View of U.S. Foreign Policy.* Philadelphia, 1951.

———. *Toward Security through Disarmament.* Philadelphia, 1952.

———. *Speak Truth to Power: A Quaker Search for an Alternative to Violence.* Philadelphia, 1955.

———. *A New China Policy: Some Quaker Proposals.* Philadelphia, 1965.

———. *Search for Peace in the Middle East.* Philadelphia, 1970.

———. *A Compassionate Peace-a Future for the Middle East.* New York: Hill and Wang, 1982.

Anderson, Betty S. *The American University of Beirut: Arab Nationalism and Liberal Education.* Austin: University of Texas Press, 2011.

Arzt, Donna and Karen Zughaib "Return to the Negotiated Lands: The Likelihood and Legality of a Population Transfer between Israel and a Future

Palestinian State." *New York University Journal of International Law and Politics* 24 (1991–92): 1399–1513.

Ateek, Naim Stifan, Cedar Duaybis, and Maurine Tobin. *Challenging Christian Zionism: Theology, Politics and the Israel-Palestine Conflict.* London: Melisende, 2005.

Austin, Allan W. "'Let's Do Away with Walls!': The American Friends Service Committee's Interracial Section and the 1920s United States." *Quaker History* 98, no. 1 (2009): 1–34.

de Azcárate, Pablo. *Mission in Palestine, 1948–1952.* Washington, DC: Middle East Institute, 1966.

Bailey, Clinton. "The Ottomans and the Bedouin Tribes of the Negev." In *Ottoman Palestine 1800–1914, Studies in Economic and Social History*, ed. Gad C. Gilbar, 321–32. Haifa: Gustav Heinemann Institute of Middle Eastern Studies, University of Haifa, 1990.

Bailey, Sydney D. "Review of D. P. Forsythe, the Humanitarians: The International Committee of the Red Cross, Cambridge: Cambridge University Press." *International Affairs* 55, no. 2 (1979): 269–70.

———. "Non-Official Mediation in Disputes: Reflections on Quaker Experience' in Royal Institute of International Affairs." *International affairs* 61 (1985): 205–22.

Bar-On, Mordechai. "Cleansing History of Its Content: Some Critical Comments on Ilan Pappé's the Ethnic Cleansing of Palestine.'" *Journal of Israeli History* 27, no. 2 (2008): 269–275.

Barnett, David and Efraim Karsh. "Azzam's Genocidal Threat." *Middle East Quarterly* 18 (2011): 85–88.

Bartholomeusz, Lance. "The Mandate of UNRWA at Sixty." *Refugee Survey Quarterly* 28, nos. 2–3 (2009): 452–74.

Barton, Gregory A. "Environmentalism, Development and British Policy in the Middle East 1945–65." *The Journal of Imperial and Commonwealth History* 38, no. 4 (2010): 619–639.

Baumgartner, Jody C, Peter L. Francia, and Jonathan S. Morris. "A Clash of Civilizations? The Influence of Religion on Public Opinion of U.S. Foreign Policy in the Middle East." *Political Research Quarterly* 61, no. 2 (2008): 171–179.

Bawardi, Hani J. "Arab American Political Organizations from 1915 to 1951: Assessing Transnational Political Consciousness and the Development of Arab American Identity," Doctoral dissertation. Wayne State University, 2009.

Baylin, Catherine C. B. "Quaker Activity in Ramallah: 1869–1914." Masters thesis. American University in Cairo, 2010.

Bennett, Gill. *Churchill's Man of Mystery: Desmond Morton and the World of Intelligence.* London: Routledge, 2007.

Benthall, Jonathan. *Disasters, Relief and the Media.* New York: I.B. Tauris, 1993.

Bingham, Jonathan B. *Shirt Sleeve Diplomacy-Point 4 in Action.* New York: John Day Company, 1954.

Blandford, John B. "Wanted: 12 Million New Houses." *National Municipal Review* 34, no. 8 (1945): 376–385.

Blanks, W. D. "Herbert Hoover and the Holy Land: A Preliminary Study Based Upon Documentary Sources in the Hoover Presidential Library." In *With Eyes toward Zion, Scholar Colloquium on America-Holy Land Studies*, edited by M. Davis, 163–76. New York: Arno Press, 1977.

Bligh, Alexander. "Israel and the Refugee Problem: From Exodus to Resettlement, 1948–52." *Middle Eastern Studies* 34, no. 1 (1998): 123–147.

Bocco, Riccardo. "UNRWA and the Palestinian Refugees: A History within History." *Refugee Survey Quarterly* 28, no. 2–3 (2009): 229–252.

Bovey, René. "L'aide Du Comité International Aux Réfugiés De Palestine." *International Review of the Red Cross* 31, no. 364 (1949): 265–270.

Bovis, H. Eugene *The Jerusalem Question, 1917–1968.* Palo Alto: The Hoover Institution, 1971.

Breger, Marshall J., and Thomas A. Idinopulos. *Jerusalem's Holy Places and the Peace Process.* Washington, DC: Washington Institute for Near East Policy, 1998.

Brinton, Howard Haines. *A Religious Solution to the Social Problem.* Wallingford, PA: Pendle Hill, 1934.

Brynen, Rex, and El-Rifai, Roula, eds. *Palestinian Refugees: Challenges of Repatriation and Development.* London: I.B. Taurus, 2007.

Buckingham, Clyde E. *Red Cross Disaster Relief, Its Origin and Development.* Washington, DC: Public Affairs Press, 1956.

———. *For Humanity's Sake: The Story of the Early Development of the League of Red Cross Societies.* Washington, DC: Public Affairs Press, 1964.

Buehrig, Edward H. *The UN and the Palestinian Refugees; a Study in Nonterritorial Administration.* Bloomington: Indiana University Press, 1971.

Burton, William L. "Protestant America and the Rebirth of Israel." *Jewish Social Studies* 26, no. 4 (1964): 203–214.

Byrd, Robert O. *Quaker Ways in Foreign Policy.* Toronto: University of Toronto Press, 1960.

Cadbury, Henry Joel. *The Peril of Modernizing Jesus.* New York: Macmillan, 1937.

Cameron, John. "Development Economics, the New Institutional Economics and NGOs." *Third World Quarterly,* 21 (2000): 627–35.

Caplan, Neil. "A Tale of Two Cities: The Rhodes and Lausanne Conferences, 1949." *Journal of Palestine Studies* 21, no. 3 (1992): 5–34.

———. *Futile Diplomacy III, the United Nations, the Great Powers, and Middle East Peacemaking, 1948–1954.* London: Frank Cass, 1997.

Carenen, Caitlin. "The American Christian Palestine Committee, the Holocaust, and Mainstream Protestant Zionism, 1938–1948." *Holocaust and Genocide Studies* 24, no. 2 (2010): 273–296.

Castle, Edgar B. *Palestine Pamphlets: A Constitution for Palestine; Reconciliation in Palestine.* London: Friends' Book Centre, 1945.

Clapp, Gordon R. "Adventures in Faith and Works." *Ethics* 58 (1947): 57–62.

Clarke, Duncan L., and Eric Flohr. "Christian Churches and the Palestine Question." *Journal of Palestine Studies* 21, no. 4 (1992): 67–79.

Cohen, Michael J. "William A. Eddy, the Oil Lobby and the Palestine Problem." *Middle Eastern Studies* 30, no. 1 (1994): 166–180.

Cohen, Michael Joseph. *Fighting World War Three from the Middle East: Allied Contingency Plans, 1945–1954.* London: Frank Cass, 1997.

Colignon, Richard A. *Power Plays: Critical Events in the Institutionalization of the Tennessee Valley Authority.* Albany: State University of New York Press, 1997.

Cordier, Andrew W. and Wilder Foote eds. *Public Papers of the Secretaries General of the United Nations.* New York: Columbia University Press, 1974.

Dandelion, Pink. *The Quakers: A Very Short Introduction.* New York: Oxford University Press, 2008.

DeNovo, John A. "The Culbertson Economic Mission and Anglo-American Tensions in the Middle East, 1944–1945." *The Journal of American History* 63, no. 4 (1977): 913–936.

Dodge, Bayard "American Educational and Missionary Efforts in the Nineteenth and Early Twentieth Centuries." *Annals of the American Academy of Political and Social Science* 401 (1972): 15–22.

Doumani, Beshara. *Rediscovering Palestine: Merchants and Peasants in Jabal Nablus, 1700–1900.* Berkeley: University of California Press, 1995.

Ekbladh, David. "Mr. TVA: Grass-Roots Development, David Lilienthal, and the Rise and Fall of the Tennessee Valley Authority as a Symbol for U.S. Overseas Development, 1933–1973." *Diplomatic History* 26, no. 3 (2002): 335–374.

El-Abed, Oroub. *Unprotected: Palestinians in Egypt since 1948.* Washington, DC: Institute for Palestine Studies, 2009.

Ellwood, Robert S. *The Fifties Spiritual Marketplace: American Religion in a Decade of Conflict.* New Brunswick, NJ: Rutgers University Press, 1997.

Elpeleg, Zvi. *The Grand Mufti, Haj Amin Al-Hussaini, Founder of the Palestinian National Movement.* London: Frank Cass, 1993.

Esber, Rosemarie M. *Under the Cover of War: The Zionist Expulsion of the Palestinians.* Alexandria Virginia: Arabicus Books & Media, 2008.

Evans, Thomas. *A Concise Account of the Religious Society of Friends.* Philadelphia: Religious Society of Friends, 1856.

Farah, Randa. "UNRWA: Through the Eyes of Its Refugee Employees in Jordan." *Refugee Survey Quarterly* 28, no. 2–3 (2009): 389–411.

Farrell, James J. *The Spirit of the Sixties: Making Postwar Radicalism.* New York: Routledge, 1997.

Favez, Jean-Claude. *The Red Cross and the Holocaust.* New York: Cambridge University Press, 1999.

Feldman, Ilana. "Everyday Government in Extraordinary Times: Persistence and Authority in Gaza's Civil Service, 1917–1967." *Comparative Studies in Society and History* 47, no. 4 (2005): 863–891.

————. "Government without Expertise?: Competence, Capacity, and Civil Service Practice in Gaza (1917–67)." *International Journal of Middle East Studies* 37, no. 4 (2005): 485–507.

————. "Difficult Distinctions: Refugee Law, Humanitarian Practice, and Political Identification in Gaza." *Cultural Anthropology* 22, no. 1 (2007): 129–169.

————. "The Quaker Way: Ethical Labor and Humanitarian Relief." *American Ethnologist* 34, no. 4 (2007): 689–705.

————. "Mercy Trains and Ration Rolls between Government and Humanitarianism in Gaza (1948–67)." In *Interpreting Welfare and Relief in the Middle East*, edited by N. Naguib and I. M. Okkenhaug, 175–94. Leiden: Brill, 2008.

Fisher, Fedora Gould. *Raphael Cilento: A Biography*. Brisbane: University of Queensland Press, 1994.

Fishman, Hertzel. *American Protestantism and a Jewish State*. Detroit, MI: Wayne State University Press, 1973.

Fischbach, Michael R. *Records of Dispossession: Palestinian Refugee Property and the Arab-Israeli Conflict*. New York: Columbia University Press, 2003.

————. *The Peace Process and Palestinian Refugee Claims: Addressing Claims for Property Compensation and Restitution*. Washington, DC: United States Institute of Peace Press, 2006.

Forsythe, David P. "UNRWA, the Palestine Refugees, and World Politics: 1949–1969." *International Organization* 25, no. 1 (1971): 26–45.

————. "Further on the United Nations Relief and Works Agency: Refugees from Objectivity: Comment." *International Organization* 25, no. 4 (1971): 950–952.

————. *United Nations Peacemaking: The Conciliation Commission for Palestine*. Baltimore: Johns Hopkins University Press, 1972.

————. *Humanitarian Politics: The International Committee of the Red Cross*. Baltimore: Johns Hopkins University Press, 1977.

Fox, Frank. "Quaker, Shaker, Rabbi: Warder Cresson, the Story of a Philadelphia Mystic." *The Pennsylvania Magazine of History and Biography* 95 (April 1971): 146–193.

Fox, George. *Journal of George Fox*. Glasgow: W.G. Mackie and Co., 1852.

Gabbay, Rony E. *A Political Study of the Arab-Jewish Conflict. The Arab Refugee Problem (a Case Study)*. Paris: Librairie Minard, 1959.

Gallagher, Nancy. *Quakers in the Israeli-Palestinian Conflict: The Dilemmas of NGO Humanitarian Activism*. Cairo: American University in Cairo Press, 2007.

Gat, Moshe. "Between Terror and Immigration: The Case of Iraqi Jewry." *Israel Affairs* 7, no. 1 (2000): 1–24.

Gazit, Mordechai. "Ben-Gurion's 1949 Proposal to Incorporate the Gaza Strip with Israel." *Studies in Zionism* 8, no. 2 (1987): 223–243.

Gelber, Yoav. *1948: War, Escape and the Emergence of the Palestinian Refugee Problem*. Brighton: Sussex Academic Press, 2006.

———. "The History of Zionist Historiography, from Apologetics to Denial." In *Making Israel*, edited by Benny Morris, 47–80. Ann Arbor: University of Michigan Press, 2007.

Giacaman, Rita, Harry S. Shannon, Hana Saab, Neil Arya, and Will Boyce. "Individual and Collective Exposure to Political Violence: Palestinian Adolescents Coping with Conflict." *European Journal of Public Health* 17, no. 4 (2007): 361–368.

Golan, Arnon. "Postwar Spatial Reorganization: The Resettlement of Greek Refugees, 1922–1930." In *Population Resettlement in International Conflicts: A Comparative Study*, edited by Arie Marcelo Kacowicz and Pawel Lutomski, 21–40. Lanham, MD: Lexington Books, 2007.

Gorfinkel, Claire. *I Have Always Wanted to Be Jewish: And Now, Thanks to the Religious Society of Friends, I Am*. Wallingford, PA: Pendle Hill Publications, 2000.

Gottheil, Fred M. "UNRWA and Moral Hazard." *Middle Eastern Studies* 42, no. 3 (2006): 409–421.

Grabill, Joseph L. *Protestant Diplomacy and the Near East; Missionary Influence on American Policy, 1810–1927*. Minneapolis, MN: University of Minnesota Press, 1971.

Greenberg, Ela. *Preparing the Mothers of Tomorrow: Education and Islam in Mandate Palestine*. Austin: University of Texas Press, 2009.

Greenberg, Gershon. *The Holy Land in American Religious Thought, 1620–1948: The Symbiosis of American Religious Approaches to Scripture's Sacred Territory*. Lanham, MD, and Jerusalem: University Press of America and the Avraham Harman Institute of Contemporary Jewry, The Hebrew University of Jerusalem, 1994.

Gulley, Emmett, W. *Tall Tales by a Tall Quaker*. Privately published, 1973.

Hahn, Peter L. "Containment and Egyptian Nationalism: The Unsuccessful Effort to Establish the Middle East Command, 1950–53." *Diplomatic History* 11, no. 1 (1987): 23–40.

———. *The United States, Great Britain, and Egypt, 1945–1956: Strategy and Diplomacy in the Early Cold War*. Chapel Hill: University of North Carolina Press, 1991.

———. "The View from Jerusalem: Revelations About U.S. Diplomacy from the Archives of Israel." *Diplomatic History* 22, no. 4 (1998): 509–532.

———. *Caught in the Middle East: U.S. Policy toward the Arab-Israeli Conflict, 1945–1961*. Chapel Hill: University of North Carolina Press, 2004.

Hamm, Thomas D. *How the Quakers Invented America*. Lanham, MD: Rowman & Littlefield, 2007.

Hanafi, Sari, and Linda Tabar. *The Emergence of a Palestinian Globalized Elite, Donors, International Organisations, and Local NGOs*. Jerusalem: Institute of Jerusalem Studies, 2005.

Harris, Ian M., Larry J. Fisk, and Carol Rank. "A Portrait of University Peace Studies in North America and Western Europe at the End of the Millennium." *International Journal of Peace Studies* 3 (1998). www.gmu.edu/programs/icar/ijps/vol3_1/Harris.htm. Last accessed June 12, 2013.

Hays, James B. *T.V.A. On the Jordan, Proposals for Irrigation and Hydro-Electric Development in Palestine.* Washington, DC: Public Affairs Press, 1948.

Heller, Joseph. "Alternative Narratives and Collective Memories: Israel's New Historians and the Use of Historical Context." *Middle Eastern Studies* 42, no. 4 (2006): 571–586.

Herzog, Chaim, and Shlomo Gazit. *The Arab-Israeli Wars: War and Peace in the Middle East from the 1948 War of Independence to the Present.* London: Greenhill Books, 2004.

Heusel, Lorton. *Friends on the Front Line the Story of Delbert and Ruth Replogle.* Greensboro, NC: Friends Historical Society, 1985.

Hinshaw, David. *Rufus Jones, Master Quaker.* New York: G. P. Putnam's Sons, 1951.

Hocking, William Ernest, ed. *Re-Thinking Missions, a Layman's Inquiry after One Hundred Years.* New York: Harper & Brothers Publishers, 1932.

Hopgood, Stephen. "Saying No to Wal-Mart? Money and Morality in Professional Humanitarianism." In *Humanitarianism in Question: Politics, Power, Ethics,* edited by Michael Barnett and Thomas G. Weiss, 98–123. Ithaca, NY: Cornell University Press, 2008.

Hurewitz, J. C. "The United Nations Conciliation Commission for Palestine: Establishment and Definition of Functions." *International Organization* 7, no. 4 (1953): 482–497.

———. *The Struggle for Palestine.* New York: Schocken Books, 1976.

Al-Husseini, Jalal. "Red Cross Palestinian Refugee Archives 1948–1950." In *Reinterpreting the Historical Record. The Use of Palestinian Refugee Archives for Social Science Research and Policy Analysis* edited by Salim Tamari & Elia Zureik, 145–71: Jerusalem: Institute of Jerusalem Studies, 2001.

———. "Arab States and the Refugee Issue: A Retrospective View." In *Israel and the Palestinian Refugees,* edited by Eyal Benvenisti et al., 435–63. Berlin: Springer, 2007.

Ingle, H. Larry. "'Speak Truth to Power': A Thirty Years' Retrospective." *Christian Century* 102 (1985): 383–385.

———. "Can We Be Friends." *Christian Century* 112 (1995): 412–413.

———. "The American Friends Service Committee, 1947–49: The Cold War's Effect." *Peace & Change* 23, no. 1 (1998): 27–48.

Isaac, R. Jean. "From Friendly Persuasion to PLO Support." *Midstream* 25 (1979): 23–29.

Jackson, Elmore. "The Developing Role of the Secretary-General." *International Organization* 11, no. 3 (1957): 431–445.

———. *Middle East Mission, the Story of a Major Bid for Peace in the Time of Nasser and Ben Gurion.* New York: W.W. Norton & Company, 1983.

Joffe, Alexander H. "UNRWA Resists Resettlement." *Middle East Quarterly* 19 (2012): 11–25.

Jones, Christina. *Friends in Palestine*. Richmond, IN: American Friends Board of Missions, 1944.

Jones, Mary Hoxie. *Swords into Ploughshares; an Account of the American Friends Service Committee, 1917–1937*. New York: Macmillan, 1937.

———. "Henry Joel Cadbury: A Biographical Sketch." In *Then and Now, Quaker Essays: Historical and Contemporary*, edited by Anna Cox Brinton 11–70. Philadelphia: University of Pennsylvania Press, 1960.

Jones, Rufus M. *A Service of Love in War Time, American Friends Relief Work in Europe, 1917–1919*. New York: Macmillan, 1920.

Junod, Dominique-D. *The Imperiled Red Cross and the Palestine-Eretz-Yisrael Conflict, 1945–1952: The Influence of Institutional Concerns on a Humanitarian Operation*. London: Keegan Paul International, 1996.

Kagan, Michael. "The (Relative) Decline of Palestinian Exceptionalism and Its Consequences for Refugee Studies in the Middle East." *Journal of Refugee Studies* 22, no. 4 (2009): 417–438.

Kahoe, Walter. *Clarence Pickett, a Memoir*. Privately printed: 1966.

Kaplan, Robert D. *The Arabists: The Romance of an American Elite*. New York: Free Press, 1993.

Karsh, Efraim. "Benny Morris and the Reign of Error." *Middle East Quarterly* 4 (1999): 15–28.

———. *Fabricating Israeli History: The "New Historians"*. London: Frank Cass, 2000.

———. "Nakbat Haifa: The Collapse and Dispersion of a Major Palestinian Community." *Middle Eastern Studies* 37, no. 4 (2001): 25–70.

———. "How Many Palestinian Arab Refugees Were There?" *Israel Affairs* 17, no. 2 (2011): 224–246.

Kedourie, Elie. "Britain, France, and the Last Phase of the Eastern Question." In *Soviet-American Rivalry in the Middle East*, edited by J. C. Hurewitz, 189–97. New York: Praeger, 1969.

———. "The Bludan Congress on Palestine." *Middle Eastern Studies* 17, no. 1 (1981): 107–125.

Khadduri, Majid "The Anglo-Egyptian Controversy." *Proceedings of the Academy of Political Science* 24, no. 2 (1952): 82–100.

Khalidi, Rashid. *Palestinian Identity: The Construction of Modern National Consciousness*. New York: Columbia University Press, 1997.

Khalidi, Walid. *From Haven to Conquest; Readings in Zionism and the Palestine Problem until 1948*. Beirut: Institute for Palestine Studies, 1971.

———. "Plan Dalet: Master Plan for the Conquest of Palestine." *Journal of Palestine Studies* 18, no. 1 (1988): 4–33. (Originally published in *Middle East Forum*, November 1961.)

———. *All That Remains: The Palestinian Villages Occupied and Depopulated by Israel in 1948*. Washington, DC: The Institute for Palestine Studies, 1992.

Khoury, Ghada Yusuf. *The Founding Fathers of the American University of Beirut.* Beirut: American University of Beirut, 1992.

Khoury, Philip S. "Review of a *Compassionate Peace-a Future for the Middle East.*" *Journal of Palestine Studies* 12 (1983): 72–76.

Kingston, Paul W. T. *Britain and the Politics of Modernization in the Middle East, 1945–1958.* Cambridge: Cambridge University Press, 1996.

Kirk, H. David. *The Friendly Perversion. Quakers as Reconcilers: Good People and Dirty Work.* New York: Americans for a Safe Israel, 1979.

Kolinsky, Martin. "The Efforts of the Truman Administration to Resolve the Arab-Israeli Conflict." *Middle Eastern Studies* 20 (1984): 81–94.

Kolsky, Thomas A. *Jews against Zionism: The American Council for Judaism, 1942–1948.* Philadelphia: Temple University Press, 1990.

Kushner, Arlene. "UNRWA, the United Nations Relief and Works Agency for Palestine Refugees in the near East, a Report." Jerusalem: Israel Resource News Agency, 2003.

———. "The UN's Palestinian Refugee Problem." *Azure* 22 (2005): 57–77.

———. "UNRWA, Overview and Policies." Jerusalem: Center for Near East Policy Research, 2008.

Lacey, Thomas Alexander. *The Acts of Uniformity: Their Scope and Effect.* London: Rivingtons, 1900.

Landis, Joshua. "Early U.S. Policy toward Palestinian Refugees: The Syria Option." In *The Palestinian Refugees: Old Problems – New Solutions,* edited by Joseph Ginat and Edward J. Perkins, 77–87. Norman, OK: University of Oklahoma Press, 2001.

Lapidoth, Ruth. "The Right of Return in International Law, with Special Reference to the Palestinian Refugees." *Israel Yearbook on Human Rights* 16 (1986): 103–125.

Ledermann, Laszlo. "The International Organization of the Red Cross and the League of Red Cross Societies." *American Journal of International Law* 42, no. 3 (1948): 635–644.

Lerner, Daniel. *The Passing of Traditional Society: Modernizing the Middle East.* Glencoe IL: The Free Press, 1958.

Lewis, N. *Nomads and Settlers in Syria and Jordan, 1800–1980.* Cambridge: Cambridge University Press, 1987.

Lewy, Guenter. *Peace and Revolution: The Moral Crisis of American Pacifism.* Grand Rapids, MI: William B. Eerdmans Publishing Company, 1988.

Likhovski, Assaf. "Post-Post-Zionist Historiography." *Israel Studies* 15, no. 2 (2010): 1–23.

Lindsay, James G. *Fixing UNRWA: Repairing the UN's Troubled System of Aid to Palestinian Refugees.* Washington: Washington Institute for Near Eastern Policy, 2009.

Lippman, Thomas. "The View from 1947: The CIA and the Partition of Palestine." *Middle East Journal* 61, no. 1 (2007): 17–28.

———. *Arabian Knight: Colonel Bill Eddy USMC and the Rise of American Power in the Middle East*. Vista, CA: Selwa Press, 2008.

Lipset, Seymour Martin. "Some Social Requisites of Democracy." *American Political Science Review* 53, no. 1 (1959): 69–105.

Livingston, Steven. "Clarifying the CNN Effect: An Examination of Media Effects According to Type of Military Intervention." *Research Paper R-18*. Cambridge, MA: The Joan Shorenstein Center on the Press, Politics and Public Policy, Harvard University, 1997.

Louis, William Roger. *The British Empire in the Middle East, 1945–1951: Arab Nationalism, the United States, and Postwar Imperialism*. Oxford: Oxford University Press, 1984.

Lowi, Miriam R. *Water and Power. The Politics of a Scarce Resource in the Jordan River Basin*. Cambridge: Cambridge University Press, 1993.

Marx, Emmanuel, and Nitza Nachmias "Dilemmas of Prolonged Humanitarian Aid Operations: The Case of UNRWA (UN Relief and Works Agency for Palestinian Refugees." *Journal of Humanitarian Assistance* (2004).

Mattar, Philip. "The Mufti of Jerusalem: Muhammad Amin Al-Husayni, a Founder of Palestinian Nationalism." Doctoral dissertation, Columbia University, 1981.

Maurer, Marvin. "Quakers in Politics: Israel, PLO, and Social Revolution." *Midstream* 23 (1977): 36–44.

May, Ernest R., ed. *American Cold War Strategy: Interpreting NSC 68*. New York: Bedford/St. Martin's, 1993.

McDonald, James G. *My Mission to Israel 1948–1951*. New York: Simon and Schuster, 1951.

McGhee, George Crews. *On the Frontline in the Cold War: An Ambassador Reports*. Westport, CT: Praeger, 1997.

Mechling, Elizabeth Walker, and Jay Mechling. "Hot Pacifism and Cold War: The American Friends Service Committee's Witness for Peace in 1950s America." *Quarterly Journal of Speech* 78, no. 2 (1992): 173–96.

Medoff, Rafael. "Herbert Hoover's Plan for Palestine: A Forgotten Episode in American Middle East Diplomacy." *American Jewish History* 79 (1990): 449–476.

Mendlesohn, Farah. "Denominational Difference in Quaker Relief Work During the Spanish Civil War: The Operation of Corporate Concern and Liberal Theologies." *Journal of Religious History* 24, no. 2 (2000): 180–96.

Miller, Larry. "Clarence Pickett and the Alger Hiss Case." *Friends Journal*, November, December (1994): 9–13, 12–15.

Miller, Lawrence. *Witness for Humanity: The Biography of Clarence E. Pickett*. Wallingford, PA: Pendle Hill Publications 1999.

Miller, Robert M. *Harry Emerson Fosdick: Preacher, Pastor, Prophet*. New York: Oxford University Press, 1985.

Miller, Rory. "Sir Edward Spears' Jewish Problem: A Leading Anti-Zionist and His Relationship with Anglo-Jewry, 1945–1948." *Journal of Israeli History* 19, no. 1 (1998): 41–60.

————. "Bible and Soil: Walter Clay Lowdermilk, the Jordan Valley Plan and the Battle over Palestine in the Final Mandatory Era." *Middle Eastern Studies* 39, no. 2 (2003): 55–81.

Mitchell, Timothy. "The Middle East in the Past and Future of Social Science." In *The Politics of Knowledge: Area Studies and the Disciplines*, edited by David L. Szanton, 74–118. Berkeley: University of California Press, 2002.

Morag, Nadav. "Water, Geopolitics and State Building: 'The Case of Israel.'" *Middle Eastern Studies.* 37, no. 3 (2001): 179–198.

Moranian, Suzanne E. "The Armenian Genocide and American Missionary Relief Efforts." In *America and the Armenian Genocide of 1915*, edited by J. M. Winter, 185–213. Cambridge: Cambridge University Press, 2003.

Morgan, Arthur Ernest. *The Making of the TVA*. Buffalo, NY: Prometheus Books, 1974.

Morris, Benny. *The Birth of the Palestinian Refugee Problem, 1947–1949*. Cambridge: Cambridge University Press, 1988.

————. *The Birth of the Palestinian Refugee Problem Revisited*. Cambridge: Cambridge University Press, 2004.

————. "The Historiography of Deir Yassin." *Journal of Israeli History* 24, no. 1 (2005): 79–107.

————. *One State, Two States: Resolving the Israel/Palestine Conflict*. New Haven: Yale University Press, 2009.

Muslih, Muhammad Y. *The Origins of Palestinian Nationalism*. New York: Columbia University Press, 1988.

Myer, Dillon S. . *An Autobiography of Dillon S. Myer*. University of California, Berkeley: Bancroft Library, Regional Oral History Office, 1970.

Nafi, Basheer M. *Arabism, Islamism and the Palestine Question, 1908–1941: A Political History*. London: Ithaca Press, 1998.

Naveh, Eyal. "Unconventional "Christian Zionist": The Theologian Reinhold Niebuhr and His Attitude toward the Jewish National Movement." *Studies in Zionism* 11 (1990): 183–196; 12 (1991): 85–88.

*Nebraska Yearly Meeting of Friends, Thirteenth Annual Assembly*. Central City: Nebraska, 1920

Newman, Daisy. *A Procession of Friends: Quakers in America*. New York: Doubleday, 1972.

Nitze, Paul. "The Development of NSC-68." *International Security* 4, no. 4 (1980): 170–176.

Obenzinger, Hilton. *American Palestine, Melville, Twain, and the Holy Land Mania*. Princeton: Princeton University Press, 1999.

Oren, Michael B. "The Tripartite System and Arms Control in the Middle East: 1950–1956." In *Arms Control in the Middle East*, edited by Dore Gold, 77–87. Boulder, CO: Westview, 1990.

Ovendale, Ritchie. *The Foreign Policy of the British Labour Governments, 1945–1951*. Leicester, Leicestershire: Leicester University Press, 1984.

Owen, Nicholas. "Britain and Decolonization: The Labour Governments and the Middle East, 1945–1951." In *Demise of the British Empire in the*

*Middle East: Britain's Responses to Nationalist Movements, 1943–55*, edited by Michael Joseph Cohen and Martin Kolinsky, 3–22. London: Frank Cass, 1998.

Pappé, Ilan. *The Making of the Arab-Israeli Conflict, 1947–1951.* London: I.B. Tauris, 1992.

———. *The Ethnic Cleansing of Palestine.* Oxford: Oneworld, 2006.

Peteet, Julie M. "AFSC Refugee Archives on Palestine, 1948–50." In *Reinterpreting the Historical Record. The Use of Palestinian Refugee Archives for Social Science Research and Policy Analysis*, edited by Salim Tamari and Elia Zureik, 109–128: Jerusalem: Institute of Jerusalem Studies, 2001.

———. *Landscape of Hope and Despair: Palestinian Refugee Camps.* Philadelphia, PA: University of Pennsylvania Press, 2005.

Petschnigg, Lilli. "The League of Red Cross Societies." *American Journal of Nursing* 50, no. 9 (1950): 516–517.

Peretz, Don. "Israel and the Arab Refugees." Doctoral dissertation, Columbia University, 1955.

———. *Israel and the Palestine Arabs.* Washington, DC: Middle East Institute, 1958.

———. *The Rights of the Palestinians.* Middle East Problem Paper. Washington, DC: Middle East Institute, 1974.

———. *The West Bank: History, Politics, Society, and Economy.* Boulder: Westview Press, 1986.

———. *Palestinians, Refugees, and the Middle East Peace Process.* Washington, DC: United States Institute of Peace Press, 1993.

———. "Vignettes – Bits and Pieces." In *Paths to the Middle East: Ten Scholars Look Back*, edited by T. Naff, 231–61. Albany: SUNY Press, 1993.

Perlmutter, Amos. "Patrons in the Babylonian Captivity of Clients: UNRWA and World Politics." *International Organization* 25, no. 2 (1971): 306–308.

———. "The Post-Zionist War against Israel." *Totalitarian Movements and Political Religions* 1, no. 2 (2000): 93–112.

Peterson, Merrill D. *"Starving Armenians": American and the Armenian Genocide, 1915–1930 and After.* Charlottesville, VA: University of Virginia Press, 2004.

Pickett, Clarence. *For More Than Bread, an Autobiographical Account of Twenty-Two Years' Work with the American Friends Service Committee.* Boston: Little, 1953.

Quandt, William B., Paul Jabber, and Ann Mosely Lesch. *The Politics of Palestinian Nationalism.* Berkeley: University of California Press, 1973.

Quigley, John B. "Repatriation of the Displaced Arabs of Palestine: The Legal Requirement as Seen from the United Nations." *Moritz College of Law, Public Law and Legal Theory Working Paper Series 60* (2006).

Radley, Kurt René. "The Palestinian Refugees: The Right to Return in International Law." *American Journal of International Law* 72 (1978): 586–614.

Reid, Fiona, Gemie, Sharif. "The Friends Relief Service and Displaced People in Europe after the Second World War, 1945–48." *Quaker Studies 7*, no. 2 (2013): 223–43.

Radai, Itamar. "The Collapse of the Palestinian-Arab Middle Class in 1948: The Case of Qatamon." *Middle Eastern Studies* 43 no. 6 (2007): 961–982.

Rey-Schyrr, Catherine. "Le CICR Et L'assistance Aux Réfugiés Arabes Palestiniens (1948-11950)." *International Review of the Red Cross* 83, no. 843 (2001): 739–761.

Reynier, Jacques de. *1948 À Jérusalem*. Paris: Éditions de la Baconnière, 1969.

Richardson, Channing B. "The United Nations and Arab Refugee Relief, 1948–1950; a Case Study in International Organization and Administration." Doctoral dissertation, Columbia University, 1951.

———. "The United Nations Relief for Palestine Refugees." *International Organization* 4, no. 1 (1950): 44–54.

———. "The Refugee Problem." *Proceedings of the Academy of Political Science* 24, no. 4 (1952): 43–50.

Richardson, John P. "Tug-of-War: American Voluntary Organizations in the West Bank." *Journal of Palestine Studies* 14, no. 2 (1985): 137–148.

Ricks, Thomas M. "Khalil Totah, the Unknown Years." *Jerusalem Quarterly* 34 (2008): 51–77.

Rieff, David. "The Humanitarian Trap." *World Policy Journal* 12, no. 5 (1995): 1–11.

Rieker, Martia. "Uses of Refugee Archives for Research and Policy Analysis." In *Reinterpreting the Historical Record. The Use of Palestinian Refugee Archives for Social Science Research and Policy Analysis,* edited by S. Tamari & E. Zureik, 11–23. Jerusalem: Institute of Jerusalem Studies, 2001.

Ringland, Arthur R. "The Organization of Voluntary Foreign Aid: 1939–1953." Washington, DC: Department of State Bulletin, 1954.

Robson, Laura C. "Palestinian Liberation Theology, Muslim-Christian Relations and the Arab-Israeli Conflict." *Islam and Christian-Muslim Relations* 21, no. 1 (2010): 39–50.

———. "Church, State, and the Holy Land: British Protestant Approaches to Imperial Policy in Palestine, 1917–1948." *The Journal of Imperial and Commonwealth History* 39, no. 3 (2011): 457–477.

Rondot, Philippe. "France and Palestine: From Charles De Gaulle to Francois Mitterand." *Journal of Palestine Studies* 16, no. 3 (1987): 87–100.

Roosevelt, Kermit, Jr. "Partition of Palestine: A Lesson in Pressure Politics." *Middle East Journal* 2 (1948): 1–16.

Rosenfeld, Maya. "From Emergency Relief Assistance to Human Development and Back: UNRWA and the Palestinian Refugees, 1950–2009." *Refugee Survey Quarterly* 28, no. 2–3 (2009): 286–317.

Rostow, Walt W. *The Stages of Economic Growth*. Cambridge: Cambridge University Press, 1960.

Rubin, Barry M. *The Arab States and the Palestine Conflict*. Contemporary Issues in the Middle East. Syracuse, NY: Syracuse University Press, 1981.

Schechtman, Joseph B. *The Mufti and the Fuehrer; the Rise and Fall of Haj Amin El-Husseini*. New York: T. Yoseloff, 1965.

Schiff, Benjamin N. *Refugees Unto the Third Generation: UN Aid to Palestinians*. Syracuse, NY: Syracuse University Press, 1995.

Schmitt, Hans A. *Quakers and Nazis: Inner Light in Outer Darkness*. Columbia: University of Missouri Press, 1997.

Segev, Zohar. "Struggle for Cooperation and Integration: American Zionists and Arab Oil, 1940s." *Middle Eastern Studies* 42, no. 5 (2006): 819–830.

Seliktar, Ofira. *Divided We Stand: American Jews, Israel, and the Peace Process*. Westport, CT.: Praeger, 2002.

———. *Doomed to Failure?: The Politics and Intelligence of the Oslo Peace Process*. Santa Barbara, CA: Praeger Security International, 2009.

Shapira, Anita. "Historiography and Politics: The Debate of the New Historians." *History and Memory* 7, no. 1 (1995): 9–40.

Shattuck, Gardiner H., Jr. ""True Israelites": Charles Thorley Bridgerman and Anglican Missions in Palestine, 1922–1948." *Anglican and Episcopal History* 77, no. 2 (2008): 115–149.

———. "Weeping over Jerusalem: Anglicans and Refugee Relief in the Middle East, 1895–1950." *Anglican and Episcopal History* 80, no. 2 (2011): 117–41.

Shlaim, Avi. *The Politics of Partition: King Abdullah, the Zionists, and Palestine, 1921–1951*. New York: Columbia University Press, 1990.

Simons, Chaim. *International Proposals to Transfer Arabs from Palestine 1895–1947: A Historical Survey* Hoboken, NJ: Ktav Publishing, 1988.

Slonim, Shlomo. "Israeli Policy on Jerusalem at the United Nations, 1948 ." *Middle Eastern Studies* 30, no. 3 (1994): 579–596.

———. "Origins of the 1950 Tripartite Declaration on the Middle East." *Middle Eastern Studies* 23 (1987): 135–149.

Smith, Allen. "Mass Society and the Bomb." *Peace & Change* 18, no. 4 (1993): 347–372.

———. "The Renewal Movement: The Peace Testimony and Modern Quakerism." *Quaker History* 85, no. 2 (1996): 1–23.

———. "The Peace Movement at the Local Level: The Syracuse Peace Council, 1936–1973." *Peace & Change* 23, no. 1 (1998): 1–26.

———. "Comments on Ingle." *Peace & Change* 29, no. 3 (1998): 399–401.

Soloway, Arnold and Edwin Weiss. *Truth and Peace in the Middle East: A Critical Analysis of the Quaker Report*. New York: Friendly House, 1971.

Spiegel, Steven L. *The Other Arab-Israeli Conflict: Making America's Middle East Policy, from Truman to Reagan*. Chicago: University of Chicago Press, 1985.

de St. Aubin, W. "Peace and Refugees in the Middle East." *Middle East Journal* 3, no. 2 (1949): 249–259.

Steinberg, Gerald M. "The Thin Line between Peace Education and Political Advocacy: Towards a Code of Conduct." In *Educating toward a Culture of Peace*, edited by Hillel Wahrman Yaacov Iram, and Zehavit Gross, 13–22. Charlotte, NC: Information Age Publishing, 2006.

———. "Postcolonial Theory and the Ideology of Peace Studies." *Israel Affairs* 13, no. 4 (2007): 786–796.

Strindberg, N. T. Anders. "'From the River to the Sea?' Honour, Identity and Political in Historical and Contemporary Palestinian Rejectionism." Doctoral dissertation. University of St. Andrews, 2001.

Tal, David. *War in Palestine, 1948: Strategy and Diplomacy*. London: Routledge, 2004.

———. "Weapons without Influence: British Arms Supply Policy and the Egyptian-Czech Arms Deal, 1945–55." *The Journal of Imperial and Commonwealth History* 34, no. 3 (2006): 369–388.

Takkenberg, Lex. "UNRWA and the Palestinian Refugees after Sixty Years: Some Reflections." *Refugee Survey Quarterly* 28, no. 2–3 (2009): 253–59.

Tamari, Salim, and Elia Zureik, eds. *Reinterpreting the Historical Record. The Use of Palestinian Refugee Archives for Social Science Research and Policy Analysis*. Jerusalem: Institute of Jerusalem Studies, 2001.

Tauber, Eliezer. "The Jewish and Arab Lobbies in Canada and the UN Partition of Palestine." *Israel Affairs* 5, no. 4 (1999): 229–244.

Terry, Fiona. *Condemned to Repeat?: The Paradox of Humanitarian Action*. Ithaca: Cornell University Press, 2002.

Teveth, Shabtai "The Palestine Arab Refugee Problem and Its Origins." *Middle East Studies* 26, no. 2 (1990): 214–249.

Tibawi, Abdul Latif. *American Interests in Syria, 1800–1901: A Study of Educational, Literary and Religious Work*. Oxford: Oxford University Press, 1966.

Tonini, Alberto. "International Donors, the Refugees and UNRWA: France, Britain and Italy as Case Studies, 1950–1993." In *The UNRWA Refugees and UNRWA in Jordan, the West Bank and Gaza, 1949–1999*. Beirut: Centre d'Etudes et de Recherche sur le Moyen-Orient Contemporain, 1999.

Totah, Khalil. "Education in Palestine." In *Palestine: A Decade of Development*, edited by Harry Viteles and Khalil Totah, 155–66. Philadelphia: American Academy of Political and Social Science, 1932.

———. *Dynamite in the Middle East*. New York: Philosophical Library, 1955.

Vidal, Dominique and Joseph Algazy. *Le Péché Originel D'israël: L'expulsion Des Palestiniens Revisitée Par Les "Nouveaux Historiens" Israéliens*. Paris: Editions de l'Atelier, 1998.

Vining, Elizabeth Gray. *Friend of Life: The Biography of Rufus M. Jones*. New York: J.B. Lippincott, 1958.

Vitalis, Robert. "The "New Deal" in Egypt: The Rise of Anglo-American Commercial Competition in World War II and the Fall of Neocolonialism." *Diplomatic History* 20, no. 2 (1996): 211–240.

Vogel, Lester. *To See a Promised Land, Americans and the Holy Land in the Nineteenth Century.* State College, PA: Penn State Press, 1995.

Waldmeier, Theophilus. *The Autobiography of Theophilus Waldmeier, Missionary: Being Ten Years' Life in Abyssinia; and Sixteen Years in Syria.* London: S. W. Partridge & Co., 1886.

Ward, Brian. "Broadcasting Truth to Power: The American Friends Service Committee and the Early Southern Civil Rights Movement." *Quaker Studies* 10, no. 1 (2005): 87–108.

Wark, Wesley K. "Development Diplomacy: Sir John Troutbeck and the British Middle East Office, 1947–1950." In *British Officials and British Foreign Policy, 1945–1950* edited by John Zametica, 228–49. Leicester: Leicester University Press, 1990.

Wasserstein, Bernard. *Divided Jerusalem, the Struggle for the Holy City.* New Haven: Yale University Press, 2002.

Wentling, Sonja. "The Engineer and the Shtadlanim: Herbert Hoover and American Jewish Non-Zionists, 1917–28." *American Jewish History* 88 (2000): 377–406.

Wilford, Hugh. *The Mighty Wurlitzer: How the CIA Played America.* Cambridge, MA: Harvard University Press, 2008.

Wilmington, Martin W. *The Middle East Supply Centre.* Albany: State University of New York Press, 1971.

Wilson, Mary C. *King Abdullah, Britain, and the Making of Jordan.* Cambridge: Cambridge University Press, 1987.

Wittner, Lawrence S. *The Struggle against the Bomb.* Palo Alto: Stanford University Press, 1995.

Wriggins, William Howard. *Picking up the Pieces from Portugal to Palestine: Quaker Refugee Relief in World War II, a Memoir.* Lanham, MD: University Press of America, 2004.

Wright, Melanie J. "The Nature and Significance of Relations between the Historic Peace Churches and Jews During and after the Shoah." In *Christian-Jewish Relations through the Centuries*, edited by S. E. Porter and B. W. R. Pearson, 400–25. Sheffield: Sheffield Academic Press, 2000.

Yaqub, Salim. *Containing Arab Nationalism: The Eisenhower Doctrine and the Middle East.* Chapel Hill: University of North Carolina Press, 2004.

Yarrow, C. H. Mike. *Quaker Experiences in International Conciliation.* New Haven: Yale University Press, 1978.

Yiftachel, Oren. *Ethnocracy: Land and Identity Politics in Israel/Palestine.* Philadelphia: University of Pennsylvania Press, 2006.

Yount, David. *How the Quakers Invented America.* Lanham, MD: Rowman & Littlefield, 2007.

Zachs, Fruma. "Toward a Proto-Nationalist Concept of Syria Revisiting the American Presbyterian Missionaries in the Levant." *Die Welt des Islams* 41, no. 2 (2001): 1–29.

———. "From the Mission to the Missionary: The Bliss Family and the Syrian Protestant College, 1866–1920." *Die Welt des Islams* 45, no. 2 (2005): 255–291.

Zaiotti, Ruben. "Dealing with Non-Palestinian Refugees in the Middle East: Policies and Practices in an Uncertain Environment." *International Journal of Refugee Law* 18 (2006): 333–353.

Zile, Dexter Van. "Mainline American Christian 'Peacemakers' against Israel." Jerusalem: Jerusalem Center for Public Affairs, 2009.

———. "Broadcasting a Lethal Narrative: The World Council of Churches and Israel." Jerusalem: Jerusalem Center for Public Affairs, 2011. (available at http://jcpa.org/article/broadcasting-a-lethal-narrative-the-world-council-of-churches-and-israel-6/. Last accessed June 12, 2013.

## MAGAZINES AND NEWSPAPERS

Castle, Edgar B. "Jerusalem Now," *The Spectator*, May 14, 1948, p. 578.

Jackson, Elmore. "Meeting Human Needs in the Near East," *New York Herald Tribune*, February 24, 1949.

Jones, Rufus M. "Our Day in the German Gestapo." *The American Friend* (July 10, 1947). Reprinted as a pamphlet for distribution. Available at https://afsc.org/sites/afsc.civicactions.net/files/documents/Our_Day_in_the_German_Gestapo_by_Rufus_Jones.pdf. Last accessed June 12, 2013.

Klein, W. C. "Pause in Palestine," *The Living Church*, October 3, 1948, p. 8.

Pickett, Clarence E. "Friends Feed Exiled Arabs," *Philadelphia Inquirer*, March 20, 1949.

"Proposals of the British Quakers Palestine Watching Committee, September 4, 1938, Friends Services Council, London," *The Friend* 97 (1939): 49–50.

*Chicago Daily Tribune*, "How Reds Lure Intellectuals to Their Side," June 6, 1948, p. 11.

*Chicago Daily Tribune*, "Chicago Faces Critical Housing Shortage, Builders Warn," June 14, 1942, p. 21

*Dubuque The Telegraph Herald*, "Simplified Order for War Housing," July 12, 1942, p. 4.

*Jewish Telegraph Agency*, "Former State Department Official Resigns from Holyland Emergency Liaison Program," October 13, 1949.

*Manchester Guardian*, "Aid to Palestine Refugees: U.N. Begins its Task," December 18, 1948, p. 6.

*New York Times*, "Truman is Urged to Bar Atom Bomb," August 20, 1945, p. 21.

*New York Times*, "World Needs After UNRRA," February 12, 1947, p. 24.

*New York Times*, "A Message to Our Fellow Americans Concerning World Hunger," February 19, 1947, p. C19.

*New York Times,* "Against Palestine Partition," November 21, 1947, p. 26.

*New York Times,* "Protection Asked in Loyalty Tests," January 12, 1948, p. 10.

*New York Times,* "Not by Might, Nor by Power, But by My Spirit," April 21, 1948, p. 19.

*New York Times,* "American Zionists Warned on Tactics," June 18, 1948, p. 15

*New York Times,* "Expansion by War Held Israel's Aim," August 1, 1948, p. 45.

*New York Times,* "U.N. Relief Expert Asks Aid to Arabs," August 8, 1948, p. 28.

*New York Times,* "Twenty U.S. Groups Map Palestine Relief," October 6, 1948, p. 5.

*New York Times,* "Child Fund Plans New Palestine Aid," *New York Times,* 19 October 19, 1948, p. 3.

*New York Times,* "Joint Appeal to Aid Holy Land Refugees," October 22, 1948, p. 6.

*New York Times,* "Text of Encyclical," *New York Times,* 24 October 24, 1948, p. 7.

*New York Times,* "Extra $5,000,000 on Hand," December 8, 1948, p. 18.

*New York Times,* "He Will Ask Congress to Appropriate 50% of Sum Sought from U.N. —Griffis Shapes Relief Distribution for 507,000," December 8, 1948, p. 18.

*New York Times,* "Refugees Create Big Arab Burden," December 12, 1948, E 5.

*New York Times,* "U.N. Relief Groups Sign Arab Aid Pacts," December 18, 1948, p. 7.

*New York Times,* "Arab Refugee Aid Well Under Way," January 5, 1949, p. 16.

*New York Times,* "Medical Aid Set for Arabs," January 20, 1949, p. 22.

*New York Times,* "Arab Refugees Get Food," January 22, 1948, p. 5.

*New York Times* "Epidemic of Measles Hits Arab Refugees," January 23, 1949, p. 27.

*New York Times,* "Senate Unit Urges Palestine Aid Gift," February 3, 1949, p. 10.

*New York Times,* "Arab Refugees Aided By Quaker Schools," March 20, 1949, p. 5.

*New York Times,* "$1,000,000 Waste is Bared in U.N. Middle East Relief," June 16, 1949, p. 1.

*New York Times,* "U.N. Relief Waste Denied by Griffis," June 17, 1949, p. 18.

*New York Times,* "U.N. Refugee Body Shifts Buying Plan," June 18, 1949, p. 5.

*New York Times,* "Griffis to Undergo Eye Surgery," July 15, 1949, p. 20.

*New York Times,* "Arab Chieftain is Against Resettlement of Palestinians on Newly-Developed Land," September 6, 1949, p. 11.

*New York Times,* "Liaison Body Formed for Near East Relief," September 12, 1949, p. 8.

*New York Times,* "Quakers Ask Help for Arab Refugees," November 14, 1949, p. 7.

*New York Times,* "Give Point Four Aid Through U.N., Witnesses Urge House Group," January 13, 1950, p. 3.

*New York Times,* "Theologians Assail New Bomb Decisions," February 2, 1950, p. 6.

*New York Times,* "Dorothy Thompson Gets Refugee Award," May 18, 1950, p. 27.

*New York Times,* "Sarnoff Receives Seminary Award, March 19, 1951, p. 36.

*New York Times,* "American Food Committee for India," April 6, 1951, p. 17.

*New York Times,* "Text of McCarran Statement on New Act," December 25, 1952, p. 4.

*New York Times,* "Two Laugh at Charges," December 26, 1952, p. 15.

*New York Times,* "Our Relations with India," December 17, 1953, p. 36.

*New York Times,* "Aid Sent to Suez Refugees," February 11, 1957, p. 3.

*New York Times,* "U.S. Group Helps Lebanon," July 3, 1958, p. 6.

*New York Times,* "Aid Sent to Algeria Refugees," March 1, 1959, p. 20.

*New York Times,* "Appeal on Mideast Sent to Eisenhower," December 8, 1959, p. 25.

*Washington Post and Times Herald,* "Nuclear Weapons Fought in Suit," April 5, 1958, p. 3.

*Washington Post,* "Witnesses Praise Hiss' Reputation," December 14, 1949, p. 2.

*Washington Post,* "Quakers List Mideast Plan," May 9, 1970, p. D 28.

*Washington Post,* "Paris Rally Attacks Nixon," February 12, 1972, A 11.

## GOVERNMENT REPORTS

Great Britain, Palestine Royal Commission. *Palestine Royal Commission Report, Presented by the Secretary of State for the Colonies to Parliament by Command of His Majesty, July 1937.* London: His Majesty's Stationary Office, 1937.

## GOVERNMENT PUBLICATIONS

U.S. Department of State, *Foreign Relations of the United States, 1948.* Vol. V, The Near East, South Asia, and Africa, (in two parts). Washington, DC: Government Printing Office, 1975–1976.

U.S. Department of State, *Foreign Relations of the United States, 1949.* Vol. VI, The Near East, South Asia, and Africa. Washington, DC: Government Printing Office, 1977.

U.S. Department of State, *Foreign Relations of the United States, 1951.* Vol. V. The Near East and Africa. Washington, DC: Government Printing Office, 1982.

U.S. Department of State, *Foreign Relations of the United States, 1952–1954.* Africa and South Asia, (in two parts). Washington, DC: Government Printing Office, 1983.

United States House of Representatives, Committee on Foreign Affairs, Hearings on Aid to Palestine Refugees. Eighty-First Congress, Second Session, February 16 and 17, 1950. Washington, DC: Government Printing Office, 1950.

## WEBSITES

Abrams, Irwin. "The Quaker Peace Testimony and the Nobel Peace Prize," Presented at the International Conference: "The Pacifist Impulse in Historical Perspective," University of Toronto, May 1991. http://www2.gol.com/users/quakers/quaker_peace_testimony.htm. Last accessed June 12, 2013.

AMIDEAST. "About AMIDEAST." http://www.amideast.org/about/how-amideast-making-difference. Last accessed June 12, 2013

Chris Gunness, "Exploding the myths: UNRWA, UNHCR and the Palestine refugees," http://www.unrwa.org/etemplate.php?id=1029

http://afsc.org/search/node/palestine, http://www.quakerpi.org/default.shtml, http://afsc.org/story/jean-zaru. Last accessed June 12, 2013.

http://archive.peacemagazine.org/v09n2p06.htm. Last accessed June 12, 2013.

http://www.brad.ac.uk/peace/qpst/. Last accessed June 12, 2013.

http://www.kairospalestine.ps/sites/default/Documents/English.pdf. Last accessed June 12, 2013.

Jahr, Gunnar. Award Ceremony Speech. http://www.nobelprize.org/nobel_prizes/peace/laureates/1947/press.html. Last accessed June 12, 2013.

National Portrait Gallery, Breaking Racial Barriers, African Americans in the Harmon Foundation Collection. http://www.npg.si.edu/exh/harmon/ Last accessed June 12, 2013.

Simon, Robert. "Channing Richardson, Professor of International Relations (1952–1983)." Hamilton College. http://www.hamilton.edu/history/memorial-minutes/Channing-Richardson. Last accessed June 12, 2013.

Williams College, Archives & Special Collections, Francis B. Sayre (1885–1972) Papers, 1914–1917. http://archives.williams.edu/manuscriptguides/sayre/bio.php Last accessed June 12, 2013.

http://unispal.un.org/UNISPAL.NSF/0/5840640903D5342E85257B430065EE0B Last accessed June 12, 2013.

http://www.un.org/News/Press/docs/2012/gaspd518.doc.htm Last accessed June 12, 2013.

## ORAL HISTORIES

AFSC Oral History Interview #601, Narrator: Paul Johnson, Interviewer: Joan Lowe, September 19, 1992.

AFSC Oral History Interview # 602, Narrator: Josina Vreed Burger, Interviewer: Paula Goldberg, September 19, 1992.

AFSC Oral History Interview #604, Narrator Alwin Holtz, Interviewer: Joan Lowe, September 19, 1992.
AFSC Oral History Interview #605, Narrator: Howard McKinney, Interviewer: Joan Lowe. November 11, 1992.
AFSC Oral History Interview #609, Narrator: David Walker, Interviewer: Joan Lowe, September 20, 1992.
AFSC Oral History Interview #612, Narrator: Vern Pings, Interviewer: Paula Goldberg. September 19, 1992.
Harry S. Truman Library and Museum. Oral History Interview with George C. McGhee Washington, DC, June 11, 1975 by Richard D. McKinzie. http://www.trumanlibrary.org/oralhist/mcgheeg.htm#transcript, 39. Last accessed June 12, 2013.
Harry S. Truman Library and Museum. Oral History Interview with Harry N. Howard, Washington, DC, June 5, 1975 by Richard D. McKinzie. http://www.trumanlibrary.org/oralhist/howardhn.htm Last accessed June 12, 2013.

## ARCHIVAL MATERIALS

Elmore Jackson Papers, Friends Historical Library of Swarthmore College. RG 5/202.
Elmore Jackson to Clarence Pickett and Charles Read, December 5, 1948. Box 5. Harry S. Truman Library and Museum.
Haverford College, Quaker & Special Collections, Khalil A. Totah and Eva Marshall Totah Papers.
Khalil Totah to Palestine Watching Committee, Friends House London, May 11, 1936.
Memorandum enclosing copy of letter from Charles P. Taft, Chairman of the Advisory Committee on Voluntary Foreign Aid, to Willard Thorp, Assistant Secretary for Economic Affairs, Department of State, on the Point IV Program, copied to William Datt, et al., 27 June 1950. http://www.trumanlibrary.org/oralhist/ringland.htm#appendix Last accessed June 12, 2013.

## AMERICAN FRIENDS SERVICE COMMITTEE ARCHIVE, PHILADELPHIA, PA

AFSC 1948. Report of Friends Mission to Palestine: April 15–20, 1948, James Vail, Edgar B. Castle.
AFSC 1948, Paul Sturge to Colin Bell, July 28, 1948.
AFSC 1948. Colin Bell to Paul Sturge, August 24, 1948.
AFSC 1948. Bernard G. Lawson to Colin Bell, August 25, 1948.
AFSC 1948. Colin Bell to A. Willard Jones, September 1, 1948.
AFSC 1948. Outline of a Proposed Plan for a Quaker Team in Palestine, September 28, 1948.

AFSC 1948. Statement, American Appeal for Holy Land Refugees, October 21, 1948.

AFSC 1948. Minutes of the Foreign Service Executive Committee meeting, November 17, 1948, submitted by Julia E. Branson.

AFSC 1948. Colin Bell to Paul Sturge, November 26, 1948.

AFSC 1948. Mildred E. White to Colin Bell, December 2, 1948.

AFSC 1948. John Devine to Stanton Griffis, December 13, 1948.

AFSC 1948. United Nations Relief for Palestine—A New Pattern in International Welfare Administration, December 1948.

AFSC 1949. Notes on Delbert Replogle and Douglas Cornog, Faluja, February 11, 1949.

AFSC 1949. Elmore Jackson to Clarence Pickett, et al. February 23, 1949.

AFSC 1949. Memo of Visit of Clarence Pickett and Delbert Replogle with the Grand Mufti of Jerusalem and Zamalih, Cairo, February 1949.

AFSC 1949. Delbert Replogle to Clarence Pickett February 24, 1949 (received March 21, 1949).

AFSC 1949. Clarence Pickett to Trygve Lie, March 2, 1949.

AFSC 1949. Delbert Replogle to Mohamad Abbasay, March 6, 1949.

AFSC 1949. Howard Wriggins to George Mathues et al., March 11, 1949.

AFSC 1949. Tony Meager to James Read, March 18, 1949.

AFSC 1949. George Mathues to James Read, March 28, 1949.

AFSC 1949. Press release, March 20, 1949.

AFSC 1949. Clarence Pickett to Howard Wriggins, March 29, 1949.

AFSC 1949. Suggested Draft for Submission to UN, March 1949.

AFSC 1949. Visit of the Quaker team to Faluja, February 26 to March 6 (1949), reported by Ray Hartsough, edited by Corrinne Hardesty.

AFSC 1949. Palestine AFSC/UN Agreement, April 4, 1949.

AFSC 1949. Delbert Replogle to Clarence Pickett, April 7, 1949.

AFSC 1949. Minutes of the meeting of the Coordinating Committee and Others Interested in the American Appeal for Holy Land Refugees Held in the Offices of the Near East Foundation on Friday, April 22, 1949.

AFSC 1949. M. Zaki, 'Schools of the Gaza Area,' April 14, 1949, attached to a memorandum from Corrinne Hardesty to John Kavanaugh and George Mathues, April 27, 1949.

AFSC 1949. Emmett Gulley to Colin Bell, May 5, 1949.

AFSC 1949. Elmore Jackson to Clarence Pickett. A Committee to stimulate interest in the overall settlement of the Palestine Refugee Problem, May 18, 1949.

AFSC 1949. Conference with Aubrey Eban, Israeli Representative to the United Nations on May 20, (1949).

AFSC 1949. Colin W. Bell to Clarence E. Pickett, May 25, 1949.

AFSC 1949. Colin Bell to Clarence Pickett, June 6, 1949.

AFSC 1949. Report on Meeting at New State Department Building, Washington, June 15, 1949, on the Future of the Palestine Refugee Problem.

AFSC 1949. Prospects for the Palestine Refugee Relief Program, June 24, 1949.

AFSC 1949. Letter of Byron Price, 314/3/01/PhE, July 8, 1949.

AFSC 1949. Donald Stevenson to Bronson Clark, Interview with Ambassador Eliahu Elath of Israel at the Israeli Embassy, Washington, on August 9, 1949.

AFSC 1949. Donald Stevenson to Bronson Clark. Discussions with Mr. Cordier of U.N. on August 10, 1949 at Lake Success on R.P.R.

AFSC 1949. Corrine Hardesty to Colin Bell and Tony Meager, August 22, 1949.

AFSC 1949. James Keen to Colin Bell, September 13, 1949.

AFSC 1949. Minutes of Camp Leader's Meeting, October 6, 1949.

AFSC 1949. Donald Stevenson to Bronson Clark, October 7, 1949.

AFSC 1949. Gaza Unit to Clarence Pickett, October 12, 1949.

AFSC 1949. Charles Read to AFSC headquarters, October 15, 1949.

AFSC 1949. Donald Stevenson to Colin Bell, October 15, 1949.

AFSC 1949. Colin Bell. American Friends Service Committee Program in Israel. 1. Impressions of Israel. October 17, 1949.

AFSC 1949. Colin Bell. American Friends Service Committee Program in Israel. 2. Possible Future AFSC Activity in Israel. October 17, 1949.

AFSC 1949. Colin Bell. American Friends Service Committee Program in Israel. Appendix A. Outline of Community Centre Program in Acre. October 17, 1949.

AFSC 1949. Colin Bell. American Friends Service Committee Program in Israel. Appendix B. Outline of Proposed Agricultural Project as Set Out by Mr. Palmon, Advisor to the Prime Minister on Arab Affairs.

AFSC 1949. Donald Stevenson to Bronson Clark, October 24, 1949.

AFSC 1949. Colin Bell to Clarence Pickett, October 27, 1949.

AFSC 1949. Donald Stevenson to Bronson Clark, October 27, 1949.

AFSC 1949. Clarence Pickett to Trygve Lie, November 1, 1949.

AFSC 1949. Don Peretz to Donald Stevenson, November 7, 1949.

AFSC 1949. Donald Stevenson to Bronson Clark, Re: Don Peretz's Letter of November 7th, November 25, 1949.

AFSC 1949. Cordelia Trimble to Bronson Clark, November 29, 1949.

AFSC 1949. Bronson Clark to Donald Stevenson and Charles Read, December 1, 1949.

AFSC 1949. Statement of the American Friends Service Committee for the Ad Hoc Political Committee of the United Nations on 2 December 1949.

AFSC 1949. Charles W. Bronson. Thoughts on Possible AFSC Activities in the Palestine Area after 1949. December 11, 1949.

AFSC 1950. Alwin Holtz to James Keen, January 20, 1950.

AFSC 1950. Memorandum in regard to Work Possibilities in the Gaza Area. January 26, 1950.

AFSC 1950. Donald Stevenson to Bronson Clark, January 27, 1950.

AFSC 1950. Marshall Sutton to Corrine Hardesty, January 30, 1950.

AFSC 1950. Bronson Clark to the Foreign Service Executive Committee February 9, 1950.

AFSC 1950. Donald Stevenson to Bronson Clark, March 4, 1950.

AFSC 1950. Charles Read to James Goble, March 15, 1950.

AFSC 1950. Arthur Ringland to Clarence Pickett, March 20, 1950.

AFSC 1950. Donald Stevenson, Report to the American Friends Service Committee on the position of the Arab Community in Israel, March 22, 1950.

AFSC 1950. Bronson Clark to Donald Stevenson and Paul Johnson. Meeting in New York with Blandford and Knight. March 23, 1950.

AFSC 1950. Bronson Clark to Paul Johnson. Proposed AFSC Projects in Gaza after April. April 4, 1950.

AFSC 1950. Summary Statement of the American Friends Service Committee Operation for the Period 1 August 1949 to 30 April 1950.

AFSC 1950. James Keen to Clarence Pickett, reproduced in a letter from Charles Read to Bronson Clark, May 20, 1950.

AFSC 1950. Bronson Clark to Ernest Morgan, June 9, 1950.

AFSC 1950. Paul Johnson to Clarence Pickett, June 15, 1950.

AFSC 1950. Bronson Clark to Lewis Hoskins, Bayard Dodge Luncheon, June 16, 1950.

AFSC 1950. Bronson Clark to Cassius Fenton and Corrine Hardesty, September 24, 1950.

AFSC 1950. Report on Gaza operations dated October 14, 1950, attached to a letter from James Keen to Clarence Pickett, November 15, 1950.

AFSC 1950. Alwin Holtz to Corrine Hardesty, November 10, 1950.

AFSC 1950. Cable from James Keen to Clarence Pickett, November 20, 1950.

AFSC 1950. Bronson Clark to Hugh Jenkins, November 21, 1950.

AFSC 1950. Delbert Replogle to Hugh Jenkins, November 22, 1950.

AFSC 1950. Clarence Pickett to James Keen, December 26, 1950.

AFSC 1951. Paul Johnson to Clarence Pickett, November 5, 1951.

AFSC 1951. Paul Johnson to Clarence Pickett, November 6, 1951.

AFSC 1951. Paul Johnson, November 20, 1951, letter addressed "Dear Friends."

AFSC 1951. Minutes of the Sub-committee on Social and Technical Assistance, December 3, 1951.

AFSC 1953. Newsletter #4 from Moses and Mabel Bailey, November 27, 1953.

## NATIONAL ARCHIVES, COLLEGE PARK, MARYLAND

Record Group 59, Textual Records from the Department of State. Bureau of Near Eastern, South Asian and African Affairs. Office of Near Eastern Affairs. Container 74, ARC Identifier 2507075–77, U.S. Department of State, Palestine Refugee Problem Secret Folder 1–3.

Record Group 59, Textual Records from the Department of State. Bureau of Near Eastern, South Asian and African Affairs. Office of Near Eastern Affairs. (1951–1958). ARC Identifier 2558731/MLR Number A1 1437. UNRPR. Minutes of meeting of UNRWA representatives held on Saturday 20 October and Monday 22 October 1951. The Role of the AFSC in Refugee Reintegration.

Record Group 59, Textual Records from the Department of State. Bureau of Near Eastern, South Asian and African Affairs. Office of Near Eastern Affairs. Office of the Country Director for Israel and Arab-Israel Affairs. Container 72, Folder 2, ARC Identifier 2507045, Memorandum of Donald G. Bergus, Beirut, "An American Policy for Arab-Israeli Peace," December 2, 1952.

## THE NATIONAL ARCHIVES, KEW, RICHMOND, UK

CAB 129/32, C.P. (49) 10, Memorandum by the Secretary of State for Foreign Affairs, Palestine, 15 January 1949.

CAB 131/7, D.O. (49) 23, Memorandum by the Secretary of State for War, Long Term Policy in Egypt, 22 March 1949.

CAB 129/36, C.P. (49) 188, 25 August 1949, Middle East Policy. Note by the Secretary of State for Foreign Affairs.

CAB 131/7, D.O. (4) 26, 21 March 1949, Memorandum by the Secretary of State for Foreign Affairs, Egyptian Defense Talks.

CAB 131/7. Defense Committee, Arms and Equipment for the Egyptians, Report by the Chiefs of Staff, D.O. (49) 58, 25 July 1949.

FO 371/68679. Raphael Cilento, Beirut to Foreign Office, 1, 3 October 1948, 'The Number of Arab Refugees (Revised Version).'

FO 371/75342/E7816. Sir J. Troutbeck, 'Summary of general impressions gathered during week-end visit to the Gaza District,' 16 June 1949.

FO 371/75439, E 11297/1821/131. Morton to Foreign Office, 23 September 1949.

F0 371/91417. Sir Henry Knight to Francis Evans, letter of 16 January 1951.

FO 371/91417, EE 18211/6. Sir Henry Knight to Francis Evans, letter of 20 February 1951.

FO 371/91417, EE 18211/9. Letter to Francis Evans, 4 April 1951.

FO 371/91417/345481. Sir Henry Knight to Francis Evans, April 19, 1951.

FO 371/91417/345481. Sir Henry Knight to Francis Evans, April 24, 1951.

FO 371/91426. Sir Henry Knight to Francis Evans, May 8, 1951, forwarding "Analysis of the State of Mind of the Palestinian Refugees in the Lebanon," by UNRWA Chief District Officer R. M. Courvoisier of April 26, 1951.

FO 371/91417, EE 18211/19. Sir Henry Knight to Francis Evans, letter of July 17, 1951.

FO 371/91430. "Informal Report of the Retiring Director of the United Nations Relief and Works Agency for Palestine Refugees to the Secretary-General, United Nations," 14 August 1951.

FO 371/91417/345481. Sir Henry Knight to Francis Evans, August 16, 1951.

FO 371/98512. 'Summary of Paper on UNRWA Activities.' 20 May 1952.

FO 371/127871/ VE1827/11. Minute by Rose, 11 April, 1957.

## UNITED NATIONS RESOLUTIONS AND REPORTS

United Nations General Assembly, Resolution 181 (III) of 29 November 1947.

United Nations General Assembly, Resolution 194 (III) of 11 December 1948.

United Nations General Assembly, Resolution 212 (III) of 19 November 1949.

United Nations General Assembly. Resolution 302 (IV) of 8 December 1949, Assistance to Palestine Refugees.

United Nations General Assembly Resolution 303 (IV) of 9 December 1949. Palestine: Question of an international regime for the Jerusalem area and the protection of the Holy Places.

United Nations General Assembly. Resolution 393 (V) of 2 December 1950.

United Nations General Assembly Resolution 513 (VI) of 26 January 1952.

United Nations General Assembly. A/648, Progress Report of the United Nations Mediator on Palestine Submitted to the Secretary-General for Transmission to the Members of the United Nations, 16 September 1948.

United Nations Conciliation Commission for Palestine. A/AC/25/W9 of 9 April 1949. Functions and Composition of the Technical Mission on Refugees.

United Nations Conciliation Commission for Palestine. A/AC/25/Org8 of 2 May 1949. Restricted. Text of a letter dated 14 April 1949 from M. de Rougé, Secretary-General, League of Red Cross Societies, to the Secretary-General of the United Nations, transmitted for the information of the Conciliation Commission.

United Nations Conciliation Commission for Palestine. A/AC/25/Org11 of 8 May 1949. Restricted. Letter dated 4 May 1949 addressed to the Chairman of the Conciliation Commission by Mr. Howard Wriggins, Geneva Representative, American Friends Service Committee, Enclosing an Analysis of Palestine Population Statistics.

United Nations Conciliation Commission for Palestine. SR/LM/17. Summary Record of a Meeting between the Conciliation Commission and Representatives of Relief Organizations in Geneva, 7 June 1949.

United Nations, Public Information Bureau. Press Release PAL/521. 24 August 1949.

United Nations. Draft Text, Verbatim Proceedings of the Ad Hoc Advisory Committee on Refugees on Relief to Palestine Refugees, Second Session, Held at Lake Success, New York on Tuesday, 4 October 1949, at 10:45 AM.

United Nations Conciliation Commission for Palestine. A/AC/25/W/28 of 27 October 1949. Restricted. Notes on the Secretary-General's Draft Report on the Work of U.N.R.P.R.

Final Report of the United Nations Economic Survey Mission for the Middle East, Part I, A/AC/25/6, of 28 December 1949.

United Nations Conciliation Commission for Palestine, A/AC.25/W.81/Rev.2 of 2 October 1961. Historical Survey of Efforts of the United Nations Conciliation Commission for Palestine to Secure the Implementation of Paragraph 11 of General Assembly Resolution 194 (III).

United Nations Conciliation Commission for Palestine. A/AC/25/W/28 of 27 October 1949. Restricted. Notes on the Secretary-General's Draft Report on the Work of U.N.R.P.R.

United Nations General Assembly, A/1451/Rev.1. Interim Report of the Director of the United Nations Relief and Works Agency for Palestine Refugees in the Near East, 6 October 1950.

United Nations General Assembly, A/1905. Report of the Director of the United Nations Relief and Works Agency for Palestine Refugees in the Near East of 28 September 1951.

United Nations General Assembly, A/4121. Proposals for the Continuation of United Nations Assistance to Palestine Refugees, Submitted by the Secretary General on 15 June 1959.

# Index ❧

Printed in the United States of America